ALIEN
INVESTIGATOR

ALIEN
INVESTIGATOR

THE CASE FILES OF BRITAIN'S
LEADING UFO DETECTIVE

TONY DODD

HEADLINE

First published in 1999
by HEADLINE BOOK PUBLISHING

10 9 8 7 6 5 4 3 2 1

British Library Cataloguing in Publication Data

Dodd, Tony
  Alien investigator
  1.Unidentified flying objects
  I.Title
  001.9'42

  ISBN 0 7472 2285 1 (hardback)
  ISBN 0 7472 7534 3 (softback)

Typeset by
Letterpart Limited, Reigate, Surrey

Printed and bound in Great Britain by
Clays Ltd, St Ives plc

HEADLINE BOOK PUBLISHING
A division of Hodder Headline PLC
338 Euston Road
London NW1 3BH

CONTENTS

To my wife Pauline, who could never quite understand my driving passion to reveal the truth about this enigma, yet stood shoulder to shoulder with me throughout the threats and attempted intimidation. Despite a heart attack and serious illness she never failed to support me, even from her hospital bed. Pauline, your courage is inspirational.

Also to Annette, Paul and Mandy, who were always there when needed. I am lucky to have such a family. Also to Mabel, the best mum in the world. This book is for you all.

Acknowledgements

I would like to thank all the friends and contacts who have shared information with me over the years. It would not be practical to name all the dedicated researchers and groups who have liaised with me, so I apologise in advance if your name is missing: my grateful thanks to you, anyway.

Tom Austin; Jeff Aspinall; Brian and Joyce Dinsdale; Graham and Mark Birdsall, *UFO* magazine; Armen Victorian; Roy Lake, LUFOS; Donald Cooper, SERIUS; Michael Dillon; Richard and Sue Hembury Kellow; Billy Buchanan; Margaret Fry; Joan Amos; Derek Gough; Richard Tarr; Rena McGuire; Harry Harris; David Dane; Roy and Ann Wilkinson; 'Mr Cedar'; George Wild; Jim Moor; Pat Otter; Jean Thornton; Graham Townsend; Colin Andrews; Pat Delgado.
    From the USA: Budd Hopkins; Linda Moulton Howe; Robert Dean; Wendelle Stevens; Virgil Armstrong.
    From Germany: Michael Hesseman; Brazil: A.J. Geveard; South Africa: Rosemary Howell; Russia: Marina Popavitch; Australia: Harry Mason; Denmark: Ib Lauland; Norway: Knut Running; Puerto Rico: Jorge Martin; Channel Islands: Kevin Giannoni.

To all those people who cannot be named, but who entrusted to me information which proves beyond a shadow of doubt that ETs are already here and have been for a very long time, my particular thanks. Many of you have risked your careers and your futures to get this important evidence out. Take heart from the knowledge that we are close to the whole truth being revealed, and that your efforts have contributed enormously.

INTRODUCTION

The black saloon car with CD plates pulled up against the kerb in a quiet street in Hampstead. Although it was the end of October, the weather was unseasonably mild for London, and the diplomat who stepped out of the car was wearing a suit, no overcoat. In his hand he carried a large, bulky brown envelope.

At the same moment, the door of a Ford Escort, parked in front of the saloon, opened, and a small man in his early forties with a receding hairline climbed out. He walked towards the diplomat. They exchanged a few brief words of greeting, then the diplomat handed over the package. As he turned to get back into his car he said:

'Be very careful. They are watching you.' He nodded his head in the direction of another car, parked on the opposite side of the road about fifty yards away. There were four people inside it and they were indeed watching closely, and without any attempt to disguise their interest.

The balding man jumped back into the Escort and drove off, aware, as he glanced in his mirror, that the dark blue Rover with the four figures inside was following him. Knowing the area well, he drove expertly through the traffic, smiling to himself as he saw the Rover being thwarted by buses and black cabs and the general mêlée of heavy traffic. It was Friday afternoon, when half of London seems to clock off early and throttle all the major routes out of the capital.

1

For a few minutes, the driver of the Escort forgot himself. It was like being in a spy thriller, trying to outwit his opponents. But quickly the reality dawned on him. This was real life, and he had in his possession a packet that he believed would blow the lid off the biggest cover-up in the history of mankind.

What was more, the men on his tail were not card-carrying members of Equity, recruited by the casting directors of a Bond movie. They wanted the package, and they would do everything within their power to get it. A momentary panic set in, as the driver considered his options. He knew that if he drove out of London and headed north towards my home in Yorkshire they would catch him on the motorway. His car only stood a chance against theirs in the crowded London streets, and only then because he was on home ground.

If he took the package to his own home, they would find him – and it. They had been to his house before: even the quick glimpses he had seen in his rearview mirror told him that one of the men in the car was the same man who had appeared on his doorstep a few weeks earlier, with a female colleague, warning him that he was under surveillance.

There was, he decided, one solution. If he could lose his pursuers for long enough, he could slip the package into a postbox. He doubled back through the side streets, making sudden turns without using his indicator. Eventually, he pulled into the heavy traffic of a main road and watched, with satisfaction, in his mirror as the other car was held at bay in a side street, unable to force a gap among the flow of cars and lorries. A few hundred yards further along he turned off the main route. He had successfully lost the other car. He stopped, and hastily wrote my name and address on the front of the package. At the top he scribbled the words 'This will be paid for at receiving end'. Checking again that he was not being followed, he drove on to the first postbox he saw, and double-parked for long enough to stick the package into the mouth of the box.

Breathing a sigh of relief, he took a circuitous route around the area and finally made his way back to his home. About three streets away he glanced in his mirror to see the blue Rover tucked in behind him again. The car and its occupants had obviously lain in wait for his return. He expected to be approached by the men when he reached his own front door, but instead the Rover cruised slowly past. The next morning he discovered that during the night his car had been broken into and searched, although nothing had been taken.

He rang me as soon as he got into his home, to say that the parcel was on its way. He was nervous and frightened, but at the same time happy to have evaded his pursuers. But even though I shared his relief that he had outwitted them, I was not as confident as he was that the vital parcel was safe. My fears hardened as every morning I waited expectantly for the post-man: and every morning I was fobbed off with the usual clutch of letters, bills and circulars. No package ever arrived. Despite a series of complaints to the Post Office, and investigations at every office that the envelope should have passed through on its journey north to my home in Grassington, in the Yorkshire Dales, the package, posted to me on 27 October 1997, has never turned up. The men who were tailing my friend in London had the last laugh, and the most vital evidence ever produced for the existence of UFOs and aliens has been – at least temporarily – suppressed.

I am not surprised. For more than twenty years I have been battling to have the existence of extra-terrestrial visitors recog-nised by the authorities. At first I believed that a combination of fear and ignorance led to the subject being sidelined: now, after many years as one of Britain's foremost UFO investigators, I know better. The authorities, including the governments of all major countries, not only know of the reality of UFOs, but actively cover up their existence and the contacts that take place between them and us. My missing package is just one more blow – a particularly devastating blow – to those of us who want the truth to be brought out into the open.

The package contained, amongst other things, sensational photographs showing aliens on board an American warship in the north Atlantic, a UFO on the ground at a USAF base, and a video of a UFO landing at a USAF base. The diplomat, one of a handful in the world who have been present at meetings between alien representatives and world leaders, had chosen to

3

leak this sensational material to me and my London-based friend for reasons which will be explained later in this book.

I am still confident that at least some of the material – the video is irreplaceable but there are copies of the photographs – will eventually come my way. If it does, it will be the culmination of all my work, but in particular of the project that has taken up most of my time in the last five years: my investigation into massive UFO bases under the sea off the coast of Iceland.

Yet although this is my most recent and possibly most important investigation, it is just one aspect of the work I have been doing since 1978, when I first saw a UFO and came to realise that there was life beyond the narrow horizons of this planet.

This book can only cover some of the research I have done, but I hope it gives a fair insight into how much I, and many other investigators, now know about extra-terrestrial visitors to earth. Of course, there are Hollywood movies and countless TV series which fictionalise and glamorise the life of alien investigators, and there are occasions, like my friend's car chase through north London, when we seem to be living in a film script. But the reality of alien investigation is that, like my career in the police force, it is hard, dedicated work that pays off.

When I left the police after twenty-five years, my record was 'exemplary'. I hope that the work I have done as an alien investigator can be described in the same way: I have certainly done my best to tackle the subject in a hard-headed, disciplined manner. Some of my personal experiences have made it difficult to be completely objective about the whole subject, but I have never lost sight of the need to investigate fairly and honestly.

Yes, I believe in aliens. But yes, I also have plenty of evidence to back up my belief. I believe too that the general public are being conned by senior politicians who, for a variety of reasons, want to keep us all in the dark.

I hope that this book sheds just a little light on a fascinating subject whose importance – for the future of all of us – must not be underestimated.

CHAPTER ONE

FIRST ENCOUNTER

It was 2.30 a.m. on a bitterly cold night in January 1978 when the radio in the police car I was driving crackled into life. It was a missing person report: a wife had phoned in to the police station because her husband had never arrived home from a trip to the pub. As a sergeant in the North Yorkshire Police Force with fifteen years of policing experience behind me, I instinctively knew this was not going to be a major case.

'What's the betting – another woman, or a pub landlord whose clock has conveniently stopped at ten minutes to closing time?' I said to the young police officer sitting in the passenger seat. 'Still, we've got to check it out, although I've got a feeling he'll have staggered home before we get there.'

As a sergeant, my job was to supervise the night patrols in the area around Skipton, where I was based. The beat police officers would expect to see me at some point as they patrolled the streets, and occasionally I would pick one of them up and take him around in the car with me, as I had done on this particular night.

The missing man lived in the village of Cononley, a few miles away. I turned the car on to a minor road which cuts across the moors directly to the village. I knew the roads around the North Yorkshire Dales like the back of my hand, and at this time of the night, with no tractors or milk lorries to hold us up, this narrow, unlisted lane was the quickest route we could take. The

only remarkable thing about the night was the clearness of the
sky, which stretched above us like a great black dome, with the
stars pinpointed as clearly as if we were in a planetarium.
Rabbits scurried from the road as we approached, and occasionally one froze in the beam of our headlights, causing me to slow
and cut my lights: I have always been an animal lover, and no
matter how hardened police work made me to the seamier side
of human nature, I am always upset if I inadvertently run over a
rabbit or a hedgehog.

As we approached a curve in the road we both noticed a glow
of light coming from the other side of the bend. There were no
buildings nearby, and my first thought was that another vehicle,
with lights on full beam, was coming towards us. But the light
was too big, too diffuse.

'What the . . .' my colleague was saying as we turned the bend.
The words died on his lips as we were suddenly confronted by a
huge airborne object only about 200 feet in front of us. It was a
massive disc, with a dome shape on top, small, round, dark
portholes along the side and a skirting at the bottom. Coloured
lights, red, green, blue, white, pulsed on and off, in no discernible
sequence, around the skirt, and the whole object, which was
hovering about 100 feet above the ground, glowed as if white-
hot.

I slammed on my brakes and we skidded to a halt almost
underneath the disc. I looked upwards and could see three
half-spheres protruding from underneath, in a triangle shape.
We both instinctively opened our doors and jumped out. Silently
and slowly, at no more than twenty m.p.h., the object began to
move away into the distance, until it was over a forest a few fields
from us, where it appeared to descend among the trees. From
this distance, all we could see was a glowing ball of white light,
until we lost sight of it completely below the ridge of the
treetops.

Neither of us had spoken, nor had we felt any fear. We were
both stunned: the object was as beautiful as it was strange.
Looking back, I think it exerted a mysterious power over us,
because the natural reasons would have been fear, and a desire to
stay inside the vehicle. But fear had simply not entered the

equation, and we had simultaneously climbed out of the car to get a better view of it. When we were at our closest to it, everything was quiet, but as it moved away a loud crackle of static came from the car radio, dying away as the disc moved further from us.

Still without speaking we climbed back into the car. Before I restarted the engine, we discussed what we had seen, without being able to make any sense of it. I had served in the RAF for three years, as my National Service, and while I may not have been at the cutting edge of experimental technology, my interest in aviation meant I had kept abreast of developments in commercial and military aircraft, and I had never seen or heard of anything like this. Neither of us could find adequate words to describe it.

We drove on, and as we approached a hill we could see lights on the other side. We wondered if the disc was back, but we soon realised that this was nothing more remarkable than a car approaching us. It turned out to be another police car, from a different station. Stopping alongside each other, we wound down our windows, and before I could speak the other driver blurted out:

'Did you see it? Did you see it?'

When we told him that we had, all three of us compared notes. Although he had not been as close to the disc, he had seen it moving away very clearly, and his description tallied with ours. None of us had any explanation.

Later, back at the station – after checking that the missing husband was safely at home, if a little the worse for wear for drink and a lashing from his wife's tongue – I made a few phone calls. The radar at Leeds/Bradford Airport was switched off at that time in the morning, and nothing had shown up on the radar at Manchester Airport. I was not surprised, as the object had been hugging the ground so closely that it was well below the hill lines.

I was profoundly shaken by what I had seen. It was beautiful, unearthly, and there had been something almost spiritual about the experience. Yet I am, and always have been, a hard-headed individual. I'd joined the police because of an in-built sense of

7

order, a need to sort things out and explain them. I had a policeman's cynical view of life. If someone had walked into the station and reported seeing what I'd just seen, I'd have laughed and told him to take more water with his whisky. I had never had any interest in talk of Unidentified Flying Objects, spacemen, extra-terrestrials, flying saucers.

Yet I had seen something that I could not explain – and two sane, reliable colleagues had witnessed it too. It bothered me, and before I went off duty at 6 a.m. that morning, I made a pact with myself that I was going to get to the bottom of it.

I had no idea, at that moment, that 'getting to the bottom of it' was going to turn into my life's mission. To me, it was just another, albeit unusual, investigation, and I was going to treat it exactly as I would any other case that came to me as a police sergeant.

I was born in Crystal Palace, in London, in 1935, into a solid, respectable working-class family. My father, George, worked as an undertaker. When he married my mother, Mabel, he brought with him a ready-made family: his first wife had died, leaving him with two daughters, Mavis and Pat, to bring up. He and my mother soon started to build their own family, with me arriving first and my sister, Beryl, soon afterwards. I was born on 2 January, so the New Year has always been a double celebration in my family.

The war dominates all my early memories: wailing sirens, the drone of the bombers overhead, being bundled in pyjamas out into the cold night and down into an air-raid shelter with a crowd of other terrified people. The adults complained about the conditions, but to me it was normal, all I could remember, and I had no real concept of the danger. In the mornings we would often emerge to find the streets devastated. We would have to pick our way through the rubble of bombed buildings, the streets strewn with debris and sometimes awash with water spewing from ruptured water mains. I can clearly remember one morning when we walked through a carpet of bread and cakes: the baker's had been hit. On another occasion I stooped to pick up something shiny, probably blown from the window of a cheap jewellery shop: my father grabbed my arms and repeated the litany that all war babies heard: 'Never pick anything up from the ground – it could blow up in your face.'

Even the cramped shelters were no guarantee of safety. I remember being shaken awake and pulled outside in my bare feet by my mother: the corner of the shelter had been hit. Just a few weeks later, we emerged after the all-clear siren one morning to find that the street where we lived had been hit, destroying our house almost entirely. There were unexploded bombs, so the whole area was sealed off. I have no memory of how the arrangements were made, but with fearsome speed, my sister and I found ourselves on a train, without our parents, heading for the relative safety of the Hertfordshire countryside. We were luckier than many evacuees, because we found ourselves billeted with a kind woman, even if she was a total stranger to us.

After only a few weeks, our parents turned up and collected us. We went back to London, this time to South Norwood. But they soon decided that the whole family would move to Leeds, where my father had relatives. I was seven when we arrived in Yorkshire, and from that day on the county has been my adopted home. I think of myself as a Yorkshireman: naturally, because my memories of London are very hazy and incomplete. We moved in with an aunt and then found a home for our family, which was expanding rapidly. Three boys and another four girls were born over the following years: there is a twenty-year age gap between me and my youngest sister. My father found work as a taxi driver, and my mother was obviously kept pretty busy with this stream of babies. Money was not plentiful, but we were better off than many of our peers, because my father had quite a substantial win on the football pools during the early years of the marriage. It was not the kind of lottery cheque that we hear of today, but it was a few hundred pounds, which in those days was enough to set the family up with a comfortable home. My father was always in work, so we were never short of the essentials.

Most importantly, it was a happy family. My parents were good people who cared for all their children, and, remarkably, the children got on well together. I am not saying we were little

9

angels who never fought, but there were never any major divisions in the ranks. My father died in 1958, and we have all missed him ever since, especially my mother, who is now in her eighties.

Despite coming from a large family, I was, as a child, a bit of a loner. When school was out, I'd grab my fishing rod and head off for a lake, where I'd be perfectly content to sit for hours. During the school holidays I'd take a sandwich and disappear for the whole day. I liked the challenge of catching fish, but I could never kill them and they always went straight back into the water.

I left school at fifteen, which was the normal leaving age at that time. I had always done well at school, but education was not as highly valued then as it is now, and there was no question of me staying on. Besides, I was keen to get on with my life, and I signed up for an electrical apprenticeship with a local firm.

When I was eighteen I was called up to do National Service, and spent the next three years in the RAF, serving a year more than the minimum because I enjoyed the life. I was trained at Cardington, in Bedfordshire, and then posted to a combined RAF/USAF base in Norfolk. I spent some months in Germany, patrolling the high barbed-wire fence which separated us from our new enemy, the Russians. As we walked along our side of the fence on those bitterly cold nights, we would see their patrols on the other side. Sometimes we would smile at each other: they looked just like me – young men who were cold and fed up and who had very little idea why we were there. It all seemed so pointless, after the war years in which we had been allies. I can remember thinking how futile it was to build artificial divisions between men: now, in the light of what I know about extra-terrestrial interest in this planet, it seems even more ludicrous that so much time and energy has been wasted on petty disputes.

I finished my service in Wharton, near Preston, Lancashire. I was a corporal when I left, and I might have been tempted to stay on had I not already met the reason I wanted to get back into civvy street: my future wife. Pauline was in the WRAF, working as a telephonist. She was the same age as me, and we knew almost as soon as we met that we intended to spend the rest of our lives together. We married while we were both still in the forces, but we'd seen enough of the kind of life involved to know that we did not want to become a services family. When we were both twenty-one we left the air force behind. But I did not leave behind my enthusiasm for everything to do with planes and aeronautics, and I've always read widely and kept up with developments in aviation technology: a background which would serve me well when I took up UFO research.

My first job, after leaving the RAF with 'exemplary service' recorded on my demob papers, was in the photographic laboratories of ICI at Fleetwood, in Lancashire, where we were perfecting colour film for use in ordinary family snapshots. Pauline's family came from Blackpool, which was why we chose the area. When ICI sold this part of their business, I was transferred to a power plant just a few miles away, where I worked in the office. I did not find the work satisfying, and this helped crystallise an ambition I had had for some time: to join the police. I was twenty-eight when I started training with what was then called the West Riding Constabulary (it later became West Yorkshire, and then North Yorkshire Police).

My first beat was in Skipton, North Yorkshire. Although they are only thirty miles from Leeds, where I grew up, I had never visited the North Yorkshire Dales before, and I was instantly captivated by the beauty of the area. Skipton itself is a traditional market town, with a few imposing stone buildings ranged around the wide main street, and its setting is the kind of striking moorland that has been popularised today as 'Herriot country' and '*Last of the Summer Wine* country'. But there was precious little time to enjoy the countryside, because by this time I had three little children to support: Annette, who was seven, Paul, who was four, and newborn Mandy. (Today they are all happily grown up and have given Pauline and me eight grandchildren.)

The new job was demanding, but I loved it. I knew almost immediately that I was cut out to be a policeman: I enjoyed the contact it gave me with the public, the working atmosphere was friendly, and I got a quiet satisfaction out of feeling that I was serving the community and doing some good. I started out on

11

the beat, which I loved, but I was soon recruited to join the first ever Crime Task Force set up in Britain to deal with serious crime, working in most city areas of west Yorkshire. It was demanding, as we were working at the rock face of policing: encountering murderers, drug-dealers, armed robbers and every known kind of heavy criminal. At times it was frightening. We would find ourselves knocking down a door and not knowing whether the person inside had a weapon loaded and ready to fire as soon as we appeared; or we would be involved in road chases with criminals who had so much to lose that they would stop at nothing to throw us off the pursuit. But it was always exhilarating and satisfying. I was trained in firearms, and served on the firearms team, being called in whenever it was felt necessary for armed police to be present. I was one of the team who hunted for the Black Panther, as Donald Neilson was dubbed by the press. He kidnapped and murdered heiress Lesley Whittle, as well as shooting three sub-postmasters in raids on post offices, and his capture in 1975 came as a result of one of the biggest police manhunts ever mounted in Britain.

I thrived on it, and soon left the uniform behind to become a detective constable in Keighley. Again, my work involved constant contact with the seamier side of humanity, and to do the job at all I had to be tough, decisive and able to evaluate and assess evidence – all qualities that I later transferred to my investigative UFO research.

In 1974 I was promoted to the rank of sergeant, which inevitably involved switching back into uniform. It was refreshing to be based back in Skipton, near to home, and I soon began to relish the variety of the job: again, I was dealing mostly with crime, but I was also involved with serious road traffic accidents and the rest of the rich tapestry of events that members of the public report to the police. I liked the fact that I was not looking at life through the jaundiced eyes of someone who spends every working moment thinking about, and dealing with, dedicated criminals.

My ideal job came to me six years later, when I took over the policing of six hundred square miles of the Yorkshire Dales, including the National Park. We moved to a police house in

Grassington, a picture-postcard village beloved of serious walkers and day-trippers. It really is, to me, the most beautiful place in the world, and we have been very happy living here ever since. I worked from my home base, with eight constables under me. During the summer months, when tourists flock to the area, the sparse population is boosted by over a million visitors, and our workload increased accordingly, with burglaries, serious road accidents, fell rescues and pothole rescues, where we worked alongside the volunteers of the Upper Wharfedale Fell Rescue Association. Grassington itself was the scene of a road accident involving the largest ever number of fatalities in the United Kingdom, when a tourist bus crashed through a bridge parapet and fell twenty feet to the ground below, killing thirty-two old-age pensioners.

After my first encounter with a UFO, in 1978, I quickly realised that plenty of other people were also seeing mysterious objects in the skies over the Yorkshire Dales. The police received a sporadic stream of reports of strange sights from postmen, milkmen, farm labourers and others who were out at night, and about twelve months before my sighting two other police officers had reported seeing something similar. As the encounters were benign, if inexplicable, nothing was done about them.

I also realised, as did the colleagues who were with me on the night I saw the UFO, that talking about my experience did not go down well at work. The general consensus was that we must have imagined it, or misinterpreted it: I would have dismissed it in similar terms had it happened to someone else. To talk too much about it could lead to being labelled a 'nutcase', or being thought of as gullible – not a good trait for a policeman. So I and the others would discuss it with each other and with close friends, but not openly while at work.

Privately, though, I was determined to find out more. At this stage, I did not think of it in terms of an alien craft, but simply imagined that it was some highly secret mind-blowing technology being test-flown across the Dales. My interest was soon rewarded: within weeks of the first sighting, I saw other bright objects in the skies over the moors. I narrowed the area down to three square miles of Carleton Moor, both from my own sight-ings and from the reports I pulled out of the filing cabinets at the police station, and concentrated on observing the area at night when I was off duty. Some nights I sat up there alone, but more often I was with friends, and they too witnessed strange glowing lights, configurations of small lights, and dark, shadowy triangles passing overhead.

Looking back, with the benefit of hindsight, I can see that I became rather obsessed. But I can also see, after all the experi-ence I have now had, that this is not unusual: most of the people I know who have had similar encounters feel compelled to find out more. They may not all become full-time investigators, as I have ultimately done, but they feel drawn to explore the whole subject, almost as if the encounter was deliberately engineered to fuel their curiosity. It may sound strange to those who are not as immersed in the subject as I am, but I have come to believe that I – and all the others who have had close encounters – have been *chosen*. We were not just in the right place at the right time; the event happened *because* we were there. We were *allowed* to witness it.

The more I looked for 'them', the more I saw, and I soon became eerily aware that they appeared to be looking out for me as much as I was for them. My research at this stage was highly individual: I had read no books on the subject – in the late seventies there simply were not many available – and I was not part of any organised group. Although I was beginning to consider the possibility that the lights and strange objects I was seeing were alien in origin, I think I would still have plumped for the top-secret-technology explanation if pressed.

The most common sight was a large orange ball of light which, if I was close enough, I could see had a small red pulsing light at its heart. These balls, sometimes singly and sometimes several together, would sweep past my car, and then return for another flypast, as if they were trying to assess me just as much as I was assessing them.

On one occasion I was parked on the moor late at night with two people who had asked to accompany me. I was happy for others to join me, mainly because they provided independent witnesses, but I always warned them that there was no guarantee they would see anything. I might spend four or five nights sitting in my car and see nothing at all, so I prepared them for disappointment. On this particular night, that seemed the likeliest outcome: we had been there for about three hours and seen nothing. I opened the car door and stepped outside to stretch my legs before driving us back to our warm beds, and immediately became aware that there was a large shape hovering overhead. It was brightly lit in many colours, like the fairy lights on a Christmas tree. Astonishingly, none of us had seen it arrive, although we had been keeping a watch on all sides of the car. It stayed for a few minutes, giving the others plenty of time to see it clearly, and then it shot away upwards at tremendous speed.

Another time I took my son-in-law, Anthony Grant, with me. Anthony is a hard-headed, down-to-earth individual who works as a mill chargehand, but he had been fascinated by my tales – and perhaps he was a bit concerned as to what sort of family he had married into! Anyway, I warned him not to expect too much, and that we might be in for a long, cold wait. But as we drove up to the top of the moor, it was waiting for us: a large cigar-shaped object approximately fifteen metres in length with a line of windows illuminated along its side. It was stationary, hovering above us, no more than fifty metres away, but as we approached, a bright white light was suddenly activated at the further end of the object, and it started to move slowly away from us, and then rapidly increased its speed. As it moved faster, so the light seemed to grow, both bigger and more powerful, until in the end it enveloped the whole shape. We watched as the ball of light receded until it was eventually nothing more than a pinprick which winked out into the clear dark sky. Anthony was amazed, rendered speechless, but to me it was becoming a commonplace happening – although I have never, even after all these years, lost my sense of wonder when I meet something so unearthly.

Within a year of my first encounter, I once again saw something astonishing while I was on duty, and again I had a police constable with me who also witnessed it. We were travelling along the A65 from Skipton towards Gargrave in the early hours of a bitterly cold morning, and on this occasion I was in the passenger seat. It had been snowing for several hours, and the fields and hedgerows had a deep coating. The road was dangerous, and we were travelling slowly because of the conditions. We drove to the brow of a hill, from where we could see the road bending away in front of us. Suddenly, to the left and below us, we both noticed a large light. For a few seconds it looked to me like a bungalow with all the lights on. I even said to the driver:

'What's a farmer doing up and about at this time?'

But as I said it, I realised it wasn't a house or bungalow. I know the area so well that I would, on reflection, have realised that this was an empty field, but what alerted me was the object beginning to move. The driver stopped the car, without me saying anything, and in silence we both watched, fascinated, as it glided smoothly across the field. It was soundless, because although the car windows were all tight shut against the cold, with the ignition off we would have heard the sound of an engine. It was a large object, dome-shaped, with white light coming from what looked like windows. We watched it travel across the field and a canal, and away over another field into the distance, a smooth, slow progress, rather like a hovercraft.

'So it's true what they say about working with you,' said the young police officer, turning towards me with a look of amazement on his face.

'Well, I didn't conjure it up. You saw it with your own eyes,' I said.

It was 4.30 a.m., and we were travelling to Gargrave to meet another police car, to exchange internal mail, so we carried on our way, mulling over all the possible explanations for what we had seen. Not that either of us had any explanations: it was too big, too solid and too slow-moving to rationalise away easily. When we reached Gargrave we picked up the mail, and then, with some time to spare, drove back to the field where we had seen the mysterious object. This time, we went right down to the dip where we had first spotted it, and climbed out of the car to look at the ground. The snow was virgin, untouched, without even an animal's pawprint. Whatever we had seen had not been

16

in contact with the ground, which confirmed our impression that it had been hovering.

It dawned on me gradually that the extraordinary was becoming the ordinary: it was unusual for me not to see anything when I drove out to Carleton Moor at night. I felt a need to go there: for three or four years I was up there at least four or five times a month, sometimes more frequently. If I went away on holiday, I'd be back up there as soon as I could. I went whatever the weather: although I saw more on clear nights, I have been on Carleton Moor with a cloudbase no more than 200 metres above my head, with these strange machines appearing beneath it. Years later, I can look back and see that this was all part of an important education for me, an education I was being *given* by the aliens. Yet at the time I still had no idea who built these amazing machines, who was flying them or where they were coming from.

I was able to make one or two quasi-scientific assessments. For example, I knew that the colour of light they exuded depended on the speed at which they were travelling: bright white light at high speed deepening to amber at slow speed and down to a cherry red when they were stationary. But this only applied to some of them, and by no means explained anything about their construction. I also felt, instinctively, that they were friendly.

There was only one night when I felt fear, although quite often my companions would be frightened just by the sight of the objects. On this occasion, as I and two friends drove up to the moor we saw a succession of bright lights dancing about 300 metres above us on the hills. They appeared to be doing aerobatics. We took the road that led us in the direction of the lights, and as we reached the brow of a hill we were dazzled by a huge orange ball of brilliance, only 300 metres away, hovering about a metre above the road surface. As the car crossed the summit of the road the headlights arced down to meet the orange ball. Immediately the light from the car hit it, the object started to move up the hill towards us, gaining speed. I was scared, and rammed the car into reverse, killing the lights. I drove backwards down the hill in darkness – thankfully it was a straight road, and

I knew it well. We were only a few metres down when the orange light reached the top, the position where our car had been. Instantly it shot vertically upwards at great speed. I had a distinct feeling that our presence was not wanted there that night, so I turned the car round and we drove home. This incident remains, to this day, the only time that I have been frightened by extra-terrestrial activity. (Although I have had plenty of reasons to be scared due to my investigation work, the instigators of my fear have always been human.)

The incident did not put me off visiting the moor at night, but it increased my determination to do more than just watch the aerial display. I wanted to know what was going on. I was seeing the evidence constantly, but if I viewed it in terms of a police investigation, I was getting nowhere. Others who came up to the moors with me seemed to be satisfied to gaze in awe at the incredible sights, but I wanted to make progress, to find out more.

I decided to try to make contact, and for some weeks, whenever I saw one of these objects passing overhead, I flashed the beam of a powerful torch at it. I do not know what I was expecting to happen, or how I would have reacted if I had got a response. It simply seemed a logical progression: I had seen the evidence, now I wanted to interview the suspects.

Yet when the acknowledgement came, I was unprepared for it. It was in the early hours of a cold December morning in 1982, and two friends and I were sitting in a car on the top of the moor, warming ourselves from a flask of coffee. I decided to stretch my legs. As I stepped out of the car I shouted out in alarm: hovering only fifty metres above the car was a large black triangular object with small coloured lights in the shape of a diamond on its underside. My friends had clambered out of the car as soon as I called them, and all three of us watched the craft move silently away. In an instant, I leaned back inside the car door and grabbed my torch. I flicked the beam on and off about half a dozen times, and to our amazement the craft made a sweeping U-turn in the air, gliding noiselessly back towards us, dropping its height to about seventy-five feet above the ground, and halting about fifty feet away from us.

It seemed to hang in the air. The most noticeable feature at this close range was an elliptical beam of amber light, about fifteen feet long and a foot wide at the widest part, tapering off at each end, which was coming from a window on the front of the craft. I was so close that I could see the ripple-effect opaque material of the window, similar to the obscured glass used for bathrooms. As I watched, mesmerised, the colour of the beam of light changed from amber to bright white and then back to amber, repeating the sequence several times. Then the craft slowly tilted, turned, and this time shot away into the distance at great speed, the only sound being the whoosh of the air that was displaced. I had a strong feeling that it had been answering my torch signals, although I also wondered whether it had been trying to frighten us away.

It was only when it had disappeared that I discovered it had alarmed my companions: they had both backed away and were fifty metres down the road. But although they were warier than I was, they had both witnessed everything that had happened. (Although I cannot name them, they were both off-duty police officers who had come with me out of curiosity; experienced investigators who trusted the evidence of their own eyes.) They, too, felt the lights had been an answer to my signals. Somehow, and I cannot explain how, I felt that 'it' had been reading my mind, and had returned to make contact because I was questioning it.

From that day on, my encounters with the strange flying objects increased. One night, soon after the torch contact, I was driving alone from my home in Grassington to Skipton when I became aware of a UFO travelling parallel to me, about fifteen metres away across the fields. It was keeping pace with me, and was only about five metres off the ground. It was disc-shaped, and so close to me that I could see its structure: it appeared to have seams, like welding seams, splitting it into panels. I could see no windows, but there were three or four lights of different colours. It was so close, and I was so comfortable with its presence, that I was waving to it. There was no obvious reply, but I knew that it had deliberately sought me out. There have been many occasions, both before and after this, when I saw alien craft when I was alone: by and large, I do not record and log events that have happened to me without any other witnesses being present, but this one was significant because it was the first of many such.

Up to this point Pauline had remained quite sceptical. She always said that she knew I would not lie; therefore she accepted that I did see flying objects. However, she felt that I was possibly misinterpreting them, that they were – as I had originally thought – secret military aircraft, and that I had stumbled on a section of airspace being used for experimental aeronautics. She regarded my sky-watching as a harmless hobby, but it was not one she shared any interest in.

All that changed on the night of 7 November 1983, almost five years after my first sighting. It was 7.55 p.m., and we were driving along the road which runs between Bolton Abbey and Addingham, a quiet country lane that we are both very familiar with. The road is narrow and has plenty of bends, so I was concentrating on my driving. Pauline suddenly said:

'My God, have you seen that?'

As I turned my head to the right, in the direction she was looking, I saw a large shape above us, festooned with hundreds of tiny red lights which pulsed on and off simultaneously. It swept towards us, passing close over the roof of the car, and then went behind the trees to our left. It was about four times the size of the car, and Pauline described it later as 'shaped like a child's spinning top'.

She was stunned, but for me it was nothing new, and I carried on driving, carefully negotiating the winding road. Then it reappeared, sweeping directly towards the windscreen of the car. It was not travelling as fast this time. I pulled over as quickly as I could, and grabbed my camera. I had, by this time, taken to carrying a camera and binoculars in the car at all times, and previous experience had taught me that I had to move fast. While Pauline tracked the craft through the binoculars, I clicked off a few frames of film of it receding into the distance. I had no idea, until I had the film developed, whether or not I had managed to catch it: luckily, the photographs clearly showed something, a strange image which cannot be readily identified.

I later sent the negatives to Ground Saucer Watch, an important and highly reputable UFO research organisation based in Arizona. GSW has earned the respect of serious investigators all over the world for two main reasons, the first being that they challenged, in law, the CIA for failing to release documents to the public under the Freedom of Information Act, thereby covering up a great deal of US government involvement in UFO activity. The second reason is that GSW pioneered the analysis of photographs by using computer-imaging enhancement, which eliminates many hoaxers and fraudsters trying to pass off doctored photographs as genuine records of UFOs – usually in the hope of selling them to newspapers or magazines. By a process known as 'edge enhancement' the computer can detect the thinnest of threads supporting a model.

GSW needed all the details: the type of camera, type of film, state of natural light (the sun had set at 4 p.m. that wintry day) and whether or not there were any artificial lights in the area (there was a solitary farmhouse, and a very faint glow from the town of Ilkley, which was behind a hill, about three miles away). Even though I knew, from its speed, altitude, shape and lights, that the object was not a plane or helicopter, I checked all local airports, RAF bases and a Leeds helicopter service: none of them had any air traffic in the area at the time.

GSW reported back to me that my negatives showed 'no evidence of hoax or airbrushing. We conclude the possibility of hoax in this case is nil.' The letter went on to state that my photographs were one of the few genuine sets of UFO pictures ever received from the UK: 'To date the Ground Saucer Watch computer has analysed 1100 purported UFO photographs. Of these 45 remain unknown. The photographs you submitted represent one of the few cases in the United Kingdom which fall into the unknown category.'

Despite the photographs showing little that is recognisable to the naked eye, the analysis was able to prove that the object was 'near spherical' in shape, about thirty feet in diameter, and airborne about three-quarters of a mile from my position as the photographer. It appeared to have a vapour trail, although this, somewhat anomalously, seemed to be at the side rather than behind it as it travelled. GSW cross-referenced the vapour images with hundreds of types of vapour, but failed to identify it.

The conclusion of the report was that 'This series of photographs have been analysed by GSW and represent Britain's first confirmed unidentified flying object photographs'.

It did not require this report to change Pauline's attitude. After the encounter she totally believed and supported me in my research work – although as I have become more and more involved in international cover-ups, she has often tried to persuade me to retire, not because she does not value my work, but simply because she fears for my safety. She also became very relaxed about the frequency of the sightings. It seemed that everywhere I went, strange lights would appear in the sky, day or night. If Pauline stepped outside into the garden she would often call back to me:

'Tony, your friends are here.'

I, for my part, continued to signal to the flying craft, by flashing lights at them, and they continued to respond. But I soon found there was no need to use my high-powered torch: a much more subtle telepathic communication began to develop. If I thought about them, they would appear. But it would be presumptuous to assume I was summoning them: it is more likely that they were summoning me, by planting the thought telepathically in my brain. Again, it's important to state here that I was not frightened: I felt that their interest was benign. The fact that they were extra-terrestrial in origin did not seem to me to be a cause for alarm. I understand that people are afraid of the unknown, but I have seen enough of the desperate and unpleasant side of human life to know that man can inflict terrible harm on his fellow men, and it has never seemed to me that anything from outside this earth could be worse than the damage we do to ourselves.

News of my increasing interest in the subject spread by word of mouth among colleagues, neighbours, friends and family, and a remarkable number of my acquaintances began telling me stories of their own encounters, things that they had instinctively kept quiet about for fear of being ridiculed. As word travelled, I found myself being contacted by members of the public with their own puzzling accounts of strange lights and objects in the sky. The more I heard, the more convinced I became that I was involved in a concerted attempt by extra-terrestrials to communicate with the human race. I also realised that if I was able to pick up so much evidence, it was highly unlikely that the authorities were ignorant of what was going on.

For those first three or four years after my initial encounter I researched the subject in my own individual way, starting to log in my diary some of the strange objects I had seen, and taking photographs whenever possible. I deliberately did not go out and buy lots of books on the subject, because I wanted my own experiences to remain uncontaminated, however subliminally, by other people's reports. It is a principle I have stuck to even to this day, although obviously I have to keep abreast of research being done across the world, and I deal with the experiences of others on a day-to-day basis; nonetheless, I keep a very clear distinction between what I have had reported to me, and what I have experienced myself.

But after four years in which I gradually came to realise that investigating this phenomenon was my vocation, I was invited to join the Yorkshire UFO Society, as their Director of Investigations. There were other local societies across the country where individuals interested in the subject met to have discussions, hear talks and compare notes, but the Yorkshire society was particularly thriving, mainly because the sparsely populated areas of high ground in the county have, as I have shown, been such fruitful grounds for alien encounters.

Because of my police background and my natural determination to make sense of what was happening, I was the ideal person for the society to appoint as their head of investigations. When I started attending meetings, one Sunday a month in a hall in Leeds, there were about twenty others there. Before very long the numbers had swollen until every month there were more than 100 turning up. We were drawing support from all over the north and Midlands, with people travelling over a hundred miles to be at the meetings.

Eventually, it was decided to make it a national, and then an international, group, with members all over the country and overseas. I came up with the name Quest, because that seemed to sum up what we were all on: a quest to find the truth. Today, Quest International is a flourishing organisation which publishes *UFO* magazine six times a year, and holds major conferences, attracting some of the most famous names in UFO research from all over the world.

I served as Director of Investigations from the founding of Quest until spring 1998, when I left to spend more time on my own research and writing. Ten years before that, in 1988, I retired from the police. I had enjoyed my years as a country copper, but gradually my interest in UFOs had taken over my life, and I wanted to dedicate more time to it.

As my experience has grown, I have established an international name for myself as Britain's leading authority, particularly in the subjects of alien abductions, government cover-ups, and the spate of bizarre and mysterious animal deaths and mutilations which have swept the USA and Europe, including Britain, and which I (and other experts) believe are extra-terrestrial-related.

In my office at home in Grassington I have files bulging with hundreds of cases that I have been responsible for investigating. I set up the UFO Hotline, a telephone number which members of the public could ring to report strange sightings: it brought in more than 1,000 calls each year, with great fluctuations in the flow: I have received as many as 300 in one week. Most of these sightings could be explained by weather phenomena, lasers, balloons, or aircraft lights, and many others simply did not provide enough information to merit an investigation: often the reports came in two or three days after the witness had seen the strange event, too late for other evidence to be collected. But there were a substantial number – about five per cent – which I delegated one of my team of volunteer investigators to look into. If they reported back that there was something inexplicable, I would take over the investigation myself, and I now have several hundred cases where, with more than one witness and often with photographs, there is evidence of strange craft patrolling the skies.

Even though I now no longer run the UFO Hotline, my name is so well known that I receive a constant stream of calls about strange sightings, possible abductions, and animal mutilations. I continue to investigate them, alongside the work I am doing to reveal the scale of alien interest in, and interference with, our planet. Although I was well aware that governments all over the world are united in a massive cover-up, my first real brush with the danger and intrigue that surrounds UFO investigation came with a case which I believe, one day, will be classified as important and significant as the famous Roswell Incident: the Kalahari Conspiracy.

CHAPTER TWO

THE KALAHARI CONSPIRACY

There was nothing special about the envelope that landed on my doormat one morning in July 1989. The postmark was South African, but that did not attract my attention: letters regularly arrived from all over the world. At the time, my home address was published as the contact address for Quest International, so the postman was used to delivering a large and varied assortment of mail.

It is hard to remember what made me open the South African letter first: perhaps I felt drawn to it in some way. It was a short letter, typed, and unsigned. The writer claimed that a South African Air Force fighter plane had shot down a UFO over the central Kalahari Desert. He gave a date for the incident: 7 May 1989, just a few weeks earlier. He claimed that the UFO was recovered undamaged, together with two of its occupants, who apparently survived. The extra-terrestrials and the craft had been taken to a South African Air Force base, and then, within days, a team of experts from the Wright Patterson Air Force Base in America arrived and took the UFO and its occupants back with them to the United States, amid very tight security.

The writer explained his anonymity, saying he feared the letter would be intercepted. He concluded by promising to send some government briefing notes on the incident. I was intrigued. I received lots of mail about UFO sightings, and I'm in correspondence with many other UFO investigators across the world.

But this letter was unusual, in that it was dealing with an incident about which, at this stage, I had heard no whisper. It was also dealing with the recovery of extra-terrestrials: this is the Rolls-Royce of proof, the Holy Grail that all UFO investigators are pursuing. To be able to show the world the real, concrete, analysable evidence of alien contact with earth would be to demonstrate to all the sceptics and unbelievers that we, who know about it and have been talking about it for years, are not an ill-assorted collection of nutcases, but a privileged and resourceful band of prophets. It would also galvanise world governments into openly admitting what they have been covering up and concealing from ordinary people for many years.

Despite my obvious interest in the letter, I contained my excitement. Documents were promised: until I had those, until there was something more reliable than an anonymous letter, I would withhold judgement. I showed the letter to a colleague of mine, Armen Victorian. Armen is one of the many interesting people I have met since I took up UFO research. He is Armenian by birth, but came to England in 1987, before which he held highly sensitive positions in security for both the British and American governments. Armen and I work well together: we have the same attitude towards research, and his contacts complement mine. He is a man of wide-ranging interests – one of his obsessions is with cultivating orchids. More importantly to me, he is an expert on international intelligence and military issues, having crusaded for years to bring into the open the secret weapons being developed by Western powers. He has amassed a large collection of intelligence documents, mostly from the US and Britain. As I had previously had no dealings with the South Africans, I enlisted his help and support. He was as intrigued as I was.

Two weeks later a package arrived, again with a South African postmark. I opened it with anticipation. It contained another letter, and five pages of what the writer claimed was a South African Air Force briefing document. This time, our correspondent revealed his name: James van Greunen. We were given an address in South Africa where we could contact him.

We were instantly suspicious of the authenticity of the photocopied document. It contained some surprising spelling and grammar mistakes: 'eminated', 'retreival', 'aggresive', 'canon', 'scaley', 'was' used instead of 'were'. Nevertheless these, we felt, could be excused, as the document was probably hastily produced, and for security reasons it was unlikely to have been typed by a secretary. There was also a curious mixture of metric and imperial measurements, sometimes using metres and sometimes yards. What was even more alarming was that the crest at the top of each page, the symbol of the South African Air Force, was not as crisp as the typed words, suggesting that it may have been a photocopy of a photocopy.

The contents of the document were mind-blowing, confirming the information van Greunen had précised in his original anonymous letter. With material as sensational as this we were naturally on our guard against forgery, and both Armen and I were initially prepared to dismiss the whole thing as a hoax and an elaborate fake.

Each page of the document was headed with the SAAF symbol, an eagle with wings outspread. The reproduction was so poor it was barely possible to make out the motto beneath the eagle's talons. All five pages were headed: 'CLASSIFIED TOP SECRET – DO NOT DIVULGE'. The first page had the heading 'DEPARTMENT OF SPECIAL INVESTIGATIONS AND RESEARCH (DSIR)' with 'DEPARTMENT OF AIR FORCE INTELLIGENCE (DAFI)' beneath it. It gave the date, 7 May 1989, and stated that its subject was 'Unidentified Flying Object'. It listed a code name, Silver Diamond, a file number, and a destination for the document of Valhalla Air Base, Pretoria, and assigned it a Red/Top Secret rating. It then listed the contents of the next four pages, including craft specifications and 'humanoid specifications'. The page concluded with the words 'DEFENCE COMPUTER PASS CODE – PROCEED WITH CAUTION'.

Page two gave the details of the incident, and I quote it here in full, complete with errors:

At 13H45 GMT on 7 May 1989 the naval frigate SA Tafalberg radioed Cape Town naval headquarters to report an unidentified flying object that appeared on radar scopes, heading towards the African continent in a north westerly direction at a calculated speed of 5746 nautical miles per hour. Naval headquarters acknowledged and connfirmed that the object was also tracked by air-borne radar, military ground radar stations and D.F. Malan international airport at Cape Town.

The object entered South African airspace at 13H52 GMT. Radio contact was attempted with object, but all communication to object proved futile. Valhalla air force base was notified and two armed Mirage FIIG fighters were scrambled. the object suddenly changed course at great speed which would be impossible for military aircraft to duplicate.

At 13H59 GMT squadron leader Goosen reported that they had radar and visual confirmation of the object. The order was given to arm and fire the experimental aircraft mounted thor 2 laser canon at object. This was done.

Squadron leader Goosen reported that several blinding flashes eminated from the object. The object started wavering whilst still heading in a northerly direction. At 14H02 it was reported that the object was decreasing altitude at a rate of 3000 feet per minute. Then at greater speed it dived at an angle of 25 degrees and impacted in desert terrain 80km north of South African border with Botswana, identified as the Central Kalahari Desert. Squadron leader Goosen was instructed to circle the area until retreival of the object was complete. A team of airforce intelligence officers, together with medical and technical staff were promptly taken to area of impact for investigation and retreival.

The findings were as follows:

1. A crater of 150 metres in diameter and 12 metres in depth.
2. A silver coloured disc shaped object 45 degrees embedded in side of crater.
3. Around object sand and rocks were fused together by intense heat.
4. An intense magnetic and radioactive environment around object resulted in eletronic failure in air force equipment.

5. It was suggested by team leader that object be moved to a classified air force base for further investigation and this was done.

The terrain of impact was filled with sand and rubble to disguise all evidence of this event having ever taken place.

The third page of the document was headed 'CRAFT SPECIFI-CATIONS', and included the following list:

TYPE OF CRAFT: Unknown – suspected extraterrestrial.
ORIGIN: Unknown – suspected extraterrestrial.
IDENTIFIABLE MARKINGS: None – curious insignia forged into metal on side of craft.
DIMENSIONS: Length – 20 yards approximately.
                 Height – 9.5 yards approximately.
                 Weight – 50,000 kilograms estimated.
MATERIAL OF CONSTRUCTION: Unknown – pending further laboratory results.
Outer surface of object flawless polished, smooth silver colour.
No visible seams noted inside or on outer surface of craft.
Perimeter showed 12 unevenly spaced, flush with outer surface oval shaped portholes.
SOURCE OF PROPULSION: Unknown – pending laboratory results.

NOTES:
a) A hydraulic type landing gear was fully deployed suggesting that electronic malfunction caused object to crash. This may have been due also to Thor laser canon being fired at craft.
b) While the investigating team observed the craft at classified AFC, a loud sound was heard. It was then noted that a hatch or entrance on lower side of craft had opened slightly. This opening was later prized open with heavy mechanical gear.

These notes were continued on the fourth page of the document:

c) Two humanoid entities clothed in tight fitting grey suits emerged and was promptly taken to make shift medical centre, level 6 of classified AFB.
d) Various objects inside craft were taken for analysis and we are still pending results of these findings.
e) The craft has been placed in a sterile environment.

MEDICAL REPORT ON HUMANOID ENTITIES
ORIGIN: Unknown – suspect extraterrestrial.
HEIGHT: 4 – 4.5 ft.
COMPLEXION: Greyish-blue – skin texture smooth, extremely resilient.
HAIR: Totally devoid of any bodily hair.
HEAD: Oversize in relation to human proportions. Raised cranium area with dark blue markings extended around head.
FACE: Prominent cheek bones.
EYES: Large and slanted upwards towards side of face. No pupils seen.
NOSE: Small consisting of two nostrils.
MOUTH: Small slit devoid of lips.
JAW: Wide in relation to human proportions.
EARS: None observed.
NECK: Very thin in relation to human proportions.
BODY: ARMS: Long and thin reaching just above knees.
HANDS: Consisting of 3 digits, webbed, claw like nails.
TORSO: Chest and abdomen covered in scaley ribbed skin.
HIPS: Small, narrow.
LEGS: Short and thin.
GENITALS: No exterior sexual organs.
FEET: Consisting of 3 toes, no nails and webbed.

NOTES
Due to aggresive nature of the humanoids, no samples of

blood or tissue could be taken. When offered various foods, they refused to eat.

Method of communication is not known and suspect telepathic.

Humanoids are kept in detention at classified AFB awaiting further results of investigations.

One way passage has been requested for both humanoids to Wright Patterson Air Force Base, USA for more advanced investigation and research.

The final page of the document was headed 'CONCLUSION'. It read:

A) No conclusion has been reached as yet. Awaiting results of investigations.
B) The object and humanoids will be moved to Wright Patterson AFB for more advanced investigation and research.
C) Date of passage – 23 June 1989.

NOTES:
Conclusion remains open ended.

This file contains initial findings of preliminary report and further details are expected after completion of investigation in South Africa and Wright Patterson AFB/USA.

END OF PRELIMINARY BRIEFING NOTES: PAGE 1–5.

Despite our grave misgivings about the provenance of the document, we decided to make contact with van Greunen. There was a wealth of detail provided, and we felt it merited several checks to see if any of it could be corroborated. After all, the fact that the document might not be authentic did not mean the subject matter was not worth investigating. Armen and I agreed that we would not waste a great deal of our time on it, but that we would make some initial enquiries, and only pursue the affair if we could find anything else, apart from this suspicious document, to substantiate the UFO story.

When we challenged James van Greunen by telephone, he insisted the document was genuine.

We contacted a serving South African Air Force intelligence officer with a high security clearance, whose name and details were given to us by van Greunen, but whom we checked out ourselves. To our astonishment he confirmed that a UFO had been brought down, and claimed to have four ten-inch-by-eight-inch photographs of the UFO and its occupants. He also told us that a ninety-page telex had been sent to the South African government from Wright Patterson Base, giving instructions on the handling and recovery of the UFO and the detention and treatment of the occupants.

The involvement of Wright Patterson Base in Ohio came as no surprise to us: Wright Patterson is where the debris collected at the scene of the famous Roswell UFO crash was taken. The Roswell Incident has been widely written about elsewhere, and it remains the most intensively researched UFO encounter ever.

It happened in July 1947, when a thunderstorm was raging over the scrubby desert near Corona, New Mexico. William 'Mack' Brazel, manager of a very large ranch, heard a loud crack in the middle of the night. It didn't sound like thunder, so the next day he rode out to see whether there had been lightning damage to any part of the ranch, and to check on his sheep.

What he found was a deep gouge in the earth, as if something large had skidded, and scattered over three-quarters of a mile was some odd-looking wreckage.

A neighbour joined Brazel at the site, and they took away with them samples of the debris. It included pieces of a material that looked like wood, some of them covered in strange symbols. But the wood would not burn. Other wreckage was made of a very light but tough material, that refused to be dented or cut.

Four days after his discovery Brazel – whose ranch was not linked to the outside world by phone – took the debris with him when he went into the nearest town, Roswell, and gave it to the sheriff.

For a couple of weeks before the crash, locals had been reporting seeing 'flying discs' zigzagging across the New Mexico sky, so the sheriff notified the Roswell Army Air Base.

Major Jesse Marcel, a staff intelligence officer, was sent to investigate the site, and filled the boot and back seat of his Buick with debris.

At the base, a press announcement was put out by Lieutenant Walter Haut, the public information officer:

> The many rumours regarding the flying disc became a reality yesterday when the intelligence office of the 509th Bomb Group of the Eighth Air Force, Roswell Army Air Field, was fortunate enough to gain possession of a disc through the co-operation of one of the local ranchers and the Sheriff's office.
>
> The flying object landed on a ranch near Roswell some-time last week.

The press release added that the debris had been sent to 'higher headquarters'.

As soon as the announcement was out, it was retracted. The crash site was sealed off and Brazel was held under house arrest for a week. He was told not to talk about what he had seen.

To calm press speculation – and there were calls coming in from all over the world – an official statement was put out that the wreckage was a weather balloon, and that it had been shipped to Eighth Air Force headquarters at Fort Worth in Texas, where it was paraded for photographers.

By this time, it certainly looked like the wreckage of a weather balloon.

The cover-up worked, and everything went quiet until thirty-one years later, when Marcel, on retirement from the USAF, spoke out. He was convinced, he told investigators, that the debris paraded at Fort Worth was not the debris he had retrieved.

When Marcel's story came out, it started an avalanche of speculation and information about the Roswell crash, and about the possibility that at around the same time, the USAF recovered one or more intact UFOs from other sites in New Mexico, containing the bodies of their alien crew. One hundred and fifty miles from Roswell, engineer Grady Barnett, described by everyone who knew him as a reliable witness, reported the discovery of a complete but damaged UFO, containing the dead bodies of its crew.

His description tallies almost exactly with that given in the document supplied to us by van Greunen: 'They were like humans but were not humans. The heads were round, the eyes were small and they had no hair. The eyes were oddly spaced. They were quite small by our standards, and their heads were larger in proportion to their bodies than ours. Their clothing seemed to be one piece and grey in colour.'

Some witnesses claim that at least one alien was recovered alive. There were reports from a nurse who saw several tiny bodies; a pilot flew some very small crates which he was told contained alien bodies to Wright Patterson Air Base; and a local undertaker claims he was asked for several of his smallest size coffins.

In 1994 the USAF admitted there had been a cover-up – but their version is that all they were covering up was a top-secret project to put acoustic sensors up on balloons to detect Soviet atomic weapons.

Although the Roswell Incident happened a long time ago, and many of the primary witnesses are dead, the level of scrutiny and the quality of the research that has been carried out into it means that I, and most other serious investigators, am convinced it was a spectacular UFO find, and it adds to the huge amount of evidence which points to governments across the world being united in keeping the general public in the dark.

Although I have never done any first-hand work on the case myself, I know personally many of the researchers who have devoted years of their life to it, and I have enormous respect for them.

Since then, the Wright Patterson Air Base has figured in other reports of UFOs and alien remains. The following year, 1948, there was another UFO crash in New Mexico, this time in the desert near Aztec, and again there are reliable reports of the bodies of aliens being flown by helicopter to Wright Patterson. Five years later, in 1953, more bodies were recovered after a crash in Arizona and, packed in ice, were transported to Wright Patterson.

Over the years, individuals who worked at the base have come forward, sometimes on their death beds, to talk about what they have seen: bodies stored deep-frozen, alien craft hidden in sealed hangars. The quality of these sources ranges from ordinary technicians who stumbled on things while going about their legitimate work, to senior ranks and scientists who were involved in the highly classified research. In 1954 President Eisenhower visited the base and was shown the bodies: his official timetable for that day shows a slot of several hours when his staff said he was having 'dental treatment', but no dentist has been found to corroborate this story. The comedian Jackie Gleason, who dedicated a lot of time and money to UFO research, and was a good friend of Eisenhower's, told his wife before he died that he, too, had been shown some of the research work being done at the base, and he confirmed that his friend the President had seen the bodies.

So to see Wright Patterson named in the van Greunen document was no surprise, but it did nothing to add to the authenticity of the paper: those of us who have spent any time studying this subject believe that Wright Patterson is the home of an emergency intervention team, a group of experts who are on constant alert to fly anywhere in the world to study alien contact, and to appropriate any hard evidence. Because the Americans have dominated this field for so long, and because they have the resources, most governments are happy to hand such a controversial problem over to them – although, as we will see later in this book, the British government has established a similar emergency intervention team.

Now that we had confirmation from the South African Air Force intelligence officer, we knew that we were on to something. Van Greunen may well have faked the document – we were still highly suspicious of him – but nonetheless we knew that he had based his forgery on a real incident. The intelligence officer also confirmed the code name that had been given to us: Silver Diamond. He told us he would trade off further information: he wanted material about a British development code-named TR-47 in exchange for more details about the UFO crash. TR-47 meant nothing to either me or Armen: we would later find out that it referred to the latest British Challenger tank, which was undergoing secret tests at the time on a newly developed armour plating. Having discovered the meaning of the code name, we duly notified the British security forces of the South African interest.

Immediately, we had to persuade the intelligence officer to give us more information without a trade-off. Within a few days we received more documents about the Kalahari crash from him, and these contained the names of the military officers, medical staff and scientists, from both the USA and South Africa, who took part in the retrieval and study of the UFO and the aliens.

At the same time, we had made contact with someone Armen knew, who works in an American intelligence records office. He had supplied useful information in the past: like so many of us, he shares the belief that too much important and world-threatening material is being kept secret by the Americans, and he is prepared to risk his career – if not his life – by helping to uncover it. His name is one that I will never divulge, as I know he would be in desperate trouble if the American authorities discovered he was leaking information.

He was able to confirm to us that the Kalahari crash had happened, and that the Americans had flown back the craft and the aliens. He also gave us a vital new detail: although Silver Diamond was the South African code name for the crash, the Americans had another name, Project Pantry, for the overall mission to recover and analyse the evidence. We were even more convinced that we were on to something big.

When the list of names arrived from South Africa, we had something concrete to work on. Among those named was a civilian scientist listed as working in the office of scientific intelligence at the Wright Patterson base. So we rang him. It seemed the most straightforward way of checking the veracity of the names.

The switchboard operator at Wright Patterson gave us a direct number for him, because, we were told, he worked in a special office. The telephone conversation between Armen and the named scientist was recorded, as were all the other calls we made to check out van Greunen's story, and I have copies of these tapes.

Armen was put on to the scientist so easily that he was taken by surprise: he was expecting to have to bluff his way rather more. He approached the subject directly, without giving his own name, and being duplicitous only in so far as he said he was calling from the US (not on an international line from England). He used the code name Silver Diamond, and the American one, Project Pantry. The scientist sounded nonplussed, and after fishing to establish how much Armen knew, said that he could not help. When we rang him back the following day we were told that he had gone away on assignment for a few weeks.

His manner when confronted with these unexpected questions confirmed to us that we were on the right track. We were even more heartened when a phone call to a military adviser on foreign affairs to the South African military intelligence unit, in which we again presented the information we had about the incident and asked for his confirmation of it, was rewarded with the reply: 'Absolutely.'

The next avenue of enquiry was the pilot who was named in the original document: Squadron Leader Goosen. I was discussing the case with another important contact of mine, who can obtain information from British intelligence sources. He has a background in the service and agreed to make a few phone calls to track down Goosen, posing as an old RAF acquaintance of his. The South African Air Force was happy to give this 'old friend' details of Goosen's whereabouts: interestingly, he was not stationed at Valhalla Air Base, but at a base near Pretoria.

Our next phone call was obviously to Goosen. This time, my contact adopted an American accent – not difficult, as he had lived in America at one time – and pretended to be General Brunel from Wright Patterson, a high-ranking USAF officer whose name had appeared in the documents we had received both from South Africa and from our American source. Again, the short telephone conversation was recorded, and this is a transcript of it:

Caller: Is that Squadron Leader Goosen?
Pilot: Yes.
Caller: This is General Brunel speaking from Wright Patterson, America.

Pilot: Yes, sir.

Caller: Listen, Squadron Leader, I am confused. I have the Silver Diamond file in front of me and it doesn't say how many times you fired at the object.

Pilot: Who did you say was speaking, sir?

Caller: This is General Brunel from Wright Patterson. Surely, Squadron Leader, it's a straightforward question? How many times did you fire at the damn thing?

Pilot: I fired once, sir. Could you hang on a second while I go on to another telephone?

Caller: That won't be necessary, Squadron Leader. You have answered my question.

Since the van Greunen document became public, critics and sceptics have tried to discredit the whole Kalahari incident. One of the minor points they picked on was the use of the rank of squadron leader. In the South African Air Force American rankings are used, and a pilot of squadron leader status would be called a colonel.

All I can say is that in this phone call Goosen himself answers to the title of Squadron Leader, and never tries to correct it. I have also been told that South African pilots like the British ranking system, enjoying the affiliation it gives them with the RAF, whom they rate more highly than the USAF.

Whatever his official rank, Goosen's confirmation of the incident gave us a great fillip. We were hearing from more and more sources that a UFO really was shot down in Kalahari. More telephone detective work followed, with an interesting call to the duty officer-in-charge at NORAD, the North American Aerospace Command. NORAD is the organisation set up to protect the USA from enemy air attack, and it operates a sophisticated detection and tracking system which picks up thousands of objects every day. A small percentage of these, inevitably, are UFOs, and again we know (from ex-employees and others who, out of a sense of duty to mankind, leak information) that NORAD files contain a great deal of information about alien activity.

When we rang them, we used a direct number which Armen

had obtained. Because it was assumed to be an internal call, a NORAD official willingly searched through computer records and confirmed that they had tracked an unidentified object entering the earth's atmosphere and moving towards the African continent on the day of the Kalahari crash. A further call, to the Office of Special Investigation at Wright Patterson Air Force Base, put us in contact with another of the men we were told were present when the UFO was recovered by the Americans. He refused to confirm or deny it.

By this time, 31 July 1989, van Greunen had succumbed to our constant pressure and travelled to England, staying until 16 August. It was fascinating to meet him, finally, face to face. He was young, tall and slim, with dark hair, and an obvious South African accent. He produced several identification cards and other documents, including one with a NASA heading that purported to give him NASA clearance. Another, which included his photograph, was for the Defense Intelligence Agency and recorded him as a lieutenant in the US Air Force, working at the Air Technical Intelligence Center at Wright Patterson Air Force Base. Yet another was a reference from the deputy base commander, confirming that van Greunen had served in the USAF from September 1984 to January 1989, and that he left for personal reasons. Again, like the documents he first sent us, these were almost certainly fakes. None of us who met him – and Graham and Mark Birdsall, the brothers who run Quest International, joined Armen and me in questioning him – was impressed by them. Despite being challenged about these papers, and the document, which we all believed was a forgery, he stubbornly stuck to his guns.

It was an awkward situation: it was thanks to him that we had been alerted to the Kalahari crash in the first place, and we had established that most – if not all – of the details he had given us were true. So we did not wish to make him out as a scoundrel, but it was hard to understand his motivation: if he was privy to top-secret information (and he obviously was, however he had obtained it), why had he jeopardised it by producing crude forgeries?

During his two weeks in England, which he spent mostly at

Armen's home in Nottingham, he produced a South African army uniform, but this was as unimpressive as his documents: at a time of national service in South Africa, almost every young man in the country would have been issued with one. Besides, we had now had time to research van Greunen, and we knew that he was a UFO enthusiast who had joined MUFON when he was only sixteen (MUFON is the Mutual UFO Network, an international organisation dedicated to serious scientific research into UFOs). I was not the first UFO investigator he had written to: he had a track record of corresponding with many experts in the field. But for some reason, which I have never really fathomed, he had chosen me to leak his one big true story to – and had then clouded the issue with lies and forgeries.

When Armen and I challenged him over the parts of his own story that did not add up, and the inconsistencies in the information he had given us, he would sulk and go silent, or claim that he was a pawn in some greater game and was only passing on the information he had been given. He told us that the Americans had recovered crystalline discs from the crashed UFO which were encoded with information about future UFO landing sites, and that they were now monitoring these areas. He suggested that our planet was facing imminent danger, but we have never found any substantiating information about these discs, and we believe it was most likely another flight of van Greunen's imagination.

Dealing with him was exasperating: there was obviously a great deal of truth in the original report he had sent us, because we had found so much corroboration. But he refused, despite prolonged interrogation, to budge from the parts of his story which were transparent lies. It is always possible that he had been part of South African intelligence, a large, amorphous organisation which recruited fairly indiscriminately – but none of us was inclined to believe him and BOSS (Bureau of State Security) did not hand out references.

Yet despite this exasperation we felt when dealing with him, it was clear that he was genuinely frightened of somebody or something. Armen recorded a conversation van Greunen had with a South African intelligence officer, and another with an official at the South African Embassy. Shortly afterwards, the phone rang in Armen's Nottingham home, where van Greunen was staying, and the caller asked for him by name. Again Armen recorded the conversation, which was with a man who introduced himself as a senior member of the South African intelligence service. It was all in Afrikaans, but it was obvious even before we arranged for it to be independently translated that the man was very angry with van Greunen. The subsequent translation revealed a stream of abuse aimed at him, and he was told to return immediately to South Africa.

I also realised that van Greunen was being tailed the whole time he was in Britain. As an ex-policeman trained in surveillance techniques, I know what to look out for, and I spotted one or two telltale signs. I made some enquiries among my contacts, and confirmed that he was, in fact, being watched by men who we are sure were South African operatives. This is heavyweight stuff, not something to be dismissed lightly. So although we knew van Greunen was dubious, we were sure that he was genuinely on to something: if he was a harmless nutcase these boys would not be wasting their time with him.

A few days later Armen received a phone call from the South African intelligence officer who had claimed to have photographs of the UFO crash. We had checked him out, and now knew that he was a very senior official working in the documentation department of the equivalent to the Ministry of Defence. He said he was 'very frightened' because the leaks of information had caused a great deal of trouble: he had been taken in front of his commanding officer and reprimanded. He said the South African authorities were aware of all the people involved in the investigation, by which we understood him to mean us. He felt that van Greunen had let him down by involving him, and said: 'There is absolute hell let loose here at the moment.'

Van Greunen received another call at Armen's home, this time from the South African Embassy. We recorded the conversation, which was littered with implicit threats to van Greunen, who was told he should return to South Africa or he would be in even more trouble.

We decided it was time to confront the embassy, and ask them to provide us with on-the-record information about the Kalahari incident, and about their interest in van Greunen. The first response was that they did not know what we were talking about, but when we offered to provide tapes of the phone calls made from the embassy to van Greunen, as well as that from the senior intelligence officer, they promised to look into the matter.

It was an unsatisfactory answer, a meaningless promise, but at least we had laid our cards on the table. We had another important card which we did not put down: we heard at about this time from one of our American intelligence contacts that the Wright Patterson base had received a fax from the South African Embassy in London dealing with, in part, the Kalahari crash. The fax was, we were told, from a colonel based in London. We have his name. But the South African Embassy was not supposed to have any military officials, and when we checked we found him listed in London as plain 'Mr'. This was hardly a surprise: every country across the world disguises intelligence officers on the staffs of its embassies by giving them routine clerical positions.

I talked about the Kalahari affair in public for the first time at a Quest International conference, held in Yorkshire in September 1989. By then, Armen and I felt we had enough evidence to at least be sure that something serious had happened in the desert, and that wreckage of some description had been taken to Wright Patterson. The reaction to our presentation about the case was mixed: we received a lot of enthusiastic support, but there were others who were so thrown by the palpable unreliability of van Greunen that they dismissed the whole case out of hand, without considering the other evidence.

Less than a month later I was in Frankfurt, at another UFO conference. I had been speaking about the Kalahari incident, and as I finished my lecture I was approached by a small man with white hair and a goatee beard, who introduced himself as Wendelle Stevens. I had never met Wendelle before, but had heard of him: he is a highly respected UFO researcher. He is a former lieutenant-colonel in the US Air Force, a World War II pilot, with good contacts in US intelligence. Although he is now

44

well into his seventies, he is remarkably fit, mentally as well as physically. Wendelle had not been at the conference in Yorkshire and knew nothing about the Kalahari crash, other than that I was listed as a speaker on the subject of a UFO crash in Africa. Crucially, when we spoke in Yorkshire neither Armen nor I mentioned that the South Africans traded the UFO wreckage for nuclear technology.

So when Wendelle introduced himself and told me that his sources in US Naval Intelligence had informed him that the USA had given the South Africans some advanced nuclear technology in exchange for a UFO, he was confirming, from a totally different source, what we had already been told, and adding detail to it. The South Africans were not allowed under international law to possess a nuclear force, so the Americans must have been very determined to get their hands on the UFO and its occupants.

At this time, neither Armen nor I knew where van Greunen was. He had been careering around Europe and Canada, staying with different UFO researchers, running up debts and continuing to claim that he was fleeing from South African intelligence. He owed money to quite a few people. We were fed up with him: although he had alerted us to the Kalahari UFO, his lies and prevarications made him impossible to deal with, and he was bringing discredit to all the genuine information we were receiving.

Although it was easy for those who only had minimal contact with him to dismiss him as a hoaxer, we knew that he had done real harm in the way he had handled the leak. From independent sources we heard that a South African intelligence officer had been forced to flee the country because he was in such trouble for helping van Greunen, who had covered his trail so ineptly it led straight back to this man. Those of us with experience in this kind of work know that the most important thing is never to blow out your sources, especially when doing so endangers them. There are plenty of public-spirited people working in highly sensitive jobs who put more than their careers on the line when they leak information to people like me. They do it because they believe that it is wrong of governments to suppress

45

information about UFOs, and the degree of alien contact with earth.

When I use the information they supply, I always make sure that I have checked it out from several other contacts, and I obfuscate it sufficiently to protect the source. I would rather sit on it and never release it than jeopardise one of my sources – which is why, at various points in this book, those who help me may appear as rather shadowy, ill-defined characters.

But van Greunen shared neither my scruples nor my background in police work. He was at best naive, and at worst totally cavalier about the safety of his sources. The man who had to flee South Africa has not, to this day, been able to return to his native land, and lives with the constant fear that the South African authorities may catch up with him. I know which country he lives in under an assumed name, but would never reveal the information. I can only hope, as he does, that the fall of the South African regime means that he is no longer a wanted man.

I have, in my twelve-inch-thick file on the Kalahari affair, a document that was sent to me by a contact with access to American intelligence records – a US government official who fits into the category of those altruistic people who believe it is their duty to help reveal to the world what is going on. The document says, referring to the South African authorities: 'We agree that the Pantry Project shall remain out of their hands due to the uncomfortable situation we are in, due to the security leaks by a South African Intelligence Officer who is at the moment on the run.'

The South African intelligence officer was not the only one under threat. A British contact of mine warned me that both Armen and I were under surveillance. I was aware that I was being followed at times: a car would tuck in behind mine, especially when I went out in the evening. I would deliberately lead my followers a merry dance across the North Yorkshire moors, using the unlisted roads I know so well, and leaving me in no doubt that I was their quarry. But they never approached me.

I suspected that my phone was tapped, and called in a few

favours with some old electronics experts. Soon after I asked the question, one of them arranged to meet me (after all, it was not possible to talk by phone!), and he confirmed that my calls were being monitored – by the intelligence services, we suspected.

I was also told that French intelligence agents were keeping tabs on Armen and me, and that we should make sure that we did not travel to France for the foreseeable future. Momentarily, I wondered what I had done to offend the French: then I remembered that the European operational headquarters for South African intelligence is based in France. My source told me that there had been a discussion about whether or not I should be 'taken out', but thankfully the consensus had been that if this happened on British soil it would be too much of a political embarrassment. I was also warned not to go to South Africa.

Pauline was understandably alarmed. She'd resigned herself to the fact that the quiet retirement she had planned for us was nothing more than a dream: I was working as hard as I ever had. But she had not anticipated that I would be at risk, yet here I was in a situation that was altogether more frightening than the most violent criminal cases I had been involved in. She was even more unsettled when we flew out together to Munich, where I was again booked to speak at a major international UFO conference, which ran from 22 to 24 June 1990. We were tailed from our home to Manchester Airport, and then a man boarded the same plane as us, and followed us for the whole three days we were there. He was in his late twenties and inauspicious-looking: he was unshaven, slightly scruffy, and wore jeans, a casual shirt and an anorak. I noticed him on the flight out to Germany because he was close to us all the time we were in the airport, and sat in the seat in front of me on the flight. My suspicions were confirmed when I realised that he did not produce a passport at immigration control, just a card. He attended the conference, and was in the same seat in front of us on the return flight. At passport control as we re-entered England he followed us through, and I made a point of glancing at his card: it was some sort of ID card with his photo on. Pauline and I were delayed, because our luggage had gone astray, and the rest of the passengers from our flight had gone:

yet he was sitting close at hand, casually reading a newspaper. His presence was so obvious that I am sure he wanted us to know that he was following us.

So it was against this background of suspicion and fear that I was surprised to see James van Greunen at the Munich conference, as a member of the audience. I had been wanting to speak to him for some time, to finally get to the bottom of the mysterious faked document he had produced at the very beginning of the whole enquiry, but he had been proving very elusive. He had, if you think about it, landed me in a double bind: other ufologists and researchers were scathing about the whole incident, simply because van Greunen was so blatantly unreliable, yet my life was being threatened because he had immersed me in something very serious.

I told him, as soon as I saw him, in a corridor outside the lecture hall, that we needed to talk, and took him with me to a quiet anteroom, away from the rest of the delegates and audience. He came with me without objection: he could see I meant business. He initially tried to palm me off with the old story, that the document was genuine. But I had gone beyond patience, and my temper flared.

'I want the truth, and I want it now!' I yelled at him, pinning him up against the wall. 'I've had enough of the lies, the deceit, the threats to my life and the danger to others. You've put us in a terrible position, and the least you can do is tell me the truth.'

He was shocked at being spoken to so forcefully. But after a few seconds of panic he visibly relaxed, as if he accepted that the game was up and he could no longer string me along. He nodded, and said he would tell me everything I wanted to know.

Although I sensed he meant it, I kept my hand on his arm, only loosening my grip slightly. I knew there was still a risk he would make a dash for it and although, with my adrenalin pumping as it was, I might well have been able to catch him, he was more than twenty years younger than me.

He told me how, twelve months earlier, he had been shown some classified documents by a friend who was a serving member of the South African Air Force intelligence. Knowing of van Greunen's interest in UFOs, the friend had secretly brought to him the top-secret file on the Kalahari crash. Van Greunen realised instantly that it was sensational stuff, and pleaded to be allowed to copy at least some of the documents. But his friend, with his career on the line, was adamant that the file could not leave his possession and could not be copied – the most he would do was allow van Greunen to pore carefully over each document.

Van Greunen, aware that he was on to something enormous, went home from the meeting and hurriedly wrote down everything he could remember, including dates, times, code name, and even the layout of the documents. He has a photographic memory, being able to recall the pages as if he was still holding them in his hand. And we know, from all our subsequent research, that he got it right: the dates, the code name and every other checkable detail had panned out.

Having forged the document, he then decided to send it to me. I don't know why he chose me. Perhaps he realised that, with his past track record for trying to get his name in the papers, he could not just send it to a journalist – he needed it to come out from someone else, someone like me, recently retired from the police, with an established reputation as a researcher. Perhaps he hoped eventually to make a lot of money from it: in effect, all he made were the small sums he conned out of fellow UFO enthusiasts.

Anyway, whatever his motivation, I felt at last I had the truth. I made him swear on the life of his family that he was finally being honest. I released him and went back to the conference auditorium. I have never seen James van Greunen since, although I have heard that he is still in Germany.

Before I spoke to the conference, the German organisers pointed out to the audience that there were two officials from the German South African Embassy among those who were there to hear me speak, and welcomed them to the conference. The two men concerned looked uncomfortable, but remained in their seats while I talked, taking notes. They left the conference as soon as I finished speaking: their interest confirming to me once again that van Greunen's forgery had, indeed, been based on real and very important information.

The South Africans and Americans were not the only ones showing an interest in me. It was at another German conference in Frankfurt that Pauline and I were introduced to Marina Popavitch, one of Russia's first women astronauts, and twice decorated with the greatest Soviet award, Hero of the Soviet Union, who was currently training other astronauts. She was giving a lecture and invited us to join her for a drink in her suite. I accepted, but explained that we needed to shower and change, and would see her later. While we were getting ready a note was pushed under our bedroom door, from an ex-CIA operative I know, who is also a UFO researcher. He was warning me to be careful, pointing out that any person of Popavitch's standing was bound to be a member of the KGB.

Pauline and I duly presented ourselves at her suite. It was luxurious, filled with bouquets of flowers still in their cellophane wrapping, and the hospitality was equally lavish, with champagne flowing freely. Four Russian men, the only others present, were drinking neat vodka, and there appeared to be no shortage of supplies. Popavitch, a short, plump woman in her forties, was very attentive to us, and I noticed that, although the champagne bottles were appearing at our elbows all the time, she hardly touched her own glass. But she did not ask any overt questions about my work: I would have been surprised had she been crass enough to do that. She may, however, have been assessing me, hoping that I would, in drink, let slip something of interest. Needless to say I, too, kept my alcohol consumption to a minimum.

Although Armen and I did most of the research into the Kalahari case, it was heartening to get support and corroboration from other, independent researchers. One such was Harry Harris, a Manchester solicitor, who heard from a source of his in August 1989 – before we had published anything or spoken about the crash retrieval – that there had been a UFO brought down in the Kalahari, which had subsequently been transported to the USA.

Later, after hearing Armen and me talk at the Yorkshire conference, Harry, who is an experienced and able researcher, sent a fax to Wright Patterson Air Base requesting information about the Kalahari incident. Astonishingly, he received a prompt reply signed by Ted B. Wadheim, and headed 'HQ Air Force Logistics Command, International Logistics Center, African Division'. It was a strange fax, containing phrases like 'the dark continent' and 'white supremist South African forces'. It claimed that the 'object in question' was not brought down, but crashed because of 'advanced composites fatigue', and that 'no life forms were found at the site'. It concluded with the jokey greeting: 'May the force be with you', which strengthened the impression that it was, perhaps, a hoax.

The following day Harry received another fax, again purporting to come from Ted Wadheim, this time without any strange phraseology, and stating that it was not possible 'to confirm the sighting of last May'. This communication went on to offer a possible explanation: almost exactly a year earlier a fireball or a satellite re-entry had occurred over the Kalahari and had been reported by various witnesses. We were aware of this red herring and would hear it again and again from the sceptics, but we had sufficient information on the UFO crash to be certain that there were two completely separate events, a year apart, over the desert.

What do I make of Harry's two faxes? I suspect the first one came from someone in the division working on information about the UFO, but was not official – someone was letting us know we were on the right track. It may even have been Ted Wadheim himself, although I doubt if he would have used his own name. The second fax was probably a statement of the official position, the one that would find its way into the files. When we checked out the numbers given on the fax we found that there is a South African division at Wright Patterson, a hitherto unknown nugget of information. We also verified the existence of Ted Wadheim.

A colleague from Quest also contributed another vital element to the research. The name of a South African warship, the *Tafelberg*, had been mentioned in van Greunen's document. My colleague spent many hours following this lead, initially being disappointed to find there was no warship of that name, but ultimately discovering the SA *Tafelberg* listed as a fleet replenishment vessel in a record of international merchant vessels. The ship does have sophisticated technology, and may well have been able to track and report a UFO.

When he tackled the South African Embassy directly, as a journalist, about a UFO crash in the Kalahari, he was initially greeted with derision. But when he mentioned the name of James van Greunen the embassy officials began to take him seriously.

'I have Mr van Greunen's file on my desk in front of me,' said the same official who only seconds before had been laughing about the possibility of a UFO. 'It appears he has been very troublesome.' He claimed that van Greunen owed money to several people at the embassy. The official then tried to find out if we knew van Greunen's whereabouts, and ended with a veiled warning.

Whilst the last thing I wanted was for anyone else to find themselves in the same uncomfortable position that Armen and I occupied, with real threats to our well-being, at the same time it was gratifying to have others experience the degree of paranoia that van Greunen's name triggered, and to have some important elements of our research confirmed independently.

Other researchers who took the case seriously included Dr J.J. Hurtak, an American academic and scientific director of an organisation called Scientific Adventure Inc. (whose motto is 'Using scientific methods to solve mankind's problems'), and Baron von Buttlar. They both travelled to the Kalahari, and Baron von Buttlar offered to pay for me to go with him. I was warned by my South African intelligence contact that it would be very foolish of me to set foot on South African soil, so I reluctantly had to turn the offer down. Jim Hurtak, on his return, contacted me to say that he had been able to confirm the UFO crash from military sources. He gave me no details because he, like me, was anxious to protect his informants.

But the greatest breakthrough came towards the end of 1989, when a close colleague of mine attended a diplomatic function in London. This was entirely unrelated to his UFO research, but by chance he found himself sharing a lunch table with a high-ranking Botswanan politician, Dithoko Seiso, Minister for the

Environment. The subject of UFOs came up for discussion, and my friend mentioned the Kalahari incident.

The general consensus round the table was disbelief, and my friend was ribbed for his credulity. When he insisted that there was evidence, Mr Seiso said that although he did not believe it, he would make some enquiries. It was some months before my friend encountered the Botswanan again, at another diplomatic function. This time, Mr Seiso sought him out and told him, in front of witnesses: 'I checked on what you said. This thing did happen. And what beats me is how you could possibly find out about this thing before I found out about it.' As the UFO came down on Botswanan territory, close to the border with South Africa, he would have expected to have been informed.

After I spoke publicly about the Kalahari affair, at the Yorkshire conference and later in Germany, there followed a wave of international publicity. As usual, most of it was fanciful and way off beam. I saw myself described in print in an American magazine as an MI5 officer, whereas Armen was assigned to the KGB. There were stories of American Air Force personnel being discovered inside the craft with the aliens; another report claimed a human body, in suspended animation, was found inside. There was even a report that the craft had the General Electric Company insignia on its side, proving that it was manufactured in America.

Leafing through the cuttings, Armen and I had to laugh. Our major investigation was being so discredited by this kind of reporting that, in the end, we either saw the funny side of it or we would have become disillusioned and despairing. And besides, we could see some good in it: while the whole world, including many distinguished ufologists, was treating it as a joke, we could quietly go about our investigation without too much hindrance.

If we were not being taken seriously by some other researchers, the authorities were certainly not underestimating the importance of our discoveries. I was warned by several of my good friends, men with influential and highly placed contacts in the American intelligence services, to keep a low profile. Although I knew these warnings were genuine, they were remote and I did not feel intimidated by them. But there was nothing remote about an encounter I had when Pauline and I flew to Tucson, Arizona, for the World UFO Conference in May 1991. I had delivered a lecture that day about the Kalahari incident. In the evening, Pauline and I were sitting in the lounge of the Holiday Inn, where most of the conference delegates were staying, discussing the day's events with four old friends, all of them American. They were all UFO experts, two of them with backgrounds in military service. Our group was approached by two men, who asked if they could join us.

My American friends immediately got up to leave. I could tell by their faces that they knew who these two dark-suited men were, and they had no wish to hang around. I, on the other hand, was intrigued. Perhaps because I am British not American, I refused to feel intimidated by what I guessed were CIA agents. They were both in their thirties, with short hair and a fit, healthy appearance, but they did not look out of place among the other delegates from the conference who were dotted about the room. I wanted to know what they had to say to me. They played a game that I, as a former police officer, am very familiar with. One of them was Mr Nice and the other Mr Nasty. The nice one did all the talking, while the other sat in complete silence, never taking his eyes off me. The nice one told me they were from the US Government, and that they were there to warn me.

'Be extremely careful with what you are doing. We can stop you if we want to. Be very, very careful in future,' he said.

I told them I had been around for a lot of years, that nobody was able to intimidate me, and I was certainly not afraid of them. Like him, I spoke in a reasonable voice, never raising it, and with a smile on my face. He smiled back, and said:

'Make no mistake, we have ways of stopping you.'

I told them that the ways of their organisation were well known all over the world, but that when they issued threats to me they should remember that I was not working in isolation, and that I had powerful people helping me. I said: 'I'm not frightened of you, or of your threats. I know that I am here to do something, and nobody will hurt me until I've done it.'

Accurate artist's impression of the UFO I saw on the North Yorkshire dales in January 1978 – my first encounter with an alien craft. (*Richard Brannan*)

Artist's impression of the alien-type known as a 'Grey', described by abductees under hypnosis. (*Richard Brannan*)

Tracey Jones of Yorkshire: the abductions that both she and her children repeatedly suffered followed them even when they moved to the Middle East.

Carol and Helen Thomas: the mother and daughter from Birmingham who were abducted together on their way to work one morning in 1988.

Bob Rylance, the former soldier who has had a succession of paranormal experiences over the last twenty years.

Hypnotherapist Joyce Dinsdale, who has helped many abductees come to terms with their experiences.

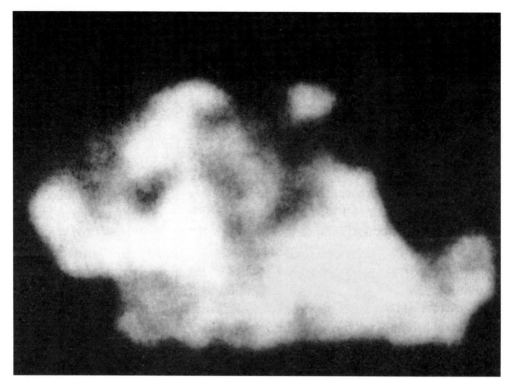

The Addingham UFO photograph I took in 1983 – still recognised by Ground Saucer Watch as 'Britain's first confirmed unidentified flying object photograph'. Above shows the UFO with the vapour trail and three glowing spheres, and below shows the true shape of the UFO after the vapour has been removed.

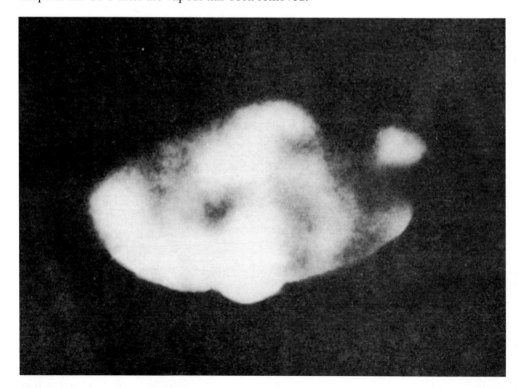

It sounds melodramatic, but again I said it with a smile on my face. If you had been observing from the other side of the room you would have thought we were all old friends. But there was a tremendous tension around the table. Pauline was really scared, but she did not show it. The nasty one never moved a muscle, but kept his eyes locked on me. Not for the first time, I quietly thanked God for my police training: I've been eyeballed by a few heavyweight villains in the past. I recognised the Americans' tactics, and refused to see their air of menace as anything more than a ploy.

Before they left, the nice one changed tack, asking us how we were enjoying our visit to America. Then he wondered whether anyone had shown us around the Tucson area, and when we said we had not yet had time to do any sightseeing, he offered to show me the desert. Perhaps foolhardily, but not wanting to show any crack in my defence, I agreed to meet them the next morning, in the hotel foyer.

After the CIA men left, my American friends were startled to hear that I had agreed to go with them, and tried to dissuade me. Pauline was also alarmed, and the next morning she insisted on coming with me, to their obvious surprise. We were shown to a four-wheel-drive vehicle bristling with aerials. As we were getting in I pretended to have forgotten something, and went back to the hotel, saying over my shoulder, 'We won't be more than an hour, will we, because my colleagues are expecting us.'

When I rejoined them they drove us out of the town into the remote desert, completely clear of any sign of civilisation. Conversation was very limited until they stopped the engine, and again the nice one spoke.

'I want to tell you again, just in case you didn't understand. Things you are telling people are not for public knowledge. We can stop you, wherever you are. Not just in this country.'

Again, although I was inwardly more nervous than the previous evening, I still knew logically that they would not risk harming us after such a public departure from the hotel. I told them once again that I was not frightened. The man who did all the talking shrugged and smiled; this time I think it was a genuine smile. Even Mr Nasty relaxed his shoulders and turned to look at me: I think they respected me for not being intimidated by them.

They drove us back to the hotel, answering Pauline's ingenuous questions about life in the States as if we were visiting cousins. As they dropped us off, Mr Nice got out and said:

'We like you both, you are good people. But please be careful.' This time he sounded as though his warning was genuinely meant, not a threat. Then he asked me, rather bizarrely, if I would like a detailed survey map of Venus and Mars. I said that of course I would.

We did not see them again during the rest of the conference. But to my astonishment, six weeks later, a tubular parcel stamped 'US Government' was delivered by our postman in Grassington. Inside were two close-up satellite maps of Mars and Venus, which I still have. We had never given the CIA men our address, but it was no surprise to find they knew it. Perhaps sending the maps to my home was a way of reminding me that they were keeping tabs on me.

Another reminder came a few weeks later. I was, as usual, upstairs in my office, dealing with calls on the UFO Hotline and a backlog of correspondence. I heard the doorbell, and then Pauline's voice and that of a man with an American accent. Before I had time to go downstairs to investigate, Pauline was showing the visitor up to my office.

He was a clean-shaven, crew-cut young man who announced that he was interested in my work, and had come along to talk to me. I asked him what an American was doing in Yorkshire, and he replied that he was working near Harrogate. I immediately said:

'Menwith Hill?'

He nodded, showing no surprise that I had instantly realised he came from the American secret communications and tracking base about fifteen miles from my home. It is part of the world's biggest listening network, run by the National Security Agency, an American organisation so secretive that UFO researchers reckon that NSA stands for 'Never Say Anything'. Compared to the NSA, the CIA are boy scouts: it is the NSA which ultimately supervises all intelligence gathering in the

USA, and consequently has a vast file on UFO reports, and on the recovery of craft and alien bodies.

We politely danced around each other verbally. I asked him if it was a coincidence that he worked at Menwith and also had an interest in UFOs, or whether he was visiting me professionally. The smile never left his face as he assured me that his interest was purely a hobby. We both knew that was not true. After only a few minutes, he left. Both he and I knew that he was there simply to warn me that they were keeping tabs on me.

I have no doubt about this. I am sometimes followed as I drive around the Yorkshire moors, often on inconsequential family business like shopping or visiting my daughter, who lives fifteen miles away. I never let my pursuers get the better of me, nor am I fazed by their presence. On one level, I regard it as a game. I double back and change my route, not just to cause them problems but to make sure, in my own mind, that they are definitely tailing me. One night Pauline and I left the farm where our daughter lives and emerged on to the road at the bottom of a quarter-of-a-mile farm track. It's a quiet spot, but no sooner had we turned on to the road than a car, parked opposite the track entrance, put its lights on and pulled out behind us. Knowing the road as well as I do, I had fun. I hurtled round a few bends and established a lead of a couple of hundred yards. As we came into a village I know well I took a sharp left-hand bend at speed and then pulled into a lay-by immediately beyond the bend, killing my lights and engine instantly. As the other car, a Jaguar XJS, came round the bend and passed us, I pulled out and tailed him. When we came to a fork at the bottom of a hill he was forced to choose a route, and I promptly took the other one. Across the fields, I could see him turning round and hurtling back to pick up my tail, so I then led him sedately to my own front door. He pulled away from us immediately before I turned into the road where we live. Pauline, in the front passenger seat, was not pleased with me: she believes that by playing games with them, I antagonise them. But how else can I treat the situation?

So I was in no doubt that our revelations about the Kalahari incident had attracted plenty of attention. There was an international conspiracy involved, as so often in major UFO cases, and Armen and I had ruffled a few feathers by getting so close to the truth of the whole affair.

The information we published – mainly obtained from the forged van Greunen document, which, as we have seen, proved to be accurate in most respects – about the speed and position of the craft which crashed in the desert provoked some interesting research, particularly by William Travis, a retired officer with the United States Air Force. From the size of the crater and the angle of impact he calculated the speed of impact as approximately 1,000 m.p.h. (the 'greater speed' referred to in the document), and from this that the UFO was at a suitable height for the Mirage to intercept it.

His research suggested that the fighter pilot would have had to be ready to take off at a moment's notice, but this does not seem unfeasible: after all, South Africa was in a state of emergency; plus we knew that NORAD had tracked the object, and may well have given prior notice to the South Africans that their airspace was about to be invaded. It only takes a Tornado pilot with the RAF six minutes to scramble from stand-by; I'm sure that the South Africans were in a greater state of readiness.

Although the van Greunen document gave us the detail which enabled these calculations to be made, it contained one fundamental error, which caused a few problems. It referred to the 'Thor 2 laser cannon'. For once, van Greunen's photographic memory let him down. However, it did not take long to establish that it was a Maser weapon, not a laser, that was used. Maser stands for Microwave Amplification by Stimulated Emission of Radiation, and has been in development since the fifties. The blinding flashes that Squadron Leader Goosen reported would be consistent with this kind of weapon being used.

I also established, from a retired colonel in the USAF, that these weapons had been developed in the States for use with their F14 Tomcat planes – and that the only other planes in the world with compatible technology (and therefore able to deploy these weapons) were Mirages. What's more, although he did not

58

know which nations had bought them, he told me that two such weapons systems had been secretly sold by the Americans to help fund further research. As France and South Africa were the only two countries flying Mirages, it is logical to assume that they were the two nations to whom the systems were sold.

Although any fresh information I receive about the Kalahari crash has, inevitably, slowed over the years to a tiny trickle, 1997 brought a surprising, and gratifying, breakthrough. I heard, from a contact of mine, about a woman scientist who was working at Groote Schuur Hospital (the hospital made world-famous by surgeon Dr Christiaan Barnard, who pioneered heart transplant surgery there) when the crash in the Kalahari desert happened. According to my friend, this woman, who now lives in Europe, had been present at the hospital when an autopsy was carried out on an alien body recovered from the crash. I was able to contact her by telephone, and after fencing verbally with me for some minutes she eventually admitted that there had been a post-mortem on an alien body, attended by specialists from several different fields. She told me that the most pronounced difference between this life form and our own was that there were no obvious gender or reproductive organs, and no immune system or digestive system. The description she gave of the body was very much in line with the classic 'grey' alien form – small; smooth grey skin; no body hair; a large head with huge, dark, oval-shaped eyes.

She said that all present at the post-mortem were warned to keep quiet about the autopsy, and she was only talking to me because she was no longer living in South Africa – she left, she told me, because she felt the running of the hospital had deteriorated. She said that soon after the autopsy, she had tried to get a printout of the results from the hospital computer but the file had been deleted. I asked if she could put me in touch with others who were present and could corroborate what she was telling me, but she said she dared not risk it. She, like so many others involved in this case, sounded afraid, even though it was more than eight years after the event.

Although what she told me flew in the face of some of the earlier information we had – that all the bodies and hardware retrieved at the crash scene were shipped out to Wright Patterson Air Base – it was a significant confirmation of the essential facts. I can only assume that either the Americans agreed to the South Africans keeping one body, or – probably the most likely explanation – the South Africans simply spirited one away quickly, before the American team arrived.

Slowly, many of the original sceptics about the Kalahari incident have been won over, particularly those who have bothered to do any real research into the crash. Once everyone who looks at the affair accepts that the van Greunen document was a forgery, but also gives it credit for setting us off on this investigation and providing a lot of information which eventually could be corroborated, perhaps the Kalahari affair will rank alongside Roswell and Rendlesham Forest as one of the most significant ever.

Which is as I believe it should be.

But major investigations of incidents like the landing in the Kalahari desert only account for some of my work. Soon after my own first sighting of a UFO, I asked myself the most fundamental question, and one that many investigators shy away from – if extra-terrestrials are visiting earth, who or what are they interested in? The inevitable conclusion has to be that they are studying us, the human race. This answer led me to what is possibly the most important – and certainly most controversial – area of my work: the investigation of human abductions.

CHAPTER THREE

THE STOLEN HOURS

From the moment I accepted that the strange craft I saw so regularly in the sky were extra-terrestrial in origin, I became fascinated by the puzzle of who or what was controlling them. There was no doubt they were being intelligently controlled, and I also knew that there was a telepathic communication between me and them – and by 'them' it was clear that I did not mean the hardware of the craft, but the beings who were piloting them.

What did they want? Buzzing across the skies at night cannot have been all they were interested in. I was convinced that they were more concerned with us, earth's inhabitants, than they were with the physical terrain of our planet. I have seen them down on the ground, and so have other people: although I am exceptional in the number of times I have seen UFOs, I am only one of many thousands of people who have witnessed their presence in the sky, and a smaller, but nonetheless substantial, number of people have also seen strange craft on the ground.

It did not take a great leap, therefore, for me to accept that they are studying the human race, and that as part of this work they have taken individuals into their ships to examine more closely. We now have a word that is in common usage for this phenomenon: abduction. And I am now Britain's leading expert in this field, having spent many hours counselling and questioning people who believe they have been abducted by aliens, checking out their stories and arranging for them to take part in regressive hypnosis sessions. But it is important to say that I did not set out to become an abduction expert: almost before I had fully established myself as an alien investigator, the first case of abduction came my way, and using hypnosis to help establish the facts was, at the time, simply a logical way forward. As with all the other investigative work I have done, one case led inevitably to others. I now have a whole filing cabinet full of abduction stories, many of which I have probed in depth. I have, however, never, ever suggested to anyone that they might be a victim of abduction. I have helped them discover the facts for themselves.

I believe that the abductees who come forward are only the tiniest tip of an extremely large iceberg. There are many, many people who have experienced disturbances in their life and have no idea of the cause. Most will never know. Others will have occasional memory flashbacks which may lead them to explore what happened, and will discover that they are abductees. A small minority will have clear memories of their abduction experiences, and will not need hypnosis to tell them what is going on.

But before I look at the nature of abduction, and the reasons for it, let me explain how I first encountered it. I was a serving police sergeant in 1982 when a young married woman came into the police station to make a complaint about what she believed was a low-flying helicopter which she said had buzzed her car as she was driving home one evening a couple of weeks previously. I knew as I listened to her that what she was describing could not possibly have been a helicopter: no pilot would have been flying so low in the dark. The woman also told me that she had arrived home an hour later than she should have done, although she was not aware of this until her husband pointed out the time to her. She had been visiting her mother, and travelling back by a familiar route, which should have taken her only about one hour. Her husband had been worried when she did not arrive, and then annoyed when she finally got back late: I think she initially came to the police because she wanted us to prove to him that something had happened.

Because by this time I had heard of abduction, and how some people involved experienced chunks of 'missing time', I was intrigued. The cases I had heard about were mainly American, and I had never met anyone who thought they had been abducted, but this young woman appeared to be reporting a classic case.

In her original statement to me she told how she had left her mother's house at about 9.30 p.m., the usual time she set off home after her weekly visit. It was a clear, wintry March evening, the temperature just above freezing, very dark, but the stars were visible. There was little traffic about, and before long she was passing across a lonely, unlit stretch of road which cuts across the top of the moorland, dropping in a straight line about three-quarters of a mile long, before the road bends away to the left. Only one vehicle passed her, travelling in the opposite direction, and she was able to watch its tail lights disappearing into the distance.

Almost immediately, she was aware that the whole of the offside of her car was bathed in a blue light. She turned round, trying to see where the light was coming from, but there was no car behind her. She then noticed in the offside mirror two lights, one red and one blue, about the size of car headlights. They were side by side, and giving off a soft, diffuse light which did not appear to have a beam, but was bright enough to light up the whole side of the car. She got the feeling that there were some smaller lights, but she was not certain.

Her first reaction was that a large lorry had somehow caught up with her and was trying to overtake. The lights, she thought for an instant, were the sort sometimes seen around the top of a lorry's rig. But at the same time she realised that she had seen no sign of a lorry approaching, nor was there any sound of an engine. She suddenly felt very hot. For a few moments the lights went out of view, but she sensed that they were above her. They appeared again on the nearside of the car, at about the height of a streetlamp. Suddenly, a very bright white light beamed downwards on to the road and adjoining field, just including the car inside the edge of the circle of light. She described the beam as cone-shaped, widening from a point at the top to a circle about thirty feet in diameter where it struck the ground. The main body of the light was white, making the grass on the field a vivid green, but at the centre the light was different, showing the grass as brown as if it had been scorched. She told me she could not describe the colour of this central beam, but could only recall the effect it had on the grass.

At this time she became aware of a deep silence, which she could sense despite the sound of her car engine, which appeared to be revving louder and louder. The light kept pace with the car until a lorry appeared in the distance coming towards her vehicle, when it shut off as if a switch had been thrown, and she did not see it again.

She calculated that she had travelled about a mile during the whole time that the light had been visible. She never felt afraid or panicky, but afterwards she felt strangely disturbed and very tired, a feeling which persisted for about a week. By the time she came to report the incident to the police, a fortnight had elapsed. She had recovered from the tiredness but was still very puzzled by the events of the night: she was obviously hoping that we would be able to give her an instant, logical explanation.

Of course, there was no such explanation, and I was as puzzled as she was. I suggested to the young woman that perhaps regressive hypnosis would help her fill the gap in her journey home. I did not mention the words 'alien' or 'abduction', simply suggesting that she may have had a memory lapse which could be helped by hypnotherapy. She was still disturbed by what had happened, and wanted to get to the bottom of it, so she agreed.

I made contact with Joyce Dinsdale, a qualified hypnotherapist. I took Joyce's name, initially, from the phone book, rang her up and questioned her about her work and experience. I could tell that she was a sympathetic person, and I was keen that the hypnotist should be a woman because I felt that would make the young subject feel more relaxed. Joyce, who is in her forties, has been a hypnotherapist for more than twenty years, with a diploma in hypnotherapy and psychotherapy. She is a member of the Council of Hypnotherapists. She has brought up her own family and now has grandchildren, which has helped to make her an empathetic person who is able to relax her subjects, at the same time inspiring them with confidence.

Although she had never dealt with a case like this, when I outlined the fact that we were trying to recover some missing time, Joyce felt she would be able to help. Her work was mostly with people who wanted to overcome phobias, to quit smoking or lose weight, so this was outside her experience, but she was happy to try.

We arranged to meet at the young woman's house, and her husband was present all the time. I had never seen anyone put under hypnosis before, and I was astonished at how simple and effective it was. As soon as our 'patient' was under, I questioned her: Joyce was, in any case, out of her depth, but I also wanted to make sure that no leading questions were asked. I know, from my police training, how vital it is not to lead a witness, and I was determined this young woman should tell her story in her own words.

She described her journey again, very much as she had told it to me before, including the description of the coloured lights following her. I asked her if she could hear anything, and she said there was a soft buzzing sound, coming from all around. She said she felt very cold all over, and started rubbing her hands together as if she was, indeed, cold, even though we were in a warm room. Then she said a beam of white light was shining on the other side of her car, coming from above. She could also see 'lights in front of me like a lot of worms going backwards and forwards, and a large green light going up and down, backwards and forwards'.

I asked how she was feeling and she said, 'I feel so tired, I want to go to sleep.' As she said this her head lolled forwards as if she had fallen into a deep sleep. She told me she could feel something soft and fluffy on her ankles and feet; it felt 'quite nice, there's a tingling feeling going up my legs towards my knees'.

I asked where she was; she didn't reply. I asked if she was in the car, and she said, 'I don't know.' She said she was not sure whether she was sitting or lying down, but that she could hear breathing. She felt as if there was a veil in front of her eyes, and there was a bright light coming through the veil.

Then she said, 'It's going round and round,' and she started to gyrate her body from the waist upwards, as if keeping time with the light. She said the soft fluffy thing was still on her feet, and it appeared to be holding her legs down. She was still very cold except for her legs, which were warm, she said.

She ignored quite a few of the questions I was asking, until eventually I enquired why she would not answer them. 'I don't know,' she said. She then stretched both her arms out, bent at the elbows, and said she could not move them because something was holding them. She could feel something touching her body but did not know what it was. When I asked if she had clothes on she said she thought so. She could still feel the tingling and hear the buzzing noise.

For ten minutes she held her arms out, which would under normal circumstances have resulted in them aching, but she appeared not to have any pain. We terminated the hypnotherapy session soon afterwards, because it was late. The young woman came out of the trance feeling very relaxed and happier than she had been since the night of the incident, so although we did not have a complete picture of what had happened, we all felt that we had achieved a lot.

In the end, she had several hypnotherapy sessions, which helped her to come to terms with what had happened. Hers was the first case I had dealt with, so I wasn't in a position to reassure her, as I did with later cases, that there were many other people who had experienced similar things. In subsequent sessions she told exactly the same story about the lights, and about lying on a table being unable to move. Every time she repeated that she felt there was a veil across her face, through which the light was filtering. After each session she seemed more relaxed.

Both Joyce and I felt the results of the sessions with this young woman were very good. I was excited at having got such amazing first-hand information about an abduction case; Joyce was fascinated by what had come out; and we both also shared a feeling that we had done some good, that the young woman was happier and better adjusted afterwards than she was before we tried hypnosis.

Until I encountered this case, I had been dealing with – and investigating the claims of – people who had seen UFOs, strange objects in the sky or on the ground. These people had all wanted to talk, and generally feared being ridiculed if they said too much to their families, friends and colleagues. They were pleased to find someone like me to take them seriously. Some of them then became fascinated by the whole subject; others simply wanted to record what had happened to them and then forget it.

But this case, my first abduction investigation, introduced me to something new, something that I would encounter more and more as my name became known as someone who was willing to help abductees: deep fear. If people who have seen UFOs become the butt of jokes when they own up to their experience, how much more difficult is it to say to others that you think you have been abducted by aliens? Even today, when the whole subject is more widely discussed and accepted, there is still a tendency to dismiss abductees as deluded, as publicity-seekers, as 'nutters'. Yet this just adds another layer of anguish to the ordeal of people who are already frightened and disturbed, either because they can remember the actual abductions or because they have been experiencing perplexing events, like losing time, waking up in strange places, finding unexplained marks on their body, or having flashbacks to their alien encounters.

From my selfish point of view as an investigator, these people are vitally important, much more important than the witnesses who have seen strange lights and shapes in the sky. They are the ones who have had direct contact with the inhabitants of the UFOs, the aliens who are piloting the craft and whose interest and involvement in life on this planet has got to be of enormous importance and significance to the human race. I want to hear what they have to say, because their testimony is as near as we can get to finding out what is going on.

But I also have a more altruistic motive. Joyce Dinsdale and I could both see how much it helped this first young woman, initially simply to be taken seriously and believed, and secondly to be helped by hypnosis to come to some understanding of what had happened to her. In all my experience of abductees – and I have now talked to a great many – the first question they ask of themselves is 'Am I going mad?' If they are ridiculed when they mention their suspicion that they have been abducted, this reinforces the idea that they may, indeed, be going mad. Meeting me and my colleagues, who can reassure them that not only are they not losing their marbles, but also that they are not alone in what they have gone through, brings back their self-esteem and hope, and, in some cases, helps repair family relationships which have come under great pressure.

When my first abduction case came to me, in 1982, it was a relatively unexplored subject. I had heard about it, of course. One of the best documented cases ever, the case of Betty and Barney Hill, happened in America in the early sixties and was the subject of a book published here a few years later. The couple, who lived in New Hampshire, were returning home at night from a short holiday. Betty noticed a bright light, close to the moon. It seemed to get brighter and brighter, and eventually they stopped the car to have a better look. Barney, using binoculars, believed it was an aeroplane. They drove on, but the object seemed to get nearer and even brighter, then appeared to be circling the car. Barney stopped again, and they watched the object drop behind some nearby trees. He got out and walked towards it, seeing a disc-shaped object with what appeared to be windows, and catching a glimpse of some strange-looking occupants. In a panic, he returned to the car and drove on home.

The journey, they then discovered, had taken two and a half hours longer than it should have done. They experienced other symptoms: they both felt exhausted, they had nightmares and high blood pressure. For several months they were tested and examined by doctors who could find nothing wrong. Eventually, with the help of a reputable psychiatrist, they were put under hypnosis and revealed a classic abduction story. They were taken aboard a craft by aliens with large black eyes, no nose and only a slit for a mouth, and were subjected to medical examinations, including a needle being inserted into Betty's stomach, which she described as 'a pregnancy test'.

By the late seventies and early eighties more and more abductees were coming forward, particularly in America, where there were an increasing number of reputable experts who took their claims seriously. Because there was still a great stigma attached, a number of self-help groups had sprung up where abductees could meet each other and share their experiences. Many of them were reporting incidents that had happened thirty or more years ago, but which still had a profound effect on their lives.

One of the most important pioneers in the field is Budd Hopkins, who in 1975 began to investigate a number of UFO sightings near his summer home in Cape Cod, and, without setting out to look into abduction, encountered a UFO witness who had a substantial chunk of 'missing time'. This prompted Budd to explore the possibility of using hypnosis to unlock hidden memories, and because his name became known, he found himself, as I did, being contacted by more and more abductees.

Recognising that the subject ought to be studied in depth and – if possible – with academic rigour, he persuaded Professor John Mack, professor of psychiatry at Harvard Medical School, to undertake an in-depth study of some abductees. Mack entered the research with the expectation of finding some logical psychological explanation, but eventually concluded that the abductees were reporting genuine experiences. He published his book, *Abduction: Human Encounters with Aliens*, in 1990, and faced a storm of protest from his own profession. Harvard Medical School held a formal enquiry into his work, but ultimately he was vindicated, and kept his post. He is just one of several respected academics who, from an initial position of scepticism, have come to accept the abduction phenomenon when they have looked into it properly.

But at the time I started to investigate abduction, Professor Mack's book had not been written, and there were no established protocols. The use of hypnosis simply seemed to me to be a logical step to help recover missing time or to make sense of incomplete and disturbing memories. I knew its use was controversial, but I could not see any other tool which could offer as much help. And although, in the years since I started using it, it has come in for even more criticism, it remains an invaluable aid.

The main objection to hypnotherapy is that it can trigger false memories, as has been demonstrated in a few sad cases where women have 'remembered' sexual abuse under hypnosis which is, in fact, nothing more than fantasy. In some cases, this has had a dire effect on the lives of those they imagine abused them, sometimes fracturing family relationships beyond repair. For this reason, the use of hypnosis has been condemned by some psychiatrists and health-care professionals, while others have urged caution in its use, which coincides with my view. I do not think we should stop using it, but I think we should be aware of its shortcomings and use it in a controlled manner.

The way it is used in forensic investigations sums this up neatly: when it was first used, in the USA, to obtain detailed statements from witnesses, it was abused, with some people being convicted of crimes purely and simply on the evidence given under hypnosis. In Britain, though, it was used much more subtly by some police forces. They arranged for witnesses to be hypnotised to release detailed memories, usually of cars and car number plates. Using this information only as a tool to aid the investigation has proved invaluable: tracing the cars has led to indisputable forensic evidence, and convictions. In other words, although it cannot be one hundred per cent relied on, it can provide some amazingly accurate details which could not be obtained in any other way.

Although it has been proven that it is possible to lie or fantasise under hypnosis, there are significant differences between those who report real abduction experiences and those who make up a version based on what they have read or heard, as an experiment in California in 1977 proved. A group of abductees and a group of non-abductees were put under hypnosis and asked to tell the story of an abduction. Although the imaginary stories contained some of the essential elements of a classic abduction, there were fundamental differences between the two groups. Those who were recalling an actual experience became agitated and distressed, and when they were brought out of hypnosis they were overwhelmed by their memories. Those who were making it up treated it lightly, and when they came round they had no feeling that it had been real in any way.

Another important piece of American research has revealed, through analysis of the personalities of abductees in comparison with a control group, that abductees are actually no more likely to have fantasy-prone personalities than the rest of society, and are of above-average intelligence. Polygraphs, or lie detectors, have also been used on abductees, and again these have demonstrated a high level of truthfulness among the victims.

All kinds of sophisticated analyses have been undertaken to try to find a common link between abductees, but to no avail. Psychiatric tests have determined that such people are not delusional or psychotic, but beyond that they are a completely mixed group of individuals, with no particular family, social or emotional problems in common.

So, while the Americans were getting on with their (often expensive and university-funded) research, I was making my own decisions about how to go forward here in Britain. As had happened with sightings of UFOs, as soon as it became known that I was interested in abductions, people began to contact me, wanting help. If using hypnotherapy was the best way forward for them, I was happy to use it. I was not, after all, doing it for any other reason than to help them deal with problems they were already aware of, and I automatically established some protocols.

First, I would never participate in a hypnosis session with a child or adolescent, even if their parents were willing. I believe the only person who can decide that they want to be put under hypnosis is a fully informed adult, and nobody else can make that decision for them. I also will not use the procedure on anyone heavily pregnant. A case I dealt with recently involved a woman in the final trimester of pregnancy, and I insisted we wait until after her baby was born and she was over the first few months of motherhood before we considered hypnosis. Hypnosis can be emotionally distressing, so I would similarly never take part in a session with someone who had a history of psychiatric problems, or who was under great stress. I also ask those volunteering for hypnotherapy to fill in a form and sign it, which ensures they know what they are undertaking.

My next inflexible rule is that I do the questioning: Joyce takes care of the hypnosis, but I do all the talking. This means I can use all the techniques I acquired as a policeman, taking statements from witnesses but not asking any leading questions.

71

I also try to video-record the sessions, although with the first ones I simply used a tape-recorder – and then not always successfully, as there is always a high rate of gadget failure around abductees. And my final unbendable rule is that I guarantee everyone their privacy and anonymity: any case included in this book has been done so with the full agreement of the abductees.

By the time Professor Mack's research was published I had investigated a substantial number of alien abduction cases. Other research was being published by various academics and researchers in different countries, all of us working independently of each other. But when I compared my work with theirs some important facts became clear.

The abductees were reporting consistently similar stories, despite coming from different backgrounds and having different levels of knowledge about the subject. One of the main arguments against the validity of the abduction experience is that the abductees have been fed their 'fantasy' by TV and other media coverage: but these stories were emerging before this was a high-profile subject, as it is today. Also, it was not simply the main publicised details that were tallying. Small things, of no significance perhaps to a newspaper or TV reporter, were appearing time after time in statements made by abductees (for example, a great many reported nosebleeds).

Many female abductees told of a thin needle being inserted into their navel, and a sample being removed. In eighty per cent of the women I have worked with, there has, afterwards, been a persistent and irritating discharge from the navel. Some males recalled having sperm surgically removed, and samples of hair and finger- and toenails were regularly taken. Most of these procedures involved no pain, as though some very effective local anaesthetic was used, but occasionally there were reports of discomfort when instruments were inserted into the nose or ears. Scars and unexplained marks appeared on the bodies of victims, but usually disappeared quickly. The marks, circular or triangular, were at the site of small depressions, as if samples of flesh had been taken, but without the skin being punctured.

Another common – and initially incredible – feature was

pregnancy, with female abductees becoming pregnant despite in many cases having no sexual contact with a partner. After about three months the pregnancy would end, mysteriously, usually without any signs of a miscarriage. Often, under hypnosis, the women could recall the growing embryo being removed from their womb by the aliens, and they frequently described seeing rooms full of jars containing what looked like human foetuses.

In most cases the description of the captors was similar: grey-skinned beings, about three and a half feet tall, with large almond-shaped black eyes, no nose, a slit for a mouth, no bodily hair and no apparent gender. In many cases these small creatures appeared to be under the supervision of a very tall humanoid figure, with long blond hair and piercing blue eyes. These two descriptions became so familiar to UFO researchers that they were dubbed 'the greys' and 'the Nordics'. Communication between the captors, and between them and their victims, always appeared to be telepathic.

Some abductees told of seeing a large number of tables in the room, with other naked humans stretched out on them, apparently asleep. The room was described as round, and lit by a white light which appeared to have no one source, but permeated the room. Some abductees recalled the walls as plain, others likened them to banks of computers with small flashing lights. Sometimes the abductees were shown large flat screens on the walls. The atmosphere was warm and humid.

There were even similarities in their descriptions of their emotions: it was common for them to feel helpless, and distressed at the lack of compassion exhibited by their captors.

There were plenty of individual variations on this scenario, but it is remarkable how many victims reported something broadly along these lines. There were also striking similarities in the abductees' experiences in the rest of their lives. Many reported waking up to find strange marks on their body; women had inflammation and discharge from the navel; strange rashes, headaches, noises in the ears and nosebleeds were common. Most victims were afraid of being alone in a dark room, and a great many had electrical disturbances in their home, with light bulbs popping, and household machines and gadgets switching on and off without anyone touching them. This heightened level of paranormal activity around an abductee is common and not just confined to the home: one woman I dealt with found that the electronic tills in shops ceased functioning when she was near them, and for whole weeks at a time she would find it embarrassing to go shopping because she was activating the shoplifting security systems of the shops, causing her to be stopped and searched so often that it added hours to every simple trip. Then, for several weeks, nothing would happen, only for it all to start again. Other abductees report car alarms going off when they pass within a few feet of them.

In households with pets, there are often reports of the animals appearing to be scared or even paralysed in the middle of the night. Strange balls of light floating around bedrooms are reported, and sometimes alien figures are seen in the bedroom before an abduction – most abductions take place at night. Abductees are occasionally not returned to exactly the right place: they may find themselves in another room of the house, or even outside their home. One woman I counselled woke up on more than one occasion in her own front garden, with no clothes on and a stream of early-morning traffic travelling along the road. A man found himself half a mile away from home, wearing only pyjamas. In another case, a young boy found himself locked in an outside shed, which he could not have achieved without someone to let him out of the house and lock the shed after him. More commonly, abductees find their night-clothes have been put on wrongly, back to front or inside out, or the clothes are simply left in the bedroom with the abductee naked. Very occasionally – and I admit this is rare – the abductee is returned with the wrong clothes.

Some victims report waking to find grass or mud on the floor of the bedroom or in the bed, and under hypnosis they tell of walking barefoot across earth to the spacecraft. Most abductions, though not all, appear to take place at night: there are, however, a substantial number who are abducted from their cars, and others who are taken in broad daylight from other places, usually only realising when they find a pocket of missing time.

In recent years, there have been many stories of abductees

having implants placed in their bodies by their abductors. I have no conclusive evidence of this, other than that there are consistent small scars on the bodies of abductees, and many report strange noises in their ears. The nose and ears seem to be the most popular locations for implants, although there have been reports of them being placed behind the knee, in the neck and in other areas of the body. The reason for them appears to be that they are a tracking device, allowing the abductors to trace their victims at any time, although it is also possible that they are monitoring the workings of the human body and providing feedback to the aliens, who are indisputably interested in the way our bodies function. These implants are, naturally, a controversial aspect of the abduction phenomenon: at first sight, they offer real, tangible proof, and a chance to get our hands on alien technology. But so far this has proved elusive: some American researchers claim to have removed implants and had them analysed, but there is, as yet, no credible scientific evidence of this.

One theory about why we are actually unable to remove and examine implants is that they are designed to self-destruct when removed from the body: there are stories of abductees actually having these small metallic objects in their possession, only to find they have vanished within a few hours. Another theory is that, to be sustained within the body, they are made of substances that would not be rejected by our tissues, and can be absorbed into our bodies. Perhaps the most important point about implants is that the victims feel they have had them inserted: whatever they are and whatever their reason, it is clear that the aliens want the abductees to know that there is some sort of ongoing link between them. Until we actually have an implant that we can demonstrate is not human technology, they will remain one of the most contentious aspects of the abduction phenomenon.

Of course, the whole subject is contentious. Even serious UFO researchers find it hard to make the leap from believing that there are alien craft in the skies around our planet to accepting that human beings are taken on board those craft for examination. To me, it seems a logical progression: just as we are more interested in the pilots of the strange craft than the spaceships themselves, then surely we can believe that they are more interested in the evolution of life on this planet than in its atmosphere and topography.

The sceptics have come up with several possible explanations, always preferring these, however tortuous and unlikely, to the overriding evidence of so many independent witnesses. At different times the culprits have been temporal lobe epilepsy induced by exposure to electro-magnetic fields; sleep paralysis; and downright lies – the assumption being that some people make up abduction stories for publicity. I can categorically rule out all of these. Tests have been carried out in America in an attempt to re-create temporal lobe epileptic fits induced by electro-magnetic fields, by using electrical apparatus fitted on to the heads of volunteers. Although some volunteers suffered hallucinations, nothing consistent with an abduction witness testimony emerged, and the volunteers, when removed from the apparatus, knew they had been hallucinating. When a leading British electronic scientist was asked for his opinion, he said that the theory was totally implausible: if it was possible to create hallucinations by being near electrical pylons, etc., a very significant percentage of the population would be experiencing them all day.

Besides, how do any of these explanations account for the abductions where more than one person is taken? Are they all simultaneously suffering from sleep paralysis or epilepsy? As for the stories coming from publicity-hungry liars, the vast majority of abductees I have met have come forward very reluctantly, because they need help, and most choose not to go public with their accounts.

Of course, there are a few hoaxers, but experienced researchers usually suss them out pretty quickly. I dealt with one case where two students from Leeds University, on their way home from a dance, claimed to have woken up together seven hours later, lying on a grass verge in a park. They contacted me, and told of being hit by a beam of light from an object which hovered over them as they walked through the park, and remembering nothing more until they woke up. It was patently obvious to me, very quickly, that they were making it up, as their story had none of the true hallmarks of an abduction. They admitted under my questioning that it was a hoax: they had been going to write about it for the college newspaper, as a great joke about how they had fooled the UFO researchers.

There are enough genuine abduction stories around for imaginary ones to be completely unnecessary. Although, in the USA, abductees are evenly split between male and female, my own files show that eighty per cent of British cases are female. I do not believe this reflects any real difference in the nature of the phenomenon: it simply means that British males find it harder to talk about. Americans, more open and upfront, are more comfortable exploring what has happened to them and finding ways to deal with it. The British, and particularly British males, suppress it and try to get on with their lives without talking about it to anyone.

Consistent with the American findings – and those reported from other countries where responsible research is going on – I have found that abduction is rarely, if ever, an isolated event. Abductees may seek help because of one individual instance which has particularly disturbed them, but as we delve into it we usually uncover a history of abduction which started in early childhood and which often runs through generations of the same family.

I have also found the people involved to be intelligent, reliable, normal citizens, people who would, without exception, have much preferred not to be singled out for what is undoubtedly a traumatic experience. The events they are reporting may fall outside the scope of present-day scientists operating within the limits of the physical world we know. But scientists believed for three hundred years that the world was flat; they denied the existence of meteorites; and they stated categorically that there could be no life on any other planet. Now the tune has changed, not just to the possibility of life on other planets but to the probability. It was one of our greatest modern physicists, Einstein, who said that 'God does not play dice', because he could not accept the entirely random nature of quantum mechanics: yet he failed to find a unifying theory that would tie the

77

behaviour of subatomic particles into our neat and tidy understanding of the universe. It is only a couple of hundred years
since innocent people were burned at the stake or drowned as
witches, simply because their views and beliefs did not fit the
conventionally accepted pattern of the time. We do not do that
any more, thank goodness. But we torture people more insidi-
ously, by refusing to accept their testimony as to what happens
to them. Their sanity is questioned, their motives, everything: is
it any wonder that many of them prefer to keep quiet, even to
their closest families, about the things they have experienced and
witnessed? I believe that the number of people who come
forward to tell even a sympathetic person like me about their
abductions is only a tiny percentage of the true number
involved. And I know, from their reactions when I assure them
that I take them seriously, and that there are many others who
have shared their experiences, that the relief is profound. I have
been told on more than one occasion that, just by offering a
listening ear, I have saved someone from a breakdown.

The cases included here are a representative cross-section of
those I have dealt with over the past fifteen years. There are
many more in my files, some of which have been investigated in
depth, others where the victims have been happy to settle for the
reassurance that they are not alone. To me, these people are
worthy of great respect. Not only have they suffered the events
that are recorded here, but they have also, almost without
exception, had to cope with their abductions alone and in secret.
Some of them are happy for me to include their names; others,
understandably, prefer to remain anonymous.

CHAPTER FOUR

TAKEN BY ALIENS

It started as just another call on the UFO Hotline, which used to ring on to an answering machine in my office. Most calls were dealt with easily, but this one, in February 1994, merited a full-scale investigation. The voice on the hotline was female, and sounded distressed and nervous: 'I read a report about you in a newspaper where some women had been abducted. Some of the things they said were very similar to what happened to my daughter and me. We have lived with this since 1988 and we didn't know who to tell. Can you help us?'

I calmed her down and reassured her, and she told me the full story. Her name was Carol Thomas, and her daughter was Helen, and in 1988 they were forty-five and twenty-four years old. They lived in Birmingham, and worked together at a mill close to both of their homes. Their normal morning routine was for Helen to call at her mother's house, and then they would walk together to the mill, which was about fifteen minutes away.

The route, which they followed every day, took them through some alleyways between houses. On the morning of 30 March 1988, they were chatting as they walked along, in darkness. They both heard a distant humming noise, and commented on it because at that time of the morning none of the local factories had started for the day, and it was normally very quiet. Carol takes up the story in her own words:

'Suddenly we were both startled by a light which was shining down on us from above. It was like somebody shining a bright torch. We both stopped and looked up, becoming frightened as the light got larger and larger until it was directly above our heads. I remember holding my daughter's hand and then starting to feel dizzy. The next thing I remember was walking along the alley with my daughter, but something was wrong. We were both in a daze, and walking erratically because we were dizzy. My daughter was wearing a leather coat which was wet, yet it hadn't been raining.

'We felt very strange, and when we reached the mill the security guard commented that we were very late for work. We don't remember much about that day at all, but since then we have been very nervous when we walk to work.'

I questioned them both, and discovered that they had suffered a reddening and blistering of the skin on their faces and arms, just like sunburn, after the incident, and that they had also both suffered from nosebleeds and a discharge from their navels. As well as this, Helen noticed a circular patch of hair was missing from the nape of her neck.

Although several years had elapsed since their strange experience, the women were both still very shaken by it, and puzzled by the fact that they had lost a chunk of time on their journey to work. They told me that if they had not been together when it happened, they would have begun to feel they had imagined it. I was familiar with the 'missing time syndrome', because it crops up regularly in encounters with aliens, and almost always masks memories of an abduction.

The majority of abductees have no conscious recollection of what happened to them: they regain their memories piecemeal over the weeks and years after the incident, or they allow themselves to be hypnotised to recover their memories.

Carol and Helen both agreed to undergo hypnosis, so I arranged for this to take place on 12 March 1994. They attended the session together, but were hypnotised separately, out of sight and earshot of each other. Carol, who was put under first, was invited to remember the events of the day of the encounter. She described their normal morning routine, and then went on to recall everything from arriving at the alleyway.

'I can hear our footsteps as we walk. Then I hear another sound, it's strange, I've never heard it before. It's like a low humming sound . . . seems to be above us. There's a light in the air, like a torch shining down on us. It's getting bigger. We're frightened, holding each other's hand. I feel strange, the light is now below us, we're looking down on the light. There's a moon above us, we're moving towards it.'

There was a long pause, then she spoke again, hesitantly, and looking bewildered.

'Where am I? A room, all white, everything is white. It seems to have a window all the way round it. I'm lying on a table, can't move, I've got no clothes on, there's a netting cloth over my legs, it feels wet. I can see Helen, she's lying on a table next to me, she has no clothes on and there's netting over her legs. What are they doing?'

At this point I asked her: 'What is who doing?'

Her answer was: 'The little men,' so I asked her to describe them.

'They're strange, only small, they've got tiny ears and big black eyes. They're very thin, they've got three long thin fingers. They're not wearing any clothes and their skin is white. There's some around my table and some around Helen's. They're touching my stomach, they feel cold. They're looking at my hands and feet. They've got a long glass tube, it's only thin. They seem to be pushing it into my stomach through my navel.'

She seemed frightened as she talked of this, but when I asked her if she could feel any pain she said no.

'But they've left the tube sticking out. They're looking at my hair. It feels as though they are pulling it. They have gone back to my stomach. They are pulling the tube out, it's got fluid in it. I think they are taking eggs from me.'

She started to show anxiety about her daughter, saying 'Please don't hurt her' several times, visibly distressed. Then she described a cup-shaped object that was placed on her head. Some time later she was allowed off the table and taken to a large screen. One of the creatures pushed some buttons, and a succession of symbols, including triangles, squares and wavy lines, appeared on the screen, followed by documentary-type film footage of wars and explosions.

Carol described the scene:

'It's strange, everything I touch feels wet. There are some other beings standing at the back of the room, tall ones, not like the little men. One is closer to me than the others: he has long blond hair, he appears to have blue eyes and is wearing a silver suit with a blue badge containing a circle, a triangle and two wavy lines.'

Then she remembered putting her clothes back on, feeling dizzy and disorientated, and then being back in the alleyway with Helen, who was asking how her leather coat had got wet.

When it was Helen's turn to be put into a hypnotic trance, she repeated the details about the walk to the alleyway, the noise and the bright light in much the same terms that her mother had used. But after that point she became very anxious, and her speech was rambling and difficult to understand. She eventually clearly described lying on a table without her clothes on, next to her mother, who was on another table. Describing it, she started to cry and repeated, 'I want my mum, I want my mum.'

The therapist and I comforted her, telling her that nothing could hurt her or her mother, and then I asked her to carry on describing what she saw. Between sobs she said: 'I've got no clothes on, I can't move . . . there's a cloth over my legs, it's wet, like netting. I can see my mum, they're looking into her mouth.'

I asked her to describe who was looking in Carol's mouth and she said: 'They are small people with big eyes, they have no clothes on. They have wrinkly skin. They walk funny: they waddle and they only have two fingers. There is something like a big camera on a long arm, it's hanging above me, there seems to be a window which goes all around the room, everything is white. The little people are round my table, looking at my hands and feet. Now they are looking into my mouth. I can feel one of them touch my stomach. One of them has a thin rod with a silver ball on the end, he's pushing it into my nose.'

She felt no pain. When the rod was removed the silver ball was missing. She described having a piece of wire inserted into her ear, and the insertion of a glass tube into her navel and the subsequent removal of fluid, just as her mother had described it. Helen also recalled having two wires inserted into her cervix and something being removed. Like Carol, she had a large glass cup-like object on her head.

'They've taken the thing off my head. They're turning me over. I can feel them examining my back and legs. They are touching my hair at the back. It feels like they've placed a small circular object on my hair at the bottom of my head, it's pulling my hair, I don't like it. They've turned me over again, they're standing near my feet. They are looking at our packets of cigarettes, they must have taken them from our pockets.'

She, too, remembered being taken to a screen, describing the touch of the 'man' who took her there as cold and wet. After seeing the symbols on the screen, she was taken to another room where there was a smell of burning. The creatures put a small wafer into her mouth, but it tasted horrible so she spat it out.

Taken back into the other room, she saw her mother standing next to a tall, beautiful blonde woman. She described the silver suit and the badge, just as Carol had. Then she was given her clothes back. One of the creatures kept rubbing her leather coat against his face as if to feel the texture. Her next memory was of being back in the alleyway with her mother.

As I questioned her further, Helen recalled other, earlier memories of abductions. I believe that all abductees are repeatedly abducted, as part of some ongoing study by the aliens, and that the first abduction is always in childhood. Helen, under hypnosis, could recall the first time she met the 'little men'.

'I was five years old and I was playing in a field full of buttercups. They took me somewhere and examined me, and then took me to a room full of strange-looking children. They asked me to draw pictures of animals and the children had to copy what I had drawn.'

She had been given a strange stone which she kept under her bed: the strange children also had these stones and she said voices could be heard coming from them. She then talked about other abductions spanning the years between the first one and the one with her mother. After the hypnosis session ended, I asked Carol if she remembered her daughter having a stone, and she said, 'Yes, she kept it under her bed for years. I don't know where she got it from.'

The case of Helen and Carol is, like many others I have dealt with, important because more than one person was abducted. The arguments used by the sceptics, that the experience is caused by sleep paralysis or temporal lobe epilepsy, or even hallucinations, mean they must both have been suffering exactly the same physical problem at exactly the same moment: and that still does not explain why, under hypnosis, they independently came up with the same story.

It was 8 p.m. on a September evening in 1996, with still enough light in the sky for children to be playing outside. Mary and her friend Jane, two mothers in their thirties, were settling down for a gossipy evening watching television together. Mary's son Peter, aged ten, and Jane's daughter Susan, fourteen, were with them. When Mary realised that she had run out of coffee, the two women decided to get into the car and drive to the nearest late-opening shop, a few miles away in another village. They took Peter with them, leaving Susan at home because she wanted to watch a programme on TV.

The route took them along a remote country road in the quiet corner of Scotland where they lived, so they were astonished to see, as dusk fell around them, two powerful beams of white light illuminating one of the fields next to the road. As they approached, they could make out a dark shape in the sky, from which the light was coming. Mary halted the car, and all three of them watched in fascination. The field and a small plantation of trees next to it were flood-lit by 'the brightest light I have ever seen in my life', according to Jane.

They all climbed out of the car to get a better look. They could make out the underside of a huge triangular-shaped craft with three red lights on each angle. It was silent, but in the distance the women suddenly detected the rumble of aeroplane engines. Suddenly the strange craft shot away, across the heads of the observers, at such speed that it appeared to jump a mile across the valley: Jane described it as disappearing and reappearing in the distance simultaneously.

Peter was upset and started to cry. The two women shepherded him back into the car and comforted him, but they were preoccupied by the strangeness of what they had seen. Their initial supposition, that the object was an aeroplane or a helicopter, had been completely demolished when they saw its size – about eighty feet across – and witnessed its silent manoeuvres at incredible speed.

They carried on with their journey, bought the coffee, and then returned along the same route, discussing who they should notify about the strange craft. When they reached the same spot on the road, Mary cut the engine again and they peered in the direction that the craft had disappeared. All three of them could make out a faint red dot of light. To their astonishment, it shot across the sky towards them and hung in the air over their car, 'as if it was aware of our presence', Jane said. Both the women were shrieking with a mixture of excitement and fear. Peter, though, was terrified, and almost hysterical. As quickly as it had arrived, the spacecraft returned to its position in the distance, with only a faint red light as evidence of its existence.

Mary drove them home. They were shaken, but determined not to let what they had seen go unreported – despite Susan scoffing and insisting that she did not believe a word of it. They called the operator, hoping to be given advice as to who to ring, and were given the number of the UFO Hotline. Many telephone operators across Britain had the special number. I was not manning the Hotline that evening, but one of my colleagues advised the women to go back as quickly as possible to the scene with binoculars and a camera. Unfortunately, they had neither. But they returned anyway, taking Susan with them. Even Peter, despite his fear, insisted on going with them. By this time it was quarter to ten, and dark.

When they reached the same area, a powerful blue glow appeared at the far end of a field, above tree-top height. There was no sign of any mysterious craft, but when they parked in a lane to watch the light they became aware that a large star-like object was visible at the top edge of the diffuse glow, and it was pulsing and growing larger and smaller. Coloured beams of light in red, green and blue were shooting up in the air from it.

Suddenly, perhaps because their eyes were growing accustomed to the dark, they all became aware of the silhouettes of several thin figures moving about on the ground. They were obviously not human, and they were all small, with the exception of one, who was about a foot taller than the rest. On the ground the observers could make out an indeterminate black shape, towards which the figures, who were emerging from the plantation of trees, appeared to be moving.

Terrified, Mary slammed the car into reverse and shot backwards up the lane until she found a place to turn round, and then drove her frightened passengers home to Jane's house. As they discussed what they had seen, and reassured each other that they were not going mad, Jane's brother arrived, on his way home from work, and offered to lend them some binoculars. Despite their fears, all four decided to go back once again to the scene.

When they got there, the blue light was still glowing, and they could see the small beings moving in and out of the trees. They took it in turns to use the binoculars, all four of them lined up against a dry-stone wall at the edge of the field where the activity was. Later, I sent one of my field investigators to interview them, and he tape-recorded the following statement from Jane:

'I could see one big star which I thought was on the ground. It was a large, transparent, illuminated capsule-type thing, rippled on the outside with indentations, like a brain. There were some very small, thin beings inside it. Next to this capsule was another smaller one, otherwise identical to the first one. This contained a tall being with brown skin. The capsule was moving, slowly rotating. I then looked toward the ground and saw the big craft we had first seen. It appeared to be on the ground near the woods. There were lots of lights around it and dozens of these small entities who seemed to be working in groups. They were going in and out of the woods. They appeared to be putting things on the ground and picking things up. Each group was carrying small boxes and canisters between the woods and the craft.

'I saw other capsules which looked like cocoons coming out

from the trees: they suddenly shot across the field to where we were standing. I was very frightened and started screaming. The objects were quite close to us, and we could see that each of the capsules contained one of the small entities. They were no more than four feet from us and there were dozens of them. Then pandemonium broke out, with Mary, Susan and Peter all screaming. I vaguely remember shouting, "Let's get out of here," and we drove back home.

'Later it was strange because I started to remember things and somehow it felt that they had taken us towards their craft. I remember this place, it was very bright, I couldn't move and they were doing things to me. They didn't hurt me so I felt happy. The little ones were smiling at me with their big eyes, and taking things from me, which they gave to a tall being. He touched them with a long probe-like rod. The little creatures were about four to five feet tall, there was nothing human about them at all. The tall one had a nose and very slanted eyes – oriental-like. There was no obvious sex gender, nor did I see a body shape or waistline. They did have two arms and two legs, and when they communicated they made strange noises – high-pitched, like whales. I didn't hear them talking, it just "happened" in my head.

'I don't think they enjoyed what they were doing, it was just work. They seemed very efficient and knew exactly what they were doing. When we got home I was very frightened and kept asking Mary, hoping that she would say I had imagined the whole thing. But she confirmed that it had really happened.'

Mary independently made a very similar statement about what they had seen, although she had no memory of being taken on board the craft or of being touched by the strange creatures. The two children, Susan and Peter, also both confirmed to my investigator that they had witnessed all the events apart from Jane's abduction.

The first time I spoke to Mary and Jane was the evening it happened, when they again rang the UFO Hotline, this time after their fourth and final encounter. It was late at night, and the Hotline had been switched through to me. Often at night we leave it on the answering machine, but when I heard the panic in

Jane's voice I switched the phone over and talked to her. She was very distressed, and it took me some time to calm her down. In the end, all four of them slept together in the same bedroom, with the light on. It took a couple of weeks before any of them were happy to sleep in the dark again.

In the weeks after their encounters, the other three also began to retrieve memories of being on board the spacecraft. Luckily, the Scottish field investigator I used, Brian Rooney, is a trained social worker, and was able to work with them and help them come to terms with their experiences. He also visited the scene of the encounter and photographed burn marks on the ground, and semi-circular impressions. Nearby trees and bushes were heavily coated with white spider-web material, as though they had been blasted with it. Although there was no motor access within 200 yards of the scene, he was convinced that a heavy vehicle had been on the land.

I have spoken to both the women many times since the incidents, and they are still profoundly shaken by them. One family has moved away from the area completely. Neither of them wants to have their name published: they are not seeking publicity, and they would much prefer it if the events of that night had not happened. But they accept that they cannot undo them, and they want an explanation. There are times when I wonder why I give so much of my life to the fight to get this whole subject out in the open; times when my own safety – and that of my family – is under threat; times when the combined forces of world governments seem too daunting. Then I think of women like Mary and Jane: ordinary people, going about their everyday business, with no interest in UFOs or aliens, who are suddenly sucked into the middle of these strange events. Not only do they face the trauma of what happened to them, but they face the frustration of not being able to speak openly about that night for fear of ridicule.

Yet another case of multiple abduction happened one warm evening in July 1995. It had been a baking-hot day, too hot to spend cooking, and so it was late on in the evening when Steve and Annie decided they would have an impromptu barbecue in their back garden. Mike and Debbie, their neighbours in their small Derbyshire home town, joined them, carrying chairs and a table out from the house. Steve lit the barbecue at about 10.15 p.m., and the sausages, burgers and chicken pieces were beginning to cook by 10.40. Lazy summer music drifted from a small portable radio, and the four friends enjoyed a glass of cider as they waited for the meal to be ready.

It was Annie who noticed it first: a large disc-shaped craft which had appeared so suddenly that none of them saw it arrive, but was now hovering only twenty feet above the garden. It had a dome above the disc, edged with oblong-shaped windows, and around the bottom were white flashing lights which appeared to be rotating in an anti-clockwise direction. It was about twenty feet in diameter, and a dark, metallic colour. Annie's scream alerted the others, who looked up in stunned silence as a door on the underside of the craft opened and a powerful shaft of light shone down into the garden. At this point, all four witnesses began to feel light-headed. They later described it as a dream-like, confused state.

'It was as if we had entered a vacuum,' said Steve. 'All sound seemed to have stopped and everything seemed to go into slow motion and we all felt disorientated. Suddenly the craft started to move slowly away and we all watched until it was just a glowing light in the distance.'

All four of them felt nauseous, and had stomach pains. Although they seemed to have been watching the spaceship for only a few minutes, they were amazed when Steve looked at his watch and it was nearly midnight. Over an hour had elapsed since the object had first appeared, and they had no memory of the missing time. The barbecue had fizzled out, and the meat on it was charred. Worried, they called the police, who treated the matter seriously and took full statements. As they looked around the garden, they realised that two of the four full glasses of cider had disappeared from the table: they were never found.

In the following few days all four suffered from acute diarrhoea and nausea. They were also all profoundly unsettled: they had nightmares, sleepless nights and found it hard to concentrate.

They were referred to me by my investigators, who realised after first interviewing the two couples that it was an important case and that I should handle it myself, as they did not know how to deal with abductions. The four victims all agreed that they would like to try regressive hypnosis in a bid to make sense of the missing chunk of time. It was a month after the encounter that we all assembled at Joyce Dinsdale's home, and they were individually hypnotised. None of them heard what the others said under hypnosis.

Debbie was the first, and she was asked to go back and relive the events of that evening. She immediately began to show signs of agitation and fear.

'We're in the garden having a barbecue, there's a flashing light coming from above, it's white, flashing down towards us. I'm looking up, I'm frightened. There's something above us, it's circular with very bright flashing lights. It's hurting my eyes, Annie is looking up as well and pointing at it. It's round with a dome on top, it's got rotating lights on the bottom, red, green, white. It's very bright, it's hurting my eyes.'

She was crying and seemed to be in great distress, but a few seconds later she started to talk again.

'I'm on my own, I'm not in the garden any more, I don't know where I am, the lights are flashing, they're hurting my eyes. Stop, stop, stop!'

She covered her eyes, rubbing them, and tears streamed down her face.

'The lights are too bright, they're hurting my eyes, I can see shadows, my eyes hurt, I can see different coloured lights, I can see eyes looking at me, they're big and black, not like ours.' She paused for a few seconds, and then continued more calmly.

'I'm lying on something hard with my back slightly raised, my feet are cold. I can see something, they're shadows, they're moving, I can't move my arms or legs.' She suddenly showed signs of great terror. 'There's something touching my knees, I can see big eyes in front of me. There's something on my legs, it's hurting me. I'm looking at the roof, it's round, it's strange, it just comes down to walls without a joining. There's a purple light in my face now.'

She became so distressed, crying and shaking, that Joyce and I agreed we should end the session, as it was obviously unleashing too much trauma for her.

Annie also showed extreme fear under hypnosis. She described the craft hovering above the garden, and the shaft of light that came from it to the ground.

'There's a small figure appeared in the garden, it's wearing a black cloak with a hood, it's got a strange, pale face with a pointed chin, and very large black eyes. There's two more of them in the garden now, I can't move. They've got hold of my arms, they're dragging me towards the light. Oh, the bright light, it's hurting my eyes, it's hurting my eyes.'

She described the craft in much the same detail as Debbie had, except that she said the windows were 'arched'. She then talked of being dragged towards the light.

'It's strange, I can't hear any sound. I'm struggling, I'm trying to break free from them but I can't. The three figures are identical to each other, about the size of a small boy. They're making strange animal-like grunting noises as if they are talking to each other. They're dragging me into the light.'

She was crying and anxious as she recounted this, but she suddenly calmed down and spoke in a hushed voice, just above a whisper.

'I'm in a round room, it's light, it's very bright, hurting my eyes. There are lots of people in here, loads of people around the sides of the room, little people, they're all wearing cloaks with hoods.'

I asked her to describe the room and she said: 'I can't see much, but it looks like a metal bench in the middle of the room. They are all looking at me, they're pulling me towards the bench, I'm frightened. I'm now lying on the bench. Oh no, they're putting their hands on me, they've only got three fingers. They're touching my face, pulling my hair. Oh no, they're taking my top off. It's horrible. They're making funny noises. I can't understand them.

'The walls are funny, they're round, like divided into squares. I can see all those little people round the walls, the lights are hurting my eyes. The lights are a peachy colour, my eyes are blurred, it's difficult to see properly. Now they've taken off my shoes, they're scraping between my toes.

'They're touching my fingers. I daren't look. He's got some-thing in his hand, it's silver, it's like a small square thing on a rod, about pencil thickness. They're touching my hair and my eyes. Please leave me alone. It's hurting, it feels like an injection into my neck. They're doing something to my belly button, I can't see. I don't like it, it's horrible, they're touching me all over, they're horrible. They won't leave me alone.

'I can see his face, he's close to me. It's really pale with long, black, slanting eyes. They're pressing down on my belly button with something. I feel warm, there's a strong sweet smell, I don't know what it is. They're pulling my hair at the back of my head, near my neck. It hurts, something sharp. Now they're touching my lips. I feel trapped. I want to go home. I don't like them.'

Once again, she suddenly became calm.

'I'm back in the garden. I'm looking up at the craft, it's moving away from us.'

Her husband Steve was then regressed, and this is his account of the events of that night:

'I'm out in the garden with Annie, Debbie and Mike, we're having a barbecue. It's a strange night, very warm. I've just thrown something up into the air, it's gone into next door's garden. There's something in the air, very close, it's coming towards me, I'm looking at it. I can hear Annie screaming, I can't move. There are flashing lights, it's very bright. Where am I? I'm not in the garden.'

There was a long pause, then he continued: 'I'm in a very bright room, there are lots of small people, like midgets, they're all wearing black cloaks with hoods, it's like black tin foil, but not tin foil. I'm in a transparent tube without seams, I can't move, the midgets are looking in at me, I can see their faces. I can't see their noses, they've got big black eyes, they've got shiny black hoods over their heads. They seem to shuffle when they move. They're all in black. I can see them staring at me, it's like being in a museum. They've taken me out of the tube, it's very bright. It's hurting my eyes. They're taking me to a hole near the windows, it's full of light, they're pushing me towards the hole.

'Where am I? God, this is big. I don't know where I am, it's like a very big room. I can see all sorts in here, it's so big. I can see there's loads of the little people in here, they seem to be all working and moving around. They've got white stuff, like balls of white stuff in their hands, they're carrying it, I don't know what it is. I'm just standing watching. I can't understand what they are saying, they just seem to mumble to each other and just shuffle along.

'I can see drawings on the wall, I can see figures of planets. I can see Saturn, earth and all the planets on a board which seems to be into the wall. Oh, my head hurts. They're touching me and prodding me. I can't move, their eyes are big and seem to be boring right into me. I can see a door. I seem to be standing in the same place all the time. I think I'm in a different craft from the first one, this one is bigger, much bigger, massive. I'm trying to move but I can't. I'm back in the tube now. I don't like it, I can't get out.'

At this juncture Steve appeared to be gasping for breath.

'I can't breathe. They're all watching me, my eyes are hurting. I'm back in the garden, I can hear Annie, she's screaming. I'm just standing looking up, it's flashing bright, it isn't spinning, the lights are going round. I can't see anybody, I feel as if I'm on my own. I can't breathe, I can't take my eyes off it, it won't let me. It's moving away now, giving off a green colour, it's moving away into the distance. Mike, Debbie and Annie are back in the garden with me, we are all confused, the girls are frightened.'

Throughout the second half of this account, Steve was breathless and we were worried that the trauma was precipitating an asthma attack, but he recovered completely as soon as Joyce brought him out of the trance.

When it was Mike's turn, both Joyce and I quickly agreed that he was too traumatised and upset to go through with the session. As soon as he was asked to go back to the night in question, he became obviously terrified and distressed, and Joyce brought him round again very quickly.

All four of them agreed that the incident had changed them profoundly, probably for ever. None of the four had had any previous interest in UFOs or aliens – in fact, before the events of that night, they would have said they did not believe in UFOs or abduction at all. The whole experience left them all feeling very uncomfortable, and they have not kept in touch with me.

One of the most striking aspects of repeated abduction cases is that they are so often surrounded by bursts of other paranormal activity, the sort of events that are normally put down to poltergeists. Things go missing and then turn up again; electricity surges and cuts out; there are strange noises like footsteps and water running. Often there are peculiar smells, sometimes pleasant and sometimes unpleasant. The abductees sometimes find they develop enhanced psychic abilities, being able to foresee events.

Another equally striking aspect is the involvement of several members of the same family in the events, with perhaps one or two of them being the main focus. Even those family members who are not abductees will witness the paranormal happenings.

One celebrated case which I have investigated is that of the Andrews family, in which it soon became apparent that Ann Andrews and her son Jason are both abductees; it is more than likely that Ann's father, who is dead, was also involved. Ann's other son, Daniel, has also had experiences linked to what has been happening to his younger brother and his mother, and Ann's husband Paul, though originally an avowed sceptic, has seen so many inexplicable events that he, too, has been forced to accept the alien explanation.

The Andrews case has received wide publicity, and it is certainly one of the most interesting ones I have dealt with. Neither Jason nor Ann has been hypnotised: I would never be party to a teenager like Jason undergoing hypnotherapy. Both of them have recovered memories of their abductions spontaneously, Jason often having them the next morning. Ann, more typically, retrieves them in flashbacks.

When they first contacted me they were scared and puzzled by what had been happening to Jason, and were very relieved when I was able to reassure them that although theirs is certainly a complex case, they are not alone. For them, as for so many of the other cases I deal with, I became a telephone counsellor, available at the end of the line to talk through with them the latest happenings. When Ann Andrews wrote a book about the family's experiences she included my name in the dedication with the tribute: 'To Tony Dodd, who is always there, for all of us.' It was a touching commendation, and it is always heartening to know that I have been able to help people.

I have recently been dealing with another case as complex and fascinating as that of Jason Andrews. Again, it involves a great deal of paranormal activity, episodes of missing time, and several members of the same family having the experiences.

Tracey Jones and her husband Darren are a young couple with four children, now living back in the UK after a short spell in Dubai. They contacted me in the summer of 1997. Like many of the cases I meet, I was their last resort. They were desperate for help.

Tracey has been psychically sensitive all her life – she described my office accurately although she has never been to my home, and she often 'senses' things about people she meets, although it is a gift that comes unbidden and she cannot do it all the time. In 1993 she, Darren and their daughter Georgina, who was then six, rented a cottage for four months from Tracey's parents. Their other children were not yet born. They stayed at the 300-year-old cottage only for a short time because they were there simply to help Tracey's parents sell it: and after the events that happened there, they were glad to move out.

One evening, at about 9 p.m., they heard a strange loud humming noise from outside. Darren's first reaction was that this was a very odd time for somebody to be mowing their lawn. Both he and Tracey went to the window, but at first could see nothing unusual. After a few moments a very bright light suddenly engulfed their cottage, leaving the neighbouring properties in darkness. It was an intense white light coming from the sky, but they could not see the source of it. It lasted for about fifteen minutes, according to the clock, although it seemed only a few seconds to the Joneses as they watched it.

The next morning, Darren discovered that the wrought-iron gates at the front of the cottage had been wrenched open and twisted, and that the three sets of stable doors, all secured with padlocks, had also been forced open. This forcing of the stable doors continued intermittently while the family lived there, usually happening about once a week.

Soon after they moved to the cottage Tracey went into hospital for a chest operation. The wound became seriously infected, to the consternation of the medical staff at the hospital in Wakefield, and Tracey was readmitted twice for treatment. When she was allowed home, she had a daily visit from a district nurse for four weeks, to change the dressing on the infected wound. She was in great pain. The bandage on the wound was secured with white surgical tape which covered the whole of her chest.

One morning she woke to find the bandage had gone. There was no sign of it anywhere in the bed, or in the room. Darren even pulled the bed out to check behind it, and when they moved out of the cottage only a few weeks later, and all the furniture was cleared, there was still no sign of it.

Astonishingly, Tracey had experienced no pain, as she invariably did when the nurse changed the dressing. The wound was clean and healthy-looking – until then, it had leaked through the bandages and stained the bedding every night. On another occasion, she woke wearing her pyjamas but the bra and knickers she had had on underneath them had vanished: this underwear also never turned up.

On one occasion, Darren woke to see a figure near the bedroom window. It was about the same size and shape as Tracey, and appeared to be looking in the box where the bandages and tapes were kept. Drowsily, Darren assumed that it was Tracey, perhaps getting herself some painkillers. It was only when he turned to go back to sleep that he discovered Tracey was sound asleep next to him. Instantly awake, he sat up and looked towards the window: there was nobody there.

Their brief stay in the house was plagued with other strange happenings: doors opening and closing on their own, ornaments and small items of furniture being moved about, voices being heard from empty rooms. They assumed the house was haunted: there was some evidence from neighbours that other residents living there previously had had problems. But, as I have discovered before, it is the family, not the place, which attracts the attention of the uninvited visitors. When the Jones family moved, to another old property, they experienced more inexplicable events.

Electrical appliances went haywire, toilets flushed when there was nobody near them, baths were filled and emptied, and Tracey once heard footsteps progressing down the hall and right past her, although she could see nobody. They contacted a local clergyman, who came and blessed every room in the house, telling them that he sensed a malign presence in the smallest of the three bedrooms. They, too, were worried about this room: it smelled constantly of lavender, it was cold even when the heating was on, and the portable TV they kept in there would switch itself on and off.

Throughout this time, Darren was waiting to land an overseas contract, so the family continued to rent temporary accommodation. For eighteen months they lived in a modern house, and were relatively free of problems. Then they moved to a large, three-bedroomed semi-detached house on the edge of the Yorkshire moors, with spectacular views from the rear of the house across the hillside. Night after night, they watched the swooping and sweeping of bright lights across the hills: the same UFOs that so many people have seen in this beautiful part of the country. They even captured one of the most spectacular aerial displays on video: the UFO remained stationary for over twenty minutes, turning on its horizontal axis every thirty seconds, so that Darren and Tracey could see the circular dark underside. They phoned Manchester Airport and my UFO Hotline. The airport put them in touch with an RAF base, and they were promised that somebody would visit them to collect the video. Mysteriously, within twenty-four hours their house was burgled and the tape taken, along with a computer and printer. Other valuables, including cash, were left untouched.

One morning, Darren went into the bathroom for a shower. Tracey followed him within a second or two, because she needed water for her baby's bottle-warmer. To her astonishment, Darren was not there. Puzzled, she looked into the shower: it was wet and had obviously been used very recently. She checked all the rooms upstairs, calling his name, but there was no sign of him. From the window she could see that his car was still on the drive, so she ran downstairs and searched the rest of the house. As she went back up the stairs she saw Darren on the landing, a towel around his waist, dabbing at a nick in his chin from shaving. He was bewildered when Tracey told him what had happened: he was adamant that she had never walked into the bathroom, and that he had been there all the time.

Shortly after this, Darren began to 'lose' time. A five-minute journey to the local garage would take half an hour, with no memory to account for the missing time. Marcus, their second child, who was two, began to have terrifying nightmares, described by the health visitor as 'night terrors'. Tracey would wake in the night feeling paralysed, unable to move anything except her eyes. On more than one occasion she saw two tall, thin old men with long white beards and wearing black habits, like a monk's, at the foot of the bed, looking at her. All the family, with the exception of the baby, Daniel, would find strange marks and bruises on their bodies, and one morning Marcus clearly had the imprint of four fingers on both sides of his torso.

Like many of the people I see, Tracey has a list of fears and phobias, some of which she cannot explain. For example, she fears that in the dark someone or something will reach out and touch her. She hates being alone, and always insists on having curtains closed 'to keep out the faces'. She told me that since she was four years old she has felt she is being watched at all times, and recently this feeling has become stronger.

In July of 1997, Darren, who worked for a shipping company, was posted to Dubai, and seven weeks later the family flew out to join him. While he had been living on his own, nothing strange had happened. But as soon as Tracey and the children arrived, life began to go haywire again. Marcus, now three, was repeatedly telling his parents about a man who lived in one of the lights in his bedroom, and who took him and his sister Georgina up into the light to talk and play. His parents were particularly worried because Marcus seemed to believe he could fly, and wanted to climb on to the villa roof. He knew, although his parents have no idea how, that there was a water tank up there. The 'man' told Marcus to repeat the letters E, R and S (neither I nor Darren and Tracey have any idea of the meaning of this, and I have no knowledge of any other case where anything like this has happened).

Georgina, who shared a bedroom with Marcus, woke in the early hours of one morning to see the light flickering violently in the hallway, and a strange fluorescent oval-shaped light on the wall at the foot of her bed. In the centre of the light was a thin grey figure with very long arms. It seemed to be moving towards her. The family's dog, Bibi, a cocker spaniel, began to whimper. Georgina glanced at Marcus, and noted that he was still soundly asleep. She remembered nothing more until the next morning, when she showed her parents marks on both her knees, which again looked like fingerprints from four fingers.

When Georgina sketched the figure she saw, Tracey did several other small sketches of faces and showed them to Marcus, who unhesitatingly selected Georgina's as the man from the light. He insisted that when he went into the light Georgina was the only person with him, apart from the man.

As the weeks in Dubai went by, Marcus became increasingly nervous and difficult. He complained that the man 'hurt his tummy', and eventually Tracey moved a mattress on to the floor next to her bed for him to sleep on. There was a succession of strange events, with electrical equipment behaving wildly, and on one occasion a mug moved across the kitchen table and smashed down on to the floor. Tracey and Georgina together lost over half an hour of time.

Because of problems with Darren's contract in Dubai, the family eventually moved back to Britain in December 1997, and rented a house in Huddersfield. Throughout their time in the Middle East they had stayed in touch with me, by e-mail and telephone, and I had encouraged Tracey to keep a diary of events as they happened. She kept this up after they returned, and her regular entries show that strange things were happening to the family on an almost daily basis.

Although they were in different surroundings, Marcus still insisted that his night visitor, the 'man', lived in the light, and

99

took him up there. He was still so badly disturbed at night that Tracey arranged an appointment with a psychologist, who told them he was suffering from nightmares. Worryingly, Daniel also began to scream in the night, and marks were found on his body.

Darren, Tracey and Georgina all heard, clearly, each other's voices when there was nobody around. Georgina, who is always referred to as Jo in the family, and Darren both heard Tracey speaking to them when she wasn't there: Georgina was particularly baffled because her mother called her by her full name, instead of Jo. For Tracey, the most moving moment was when she woke to hear the voice of a young boy, aged about eight to ten, as if he was on the pillow next to her. He was showing something to somebody, saying in amazement: 'Isn't this interesting?' For Tracey it unleashed memories: years before, she had lost a baby, a boy, who would have been nine had he lived. She carried him for the full nine months of pregnancy, but he was stillborn.

Again, the Jones household was plagued by mysterious bangs and other noises. Small items would go missing and then reappear, other objects would turn up unexpectedly in strange places: for instance, Georgina found a hammer on top of a pile of games she had just tidied up. The hammer had not been there a few minutes earlier. Darren, having fallen asleep downstairs on the settee, woke to find himself on the floor and the fire switched on, although he had no memory of moving or putting the fire on.

Significantly to me, because of what I know of other cases, Tracey woke one morning to find her right nostril bleeding slightly, and hurting. At times, like so many of the others I have counselled, Tracey felt she was going mad. Because she was pregnant with her fourth child, I was not prepared to let her be hypnotised. A few months after the birth of her son, Branden, we met at Joyce's home and Tracey was put under hypnosis. She told of waking in the middle of the night to see two very tall men at the foot of her bed, both wearing monk-like habits, and both with piercing blue eyes and white beards. Not knowing how she had got there, she then found herself lying on a white table in a room with 'rounded ends': it was not completely circular but was curved at the corners. She was unable to move, but could feel no physical restraints. There was a powerful white light shining down on her, and her chest was exposed. She saw what she described as a 'mechanical object' coming down from above, with a long silver-coloured needle at the end, and a line of red lights flashing up and down the needle. The needle came down, as if automatically, and entered the open wound on her chest, and she felt a burning sensation. She recalled seeing shadowy figures moving about the room, but she was unable to look at them properly because she could not turn her head.

This was enough for one session, but in future Tracey will be having more hypnotherapy to talk about other incidents. Like most of the others who have seen Joyce, she felt a sense of calm and relief after the session. My own belief is that Tracey, Marcus, Georgina and probably Darren are being abducted on a regular basis. They themselves have found it hard to accept the idea of abduction, but they have open minds and they believe the hypnotherapy will provide some answers. Tracey would like me to try hypnotherapy on Georgina, who is keen to have it, but I will resist until she is much older. It certainly sounds as though Georgina is the focus for a great deal of the activity: one morning in June 1998 she woke with a very clear handprint on her left thigh, a print of a palm and four very long fingers.

Their case has many parallels with that of Jason and Ann Andrews, and, like that one, illustrates how small children can give unbiased, impartial evidence about what is happening to them, without the possibility of their imaginations being polluted or seeded with what they have read or seen on television.

Both Darren and Tracey are sensible, intelligent people who ask for nothing more than a happy, normal family life. The fact that these strange events have occurred in several homes in Britain and even one in the Middle East shows that whatever is pursuing them is dogged, and is interested in them, not their surroundings.

If it is hard for those who have no experience of the abduction phenomenon to accept that it is a real experience, imagine how the victims feel. They, too, were often of the opinion before it happened to them that the only people who reported such events were, to use the words they use to me, 'lunatics', 'nutters', people 'several pennies short of the full pound'. Accepting that they themselves might fall into this category in the eyes of others is very difficult. They have had the experience, and that, in itself, is traumatic, without having to try to suppress it for fear of ridicule.

One case I dealt with involved a thirty-two-year-old nurse, Alex, who had no background knowledge of UFOs or abductions. She had never read a book on the subject, she turned the pages of newspapers and magazines when she saw a reference to such a 'bizarre' thing, she never chose to watch TV documentaries or drama series which dealt with the subject.

Then, during July 1996, something happened which she could not understand, but which troubled her. She mentioned it one evening to some friends. One of them, who knew a little about UFOs and abductions, suggested she contact me. She did, but she was apologetic and embarrassed about the nature of her call. I am used to this approach: when people talk to me they often say they have been trying to pluck up the courage for days, frightened not by me but by the nature of what they need to tell me.

With a little bit of coaxing, Alex relaxed enough to tell me that, although she did not know what had happened, she was bewildered and traumatised by it: so much so that she had moved from her home and was living with friends, because she needed to be surrounded by other people.

This is what she told me:

'I had finished work at 6 a.m. on 2 July 1996, after working the night shift. I went home, took my dogs for a walk and then went to bed. I got up at lunchtime, and when I realised it was a nice day I decided to take a book and relax in the sunshine. I often went to a field not too far from my home, where I could read and unwind in a nice sunny spot. Soon after I started reading I suddenly felt that I was being drawn up into the air. I am afraid of heights and began to feel sick. By this time I felt myself rising rapidly, I was facing upwards and vaguely remember seeing myself getting close to a large black triangular object in the air above me. I must have blacked out at this time.

'The next thing I remember was seeing a blinding white light, like an operating theatre light shining down on me. I realised that I was lying on a table without my clothes. I was terrified. I couldn't move. I felt that somehow I was being restrained. My head was turned to the left. When I began to focus properly I saw three strange-looking beings standing to my left near my legs. I was able to move my head and I turned to look right and saw another three of the same beings standing on my right side. They were very odd, small – only about three feet tall. They had very large heads, like a baby before it is born. They had no hair or eyebrows and no nose or ears. I think they were wearing white transparent one-piece suits, but I'm not sure because I could not see any seams.

'The room was very bright and looked as if it was shaped like a fifty-pence piece. Although I couldn't see anything on my chest it felt as though there was a weight holding me down. As I looked to my right I saw a young girl asleep on another table. She had no clothes on and was only fourteen or fifteen years old, with dark-brown hair and a centre parting. I felt so sorry for her. I felt maternal towards her. At the back were some large jars, like those lava lamps that were popular in the seventies, where oil moves up and down. At this moment another creature who was much taller than the others came towards me. He was about six feet tall and looked exactly like the others. He bent over the table and I saw his very big black eyes, like fluid, looking at me. I got the feeling that I should be asleep and not seeing these things. Suddenly I felt very calm and a pleasant relaxed state overcame me. It was almost like a religious experience, warm and loving. The next thing I remember was waking up in the field, but I was now several yards from the place where I had sat down. My book was on some nearby bushes. I don't know how it got there. I glanced at my watch, and saw that it had stopped at 1.10 p.m. There were marks and a rash on my left arm.

'When I got home I found that five hours had passed since arriving in the field, and I tried to rationalise what had happened. I wondered if I had fallen asleep and dreamt everything, but if it was a dream, it was very vivid. And why did I wake up in a different part of the field?

'Later I found it hard to sleep. I was very uneasy in the bedroom on my own. I kept dreaming about aliens and spaceships, and having heavy nosebleeds. I was having trouble with the television and video recorder, which kept turning themselves on and off, and the electric clock in my bedroom went haywire. I had to resort to a wind-up clock, to make sure that I left for work on time.

'Eventually I moved to a big city, so that I could live among other people. My attitude to life has altered now: how can a dream do that? I even went to a psychiatrist and he said it was just a dream, and that I was under stress.'

Alex was happy to try regressive hypnosis. She was still having disturbed nights, and wanted to be able to put her mind at rest about what had actually happened in the field. The hypnotherapy session took place in October 1996, three months after the event. I asked her to go back to the day that she was in the field, and almost immediately she showed signs of distress and fear. She talked about being drawn up into the air beneath a very large black triangular object, but then she became disorientated and could remember nothing more until she found herself in the hexagonal room. A powerful white light was shining on her from above, and she realised she was lying naked on a table, unable to move anything except her head. She was not aware of any physical restraints, apart from a pressure on her chest.

She again described the small creatures she had been able to remember, three of them on either side of her; the young girl asleep on a table near to her (and again, she re-experienced the surge of pity she had felt for the girl); and the taller creature bending over and looking into her eyes. She was clearly terrified, but then she reported hearing a voice inside her head which said, 'Don't be afraid, this is being done for your own good.' Again, she was overcome by a euphoric feeling. She said the small creatures touched various parts of her body, and she was able to communicate with them telepathically.

She said, 'Oh no, not again, why do you keep taking me?'

I asked her what this meant and she said, 'They are always taking me.'

Everything she recalled under hypnosis tallied very closely with her original incomplete memories of the event. I asked her to go back to her very first encounter with the aliens, and she told of meeting some strange 'children' when she was five. She started to talk like a five-year-old. She was upset because her mother had taken her pet guinea pig back to the shop, because she did not look after it. She had wandered out into the woods behind her home, carrying her teddy bear, and that was where she met the 'ugly-faced creatures', who said they would take her somewhere to play. She thought it was odd that they wore no clothes. They took her to a 'round house' and when she asked who would play with her, they brought another of the 'ugly-faced' creatures, but she refused to play with it. (There's no doubt in my mind, from her description, that she was in a spaceship and the creatures were the small aliens we call greys.)

She met the creatures again when she was six, and was taken to the same place, where she was examined by a creature she called 'the doctor'. She did not seem to be afraid. Her next encounter took place when she was fourteen. Her family were living in a small village, and she took the dog for a walk into some nearby woods, and found herself being drawn up in the air. She was then naked, lying on a table, unable to move. She tried to fight, but was powerless. Several strange creatures were using instruments on her body, apparently taking samples. She told of feeling very indignant with them when they said she was sterile and unable to have a baby. The next thing she knew, she was lying on the ground in the woods, but the dog was gone. She searched for the animal, fruitlessly, and eventually returned home, where she was in trouble for losing him. The dog turned up a couple of days later, but was always reluctant to go into the woods again.

She had a similar experience when she was eighteen, and this time she remembered seeing lots of tables in the same room, each one with a naked human female asleep on it. Her most traumatic abduction happened when she was twenty-seven, when she was, apparently, two months pregnant: an unexpected occurrence, but one that she was very excited and pleased about. This time she found herself in a different room, with dozens of large jars lining the walls. She said:

'The jars have wires going into the top of them. They are full of liquid and bubbles are rising in them. Oh my God, they have got babies in them. They are not full-term babies, they are very small, they are human, I don't like this.'

She was so distressed that Joyce and I decided to halt the interview until she was more relaxed. Joyce brought her out of the trance and we all had a cup of tea. But when we resumed she was just as agitated.

'Please don't take my baby, I know what you are going to do, please don't hurt my baby. They are taking my baby from me,' she said.

I asked her to move on three weeks in time, because it was obvious that this abduction was very difficult for her to deal with. I asked her to tell us about her pregnancy, and she replied in a flat, angry tone: 'I am not pregnant any more, they took my baby from me.'

'Who took it?' I asked.

'The aliens. I hate them,' she said.

Her next abduction, and the final one before the encounter in the field, happened when she was thirty, and followed the pattern of the earlier ones: once again, she found herself on the table being subjected to a medical examination. Samples of her skin, fingernails and hair were taken. She was again aware of other people on the tables around the room. She commented on the way the aliens went mechanically and unemotionally about their tasks, and she used an expression I have heard from other abductees: she described the experience as feeling 'like an animal in a cage'.

Her case was interesting to me, because not only did she describe very vividly the genetic experimentation which is going on – the removal of human foetuses at such an early stage of pregnancy that they would not be viable without a technology far in advance of ours – but she also touched forcibly on another aspect of abduction which comes up repeatedly: the spiritual part of it. She described the feeling of peace and relaxation as both 'religious' and 'euphoric'. In some way, the aliens were able to manipulate her emotions to trigger this deeply happy feeling: I believe that the two things they are most interested in, in their study of human life, are our reproductive abilities and our emotions. Theirs is not purely a disinterested scientific study: they are, for whatever reasons of their own, meddling in these aspects of our existence.

Bob Rylance, who served for twenty-four years in the Royal Signals and now works as a manager, is a good example of someone who, all his life, has struggled with a catalogue of paranormal events. Again, his testimony is strengthened by the fact that he and his wife Linda are such normal, down-to-earth people.

For many years, Bob has had night-time experiences, which start when he hears a buzzing noise in his head and experiences a floating sensation. Like other abductees, he finds himself on a table where various medical procedures are carried out: unlike most of the others, Bob has experienced pain when a triangular grille was placed on his stomach. He was told, telepathically, that it was being placed there 'to cure a diseased part of your stomach'. The next day, the marks of the grille could be seen, but faded before he could have them photographed.

He has also experienced something common to male abductees: a tube being placed over his genitals.

Bob's experiences started as a child: he remembers telling his mother that he woke up in the night paralysed, and sensed there was a face close to his. She soothed him by reassuring him that she, too, suffered the same thing.

After he married, he and Linda found themselves plagued by what sounds like poltergeist activity: doors would open and close, footsteps would be heard along the landing, both a friend who came to stay and, on another occasion, Bob's mother-in-law saw strange figures in their bedrooms. One evening they found Bob's electric razor, plugged in, lying on top of the cooker. The razor had been put away that morning after Bob had shaved and they had used the cooker to prepare a meal only an hour earlier: they were baffled.

One morning Bob found four or five large brown water blisters on each of his thighs: again, they disappeared quickly. He has several clear memories, unprompted by hypnosis, of 'little guys' taking him away in the night and him waking up on a table.

Under hypnosis, he revealed a classic story of repeated abductions, with the earliest one happening when he was twelve.

Like so many of the people I see, Bob copes very well with his ongoing experiences, but at the same time finds it very hard to, as he puts it, 'fit them in with my perception of reality'. I believe that is because we are, all of us, force-fed a version of reality from birth that does not take into account anything that cannot be explained away in straightforward scientific terms.

Bob's case is interesting because of the telepathic knowledge he was given that the aliens were curing him when they placed the triangular grille on his stomach and caused him pain. He had had no knowledge that he was ill. I have heard, from a completely separate case, a similar story.

People come to me when they are desperate. Even if they have supportive partners and families, they feel isolated and scared, especially if they know that the events which have frightened them may well happen again. I have to contain my anger when sceptics sneer at the use of hypnotherapy: I have seen it help so many people come to terms with their own fractured memories of events they do not understand.

Sharon, a woman in her thirties, married with two young children, heard my name on a radio broadcast and immediately made contact, because she heard me talking about my work, and the things I was saying seemed to match up with her experiences. Sharon, who lives in Yorkshire, was then sent an 'abduction enquiry questionnaire', a standard document I mail out to people who claim to have had abduction experiences. From the answers she gave, it was quickly apparent that she was a genuine case, and needed help.

Her answers to my questions contained many classic symptoms: she had woken to find the nightdress she went to bed in the night before completely missing; she had found blood on her pillows; there were strange marks on her body which appeared overnight; she had woken in other parts of the house, and always assumed she had been sleepwalking; she had found mud and grass in the bedroom which had not been there the previous evening, but had dismissed it as something her children had brought in. She had experienced all the paranormal activity which often surrounds abductees: electrical equipment malfunctioning, clocks running backwards, strange smells in the home, and on one occasion her car had cut out on a lonely road for no explicable reason, and then started again automatically. Significantly, she had experienced a pregnancy that 'disappeared' after about three months, and she had several times suffered from navel discharges.

She was happy to try hypnosis, and she and her husband Alan attended a session with Joyce and me. The session was videoed, and I reproduce here a transcript of what Sharon told me: it makes it clear how little I need to prompt people for them to tell their amazing stories. It wasn't until Sharon had heard me speaking about abduction on the radio programme that she knew anything about it, or that it could explain the mysteries of her life. She had never read any abduction stories in newspapers, magazines or books, and she generally knew very little about the whole UFO phenomenon. On the video, there are moments when she shows distress and fear, and yet, like everyone else who has attended a hypnotherapy session with me and Joyce, she said afterwards how much better she felt.

The session took place at Joyce's home, in a pleasant living room, which helps to make it a relaxing, cosy experience. Sharon slipped easily into a trance, and Joyce told her that she could relive, re-feel and re-enact various situations, knowing that she was safe and secure. Then I started questioning her:

Me: I'm going to ask you a few questions. I want to take you back to the 1980s, to 1989. It is 5 a.m. and you are just getting out of bed to go to work when something attracts you at the window . . .
Sharon: It's massive, greeny-brown, the length of the working men's club. Two more – one each side. They are going

towards [she names a place]. Now they are gone. I opened the curtains to see them go. It's dark, solid, green, brown, straight sides, curved across the top, no lights, no windows, solid. The others are the same. They've come and gone in the blink of my eyes, all gone. I'm upset, and crying, afraid of them. I've never seen anything like that before. Not like that.

Me: Do you know what's inside?

Sharon: Big white rooms, a ramp, two tall people on the ramp. They're nice, big, very tall, fair, arms thin, shoulders. Heads spherical, big face, thin necks, very tall, long bodies. Very big eyes. Nose, it's just down. They're powerful. Skin tanned, no hair. They're powerful, I can feel it. They're not wearing anything, just tanned. I think they're male. They don't speak how we speak, they speak into my head.

Me: What do they say?'

Sharon: Help us.

Me: What with?

Sharon: The earth, to look after it. I'm with the other people at the bottom of the ramp. With a man, not one of them, like us. He's bald, grey hair, called Nigel. He's clothed, he's got a shirt, light blue. He's about in his forties, late forties. We're in a room, a white room. There's just people there. I don't talk to the others. They're just people, like us. Some are sitting in front, at the side, at the back. Another tall person comes in. We have to listen. He tells us in our heads how we are polluted. He makes us feel sad. [She starts to cry.] He wants us to stop pollution. He's stronger than the others. He's tall, like them. We have to look out. We can see the earth from the back of the wall of the white room. We have to turn round to see it.

We've got to go. We walk up the ramp, down the long corridor. I want to touch the walls but I daren't. I can feel the power – I like the feel. I'm not afraid. It comes out every so often, the wall – I can't touch it. It's dark and light and it isn't a colour. It's like sand but it's not sand. I can't describe it, it's not metal. It's darkish, I daren't look up, I have to look forward, it's light at the top, dark at the sides. There's a room to the right, nothing to the left. We go forward, I'm having to go. We're all lined up, walking down, and there's the floor below us. I'm getting scared, I don't know what's happening.

I'm waiting, I don't know what for, that's why I'm frightened. I go down at the left, I'm not walking, I can't move. It's dark now, not like the white room. There's light in front. I'm just waiting in the dark room. Lights – orange. I can't move. I don't want to. There's three beams of orange light.

I'm lying down in the dark room. My right leg is hurting, I'm on something. I don't know if I'm floating, I feel strange. I don't want this: they're holding my leg, I can feel them. I can't see them. I have to look upwards. I can feel them on my right leg, on my thigh. I don't like this. My head . . . I can't see, I can't see, I can't see. I can feel, I can feel. I don't like it. They're holding me, I can see the light now, it's bright in my eyes. I feel numb. I know they're doing something and I can't stop it and I can't feel it and I know. I can see the white light, bright in the middle. I can lift my head now.

In the corner, on the left, there's a door with light shining through it. There's two in the door, they're different, smaller, darker. They're touching my fingers. They're just above the table, I can just see their heads, big heads with big eyes round to the side of their heads.

He's touching my fingers. He's got long fingers, four fingers, not like ours. They're looking at my fingers, checking each finger. My head's going back. Above me there's a round thing with things coming down, things coming down to me. It's going in me, in my stomach. The little ones are holding my hand. I can feel it but it doesn't hurt. It's going, it's like a long injection. The light's golden, it's coming down. They're stroking my hands. The gold light's coming down in a circle. I can move, sit on the edge of the table. I get down, I go to the door. The big people have come now. There's a triangle through the door. I feel nice, I have to go to the triangle.

They make me feel happy, I'm dancing, most of the boys and girls can't. I'm teaching them to skip, it's nice, everybody's friendly, we just have to play.

The man, a big man, comes and tells us we have to go home.

Me: Tell me about the next time.

Sharon: I'm eight, in bed, at home [she gives the address where her family were living]. The man's here again, he's woken me up. I have to go. I don't want to go, I'm tired, but I have to go. It's nice outside, the sun's coming up. The spaceship's here again, I have to go again. It's going on its side, I'm floating. I've told my friends I can fly and they don't believe me. I broke my arm – jumped off the slide to fly and I didn't.

That little man is here again, he's funny. I like him. Oh heck, the big people are there. You've got to be good. They play pop if you don't behave. We're going into the playroom. They're the teachers, you have to listen, they teach you.

Me: And the next time, how old are you?

Sharon: I'm fourteen and at my auntie's [she gives another address]. I'm in the back garden, having a fag. If she finds out she'll kill me.

I'm going straight up into the ship. It's different this ship, lighter. It's different than the others. There's panelling on the wall, it's not as nice. I can see funny writing, shapes, something like Egyptian writing. There are tubes around the panelling.

I feel funny, pins and needles all over my body. I'm on my own standing in the middle of the room. I stood up – I'm being undressed by the taller aliens. They're looking at me, touching my shoulders, one's behind, one's in front. Oh boy. I'm being taught lessons about life. I'm being taught to respect the earth. I don't believe half of this. They're making me listen but I don't want to. This is a bit heavy. They're telling me about pyramids, they put pyramids here.

We have to learn, grow, grow spiritually. We have to learn like the Indians how to respect the earth. I've got to listen. They give me energy, it's all in the room, pins and needles, all over, it's all going into my body, I feel the energy.

I'm on my own. I'm in the room. I can't understand

why they're telling me all this. Why me? Nobody wants to know me, nobody understands me, that's why I had to go to my auntie's. Nobody listens to me. [She is crying and distressed.]

Me: Can you tell me about the next time?

Sharon: I'm twenty-two, at [she gives me another address]. I'm in the bedroom. I have to have bed rest, I'm pregnant. I'm bored. Oh God, the light's here again, in the bedroom, the window's open and the light's there, I just have to walk into it. I'm cold. I've gone into the light. I go towards the corridor, I've been here before, I know where to go – down the corridor to the white room. I'm pregnant, though. The baby. Why now, when I'm pregnant? My baby.

They're taking me to the dark room again. I don't want it now, I'm pregnant. I can't move. They're taking me to the bed. I'm fighting, getting cross. I've got no clothes on. The baby.

All I can see is light above. There's a thing on my head, clamps on, I'm fighting it. I don't want them to hurt the baby, they want to check the baby. There's no need to check the baby, the baby's fine. [Her voice is distressed and she moves about in an agitated way.]

The probe. They're going in my side. There's no pain, I can feel it, it doesn't hurt. They're telling me they're checking the baby. They're doing something to my jaw, I can't move my head. They're doing something. They say my baby's going to be fine. I want to go back. They say she's going to help them like I'm helping them. I can go.

Me: How pregnant are you?

Sharon: Five months. There's a female with long dark hair, taller than the others, big eyes like the small ones, I've never seen one of these before. She's seeing me out. They only wanted to check on the baby. I'm going back into the light to come back. I'm in bed.

Me: And the next time?

Sharon: I'm twenty-four, pushing the pram, walking towards [she names a place]. Louise, she's seventeen months old, she's walking with me and I've got the pram. The light comes again. Where are they taking her? They're taking Louise. I want to go with them. They've taken me to a dark room, they're weighing me down again. They've taken my clothes off in another room. I'm back on the table – here we go again. The probe's coming down from above into my stomach. I've got the thing on my head. The little one's holding my hand, telling me I'm going to be better.

I can't see Louise or hear her. I can't move my head. They've put a thing on my hand, it's round, it's locked over my wrist. I can't see it, I can feel it, something on my forearm. The probe's going to make me better, but I'm not ill. It's putting pressure on my head, the light's above me, I've got to look into the light. Something's going into my arm, I can feel it, it's moving around in my blood.

I'm shouting for Louise. I can see something coming down, like a needle. Liquid, coming down the outside. Probe in my stomach, liquid coming down outside, dark purple, not light, dark.

I can hear Louise. They're fetching her. She's just stood there, I can move my head. The thing round my head is rotating. The pressure's gone off my head but I can feel it moving. Louise is just walking around. I can feel – it's moving down my arm, it's all happening at once. They won't let me get off the bed just yet, they're fetching Louise to me. Another bed, longer . . . there's doors. They're taking me to go home. The small ones are with me this time. Louise has just called the small one Mummy. She's going in front. Nobody's holding me, they're just letting me walk, there's one behind me.

Me: Tell me about the next occasion. How old are you?
Sharon: I'm thirty-three. I'm in the bedroom at [she gives her current address]. I'm in bed. I feel that somebody's at the door. Alan's next to me, but there's a light outside the bedroom. I can't wake him, I want him to see it. The door opens and they're there, the small aliens again. I want Alan to see, I want him to see so much. [Again, she sounds distressed.]

They're taking me on to a balcony. The light's above us.

114

You have to walk into it. It's been so long. I'm going up. There's railings.

I've got nothing for them this time. I've got no womb, no ovaries. That's what they wanted, I think. They never told me. I try to tell them.

It's not for that this time. It's for the learning. It's really nice, there's a bright light, the corridor smells damp, I've never noticed before. It's different this time. I'm going, walking, and I've turned and gone through something. I'm shouting – I don't want to go. It's a different place, I've never been in this part before. It's oval. I have to walk around the outside of the room. I just feel I have to – I daren't go in the middle. The walls are dark, the middle is lighter, the floor is shiny, there's marking on the floor. It's like an MW [i.e. the shape] with lines at the top, a triangle, a square. I don't want to walk on that. I walk around to another door. I don't want to go against the wall. They make me walk backwards. I've been naughty, fighting them, they're telling me. I'm up against an archway, I walk into it. They're trying to be nice, I'm being nasty, ignoring them.

I can't see. They come forward. They've done something to my arm. It didn't hurt. They just came forward with something. I walk around. They put me on the bed again – I didn't think I was coming for this. The lights. The thing is pressing on my head, it's covering my mouth, they're going into my mouth. I don't want this.

I'm upset. They're shining a golden light at me. I feel guilty, they're just trying to help me and I've been so nasty.

Me: Have you ever seen Alan when you have been taken?
Sharon: No.
Me: Have you ever seen them since this time?
Sharon: No.

That was the end of the session. Joyce brought Sharon out of the trance easily, and although she had been distressed while telling us about her abductions, she was very calm and relaxed when it was over. She later saw the video-recording, and was surprised by the things she had told us: she had no conscious

115

memory of them. Since the hypnotherapy session she has told me how much more at peace she feels.

Sharon's case is, in so many ways, a classic. Her abductions started when she was very young, and have gone on at odd intervals ever since. She has experienced both themes: the medical examinations, with particular emphasis on her reproductive organs; and the 'teaching', which, in common with most other abductees, seems to have given her a more spiritual approach to her own life.

The fact that she was first abducted as a young child, and feels that her own daughter is now also 'helping' the aliens, illustrates the generational nature of the phenomenon. She has, like so many abductees, found strange scoop marks on her arms, as if flesh has been removed. She has seen lights in her bedroom at night, and refuses to sleep alone.

From the transcript, it is obvious that my input into the session is minimal: I don't prompt her, ask leading questions, or in any way implant any ideas in her head. Everything she says comes from her own experience. She gave me so many details, even down to the name of a shop where she bought sweets when she was a child: I checked it, and although its name had changed twenty-five years ago, her memory under hypnosis was accurate.

All the abductees mentioned in this chapter have found hypnotherapy a benefit. I, too, have found it a great tool – and not just for the retrieval of abduction memories. It has also helped me explore another dimension to the abduction phenomenon, as we shall see in the next chapter.

CHAPTER FIVE

TALKING TO THE 'ENEMY'

When I first started working with abductees I was told, by
several other respected international figures from the UFO
research world, that it was a dangerous path to go down. They
told me I risked losing my reputation, because abduction is a
belief too far for many experts. I replied then that I had not
moved into the UFO world to build a reputation: I had come
seeking the truth. And if the pursuit of that truth lies in an
unfashionable and often discredited branch of research, that
does not bother me.

In the years since, as more and more respected scientists have
weighed in to the debate and are joining in the research, I have
been vindicated. But, if I am honest with myself, the compunc-
tion to delve into abduction accounts is not only objective – in
the pursuit of truth – but also subjective, because I have always
been aware of a very strong link between my own personal
experiences and those of the abductees.

This intuitive feeling of in some way identifying with them has
enabled me to help them more than perhaps I could have done
from a purely disinterested research stance. The cases in the
previous chapter illustrate how vital hypnotherapy is to my
work, not simply to provide me with more information but to
give peace of mind to the abductees. Knowing what has happened to them does not automatically mean that they are happy
with the experience: the vast majority would still prefer never to

have been involved. But it is much easier to cope with a situation that they know and, at least partially, understand than with an unspecified, pervasive fear which may contaminate the whole of life.

Hypnotherapy does not make the situation go away, but it gives people a handle to begin to understand it. Even more importantly, the fact that they are not alone – that my files are full of other, perfectly normal men and women, who have had similar experiences – is comforting. Any problem lessens when it is shared.

Several of the abductees I have worked with express a very strong feeling that their abductors have the facility to 'tune into' them whenever they choose, not just during an abduction. In other words, the telepathy the aliens use to communicate with each other and with their victims extends to being used at any time, as though once the link with a certain person is established it can be made without a physical abduction. Tracey Jones has an overpowering feeling that she is being watched; Jason Andrews talks of the aliens sharing his emotions. On one particular occasion he was riding his horse, galloping, and he was convinced 'they' were with him, experiencing the exhilaration of speed, yet not at all happy when the horse was spooked and he fell off: he sensed that they disliked the pain of a hard landing on the earth.

This conviction that the aliens are present – or can be present – at any time is not limited to the cases I have dealt with: it crops up in all other serious in-depth studies of abductees. It provides a possible explanation for the implant phenomenon. Although we have so far failed to remove and successfully analyse an implant, so many abductees are convinced that these small pieces of alien technology have been placed in their bodies that we have to give credence to it. One thing I have learned, from over fifteen years of studying abductees, is to listen to them: never allow your own preconceived ideas to prejudice your treatment of the information they are giving you. If they say implants are being placed in their bodies, I believe them, even though we do not – yet – have physical proof.

I also know, from my own experience, that the alien abductors

A series of three mysterious descending lights pictured over Whitchurch in Bristol on 24 July 1990 – typical of the inexplicable sightings that ordinary members of the public send to me to investigate. (*Jeffrey Woods*)

A selection of photographs of mysterious flying objects that have been sent me from other UFO investigators around the world:

Midlands, England, 1994

Winkelriet, Switzerland, 18 March 1975 (*Wendelle C. Stevens*)

Mexico City, Mexico, 12 May 1993 (*Wendelle C. Stevens*)

Portland, Oregano, USA, 17 October 1992 (*Wendelle C. Stevens*)

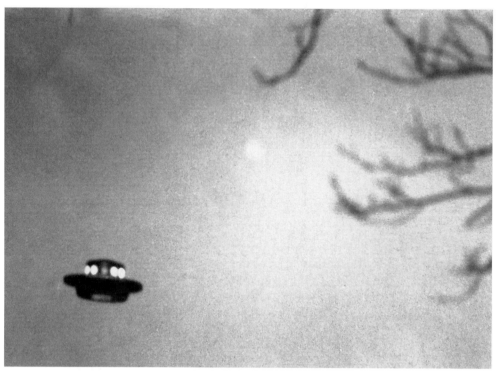

Ocotlán, Jalisco, Mexico, 27 April 1993 (*Wendelle C. Stevens*)

Himeji City, Japan, late August 1976 (*Wendelle C. Stevens*)

do communicate with their victims by telepathy, and not necessarily simply during abductions. As I question the abductees under hypnosis, on several occasions a truly remarkable event occurs: I find myself talking not to them, but to their abductors. Through their mouths come the words and messages of the aliens who are monitoring them and who are, obviously, able to be present at any time. It is as though the alien intelligence finds a voice to communicate directly with me through the hypnotised abductee. It does not happen often. The first time was also the first time that I had organised a hypnotherapy session, with the young woman who came to the police about the mysterious lights which plagued her car. I was shocked, and probably did not ask the questions I should have done: the whole subject was so new to me, and this was the very last thing I expected to happen. (Interestingly, since researching the whole subject, I have discovered I am not the only interrogator this has happened to: others have found themselves having conversations with abductors through the channel of the hypnotised victim.)

Joyce Dinsdale was as stunned as I was the first time it happened. She had many years' experience as a hypnotherapist, but had never encountered anything like this before. I was asking the young woman questions when her voice suddenly dropped a register, and she said: 'I am C [her own name] and you are talking to Zeus.'

For a few moments this strange voice continued talking about the incident, but in the third person, as though it was, indeed, no longer the young woman talking.

Then the voice changed back to her own, and the weirdest encounter of my life to that date was over. It has happened to me two or three times since, I cannot predict when it is going to happen and I cannot make it happen. The decision to talk directly to me is always theirs, never mine. Here is an account of one bizarre question-and-answer session I had with an alien abductor:

The room was quiet. The abductee was breathing slowly and steadily, and the hypnotherapist signalled to me that she was ready to be questioned. I asked the woman to tell me about her last abduction, which had taken place a few weeks earlier. She was describing it to me when her voice changed, becoming higher and acquiring a slightly metallic tone. I knew, without being told, that I was talking directly to her abductor, but the policeman in me made me ask the logical question:

'How can I be speaking to you now, when her last abduction was several weeks ago?'

The voice replied: 'You do not understand the nature of things. Time is of no consequence. Time is only something that has been devised by humanity to create an organised society, but in truth time does not exist.'

There was an air of condescension to the voice, as though it was talking down to someone of much lesser intelligence. I bristled, and again sounded as though I was back in the interview room at the police station, taking down a statement from some small-time offender.

'What gives you the right to take people without their knowledge or authority and do these things to them?' I asked.

'We have every right,' said the voice. 'Do you not do these things to your lower animals?'

Once again, the implication was that we were inferior creatures. I asked:

'Are you what we call gods?'

'This is how some of you perceive us, but you do not understand the nature of things.'

'If this is the case, do you require us to worship you?'

'No, this is not necessary.'

I asked if they were responsible for the strange machines we saw in our skies, which we called UFOs. The reply came:

'Some of these things are our vehicles.'

'Are some belonging to other entities?' I asked.

'Yes.'

'Are all these entities friendly?'

'No.'

When I asked what the purpose of abductions was, the voice avoided answering by telling me again that I did not understand the nature of things. Then the abductee was talking in her own voice again. When she came round from the hypnosis she had no memory of the conversation.

This direct contact, while baffling and fascinating, was not as surprising to me as it would have been had I not, from early on, been experiencing my own telepathic communication with the UFOs I saw over Carleton Moor. From the point that I discovered I could communicate with them – by flashing my torch – I entered into a telepathic dialogue with them which continues to this day, even though I no longer feel the need to spend cold nights in my car on the moor, waiting to see them.

So, inevitably, I had to face up to an obvious question: am I myself an abductee?

Initially, I resisted the answer: I was as much in denial as most of the abductees who come to me for help. It was not that I was afraid of being abducted: I now know enough about the subject to realise that I am far more likely to come to harm at the hands of my fellow human beings than I am during an abduction. But I felt, as most abductees do, bemused at having been selected (I now believe that a very large number of human beings are abductees, and simply do not know it).

Looking at my life, though, I have to accept that I have all the classic signs of being an abductee. As a child I suffered persistent nosebleeds; I have found strange bruises and marks on my body. I have some memories, just a few, of actually seeing creatures. The most complete memory I have is of lying on a table, unable to move. Around me were several small creatures, wearing monk's habits and with hoods over their heads. They looked very, very old: their faces were wrinkled, they looked like those ugly troll dolls which were popular a few years ago. I could sense, although I don't know how, that as well as being old they were very wise. I eventually managed to turn my head towards them, and then they looked away from me towards each other. They were communicating among themselves, telepathically. I was not frightened, but I felt irritated that I had no control of the situation, that it was being imposed on me.

Another possible memory surfaces for me in a recurrent dream I have. I am in a spacecraft, and the beings around me are both very familiar to me, and show me a lot of respect. I have a feeling of being completely at home among them. Soon I leave the craft, alone, and go through a large entryway that appears to lead straight into a hillside. I am in an enormous hall, at the far end of which there is a very old-looking being, with a white goatee beard, sitting in a high-backed chair. We communicate telepathically, but I cannot consciously remember anything that passes between us, except that I call him 'father'. I leave the hall, return to the craft, and am taken back to my home.

I can see the figure of the old man very clearly. So I was shocked when one of the people attending the Quest conference in Leeds in 1988 showed me a photograph he had taken. The subject matter was not special: my friend was simply taking shots of the whole conference, and this was a general picture of some of the audience. When the film was developed, superimposed on the shot was the figure of an old man: the same being I meet in my recurring dream. When the snap was taken, there was no sign of the figure to the naked eye.

Interestingly, one woman abductee told me that she had, during an abduction, seen another person lying on a table, and she had recognised that it was me. When she seemed upset and worried, she was told, again telepathically, not to worry, as they were taking very good care of me.

I have never been hypnotised. This is not because I am afraid to try it: I would not recommend to anyone else anything I was not prepared to undergo myself. But, since that first communication on the moor, I have received so many very strong messages, among which is a clear instruction not to interfere with my 'gift'. I have been told many times that I have an important role to play in the communication link between aliens and human beings.

These telepathic messages first started to come to me while I was still serving with the police, in the early days of my UFO research. I cannot explain how they happen, other than that some are in direct response to questions I ask, while others are spiritually uplifting messages that come into my head unbidden. They are not part of my normal, down-to-earth thought processes: I have never been a particularly religious person or someone who has studied spiritual enlightenment. I was surprised by them, but knew that they did not originate in my own brain but were put there for a purpose. Several times I have been told, telepathically, that I am a 'teacher', and I believe that my role is part of the conditioning process the aliens are following, preparing the human race for further, more open contact with them.

I record on to tape the messages I receive, as soon as I possibly can, so that I do not forget them. One tape, with a background of soft music, was borrowed by a friend to play to his young son, who was dying of cancer in a hospice. The hospice staff were so impressed by the soothing and uplifting effect of the tape that it was played to other patients. Word has spread, and now I supply copies of it to several hospices and old people's homes.

If there is no tape to hand, I scribble down the messages. The need to do this can happen at any moment: I have irritated my wife by letting my meal grow cold as I wrote down a message that had appeared, unbidden in my mind; I have pulled the car over to the side of the road to make notes on another one.

The nature of the messages is either spiritual or informative. The poetic language is not the language of my ordinary everyday speech, and anyone who knows me well will confirm that I do not normally indulge in philosophical or intellectual theorising: these messages are coming from somewhere beyond me. One of the first I received, when I was still serving in the police force, was that my word 'would become known across the world'. At the time I dismissed this: I was a serving policeman in a quiet Yorkshire town; it was preposterous to think in terms of communicating with the world. It was only in retrospect that I realised, a few years later, that the prophecy had come true. Since leaving the police I have lectured across the world, and am now regarded as an international authority on UFO research – and this in itself is surprising, because as a policeman I hated having to give any kind of public talk, even a road-safety lecture to schoolchildren, yet now I can stand with confidence in front of crowds of 1,500 and more.

But even when I am in receipt of these messages, my own pragmatic personality insists on making itself heard: I ask for proof. Normally this request is ignored, but on one occasion I was given startling evidence. My wife Pauline was seriously ill in hospital, recovering from major heart surgery. I received a

123

telepathic communication just before I visited her, and again I asked for evidence. There was no direct reply, but as I stretched out my arm to take hold of Pauline's hand at her bedside, she asked me what I had done to my watch strap. The strap, which had been gold-coloured, had changed and was now half silver-coloured. I was amazed, but realised this was the proof I had been asking for. The watch strap remains half silver to this day. (I have since heard of a similar phenomenon happening to a group of people who saw some mysterious lights in the sky in Yugoslavia.)

Another piece of tangible proof came one night. For several nights running, Pauline and I had both heard noises from my office, but on each occasion when I got out of bed to investigate there was nothing to see. Eventually I installed a closed-circuit camera, which would be activated by movement or light. The next morning we found the camera had been turned, so that it faced the wall. The following night I left a voice-operated recorder in the middle of the room: I realised there was little point in trying to conceal it. When we played back the tape there was only one word on it, in a strange metallic-sounding voice: 'Teacher.'

'Teacher' is a description that has come up several times in my telepathic communication with the aliens, and I have, after long and hard thought, accepted it. I am unsure of the reason why I was chosen, but it is clear that I have been selected to receive these messages, and pass them on. I believe mankind is being prepared for ultimate acceptance of the alien presence in our midst, but it has to be achieved slowly and with our acquiescence.

I do not think I am unique in receiving messages. To some extent, all abductees are being similarly prepared. They all report an enhanced spiritual dimension to their lives, they become more psychic, more artistic, with a deeper understanding of the environment. Research done in America shows that a large proportion actually change their lives after recognising their abductions: they give up materialist lifestyles in favour of more satisfying, if less financially successful, work, often with the sick or animals. An empathy with animals is a very normal reaction to the abduction experience: several abductees likened being the subject of medical examinations by aliens to the way we treat animals in laboratory experiments. After all, imagine being a wild animal in a big-game reserve, and being tranquillised by a dart, only to wake up with strange creatures (humans) all around, carrying out various medical procedures: would the experience not be very similar to that reported by abductees? We are, perhaps, nothing more than a race of lower animals to these beings.

But although all abductees do get some spiritual teaching from their experiences, most of them do not feel, as I do, a need to proselytise. Helping individuals cope with their own experiences is one way of doing this; lecturing is another. One of my recurrent messages is that I have an obligation to fulfil. At present I do not know what that obligation is, other than to keep passing on my messages, but I have also been told that I have a great deal more to learn, and that the more I know the more I will be misunderstood and isolated.

My telepathic communication with the aliens has helped me resolve a lot of questions about who they are and why they are involving themselves in the life of this planet. Here, in the words given to me, is one of the messages I have received in response to my mental questioning:

'Our presence within your solar systems is to observe the evolutionary progress and environmental changes occurring not only to your planet but to its people. Using this observational technique enables us to foresee potential future difficulties which may arise and if necessary give you advice on the course of action needed to overcome them. To achieve these aims we employ the use of many types of monitoring equipment, each with a responsibility for a different area of scientific investigation.

'Telemeter discs of all sizes, used as remote-controlled sophisticated recording and analysing vehicles, are one of many types of drones. We observe every aspect of your world and its inhabitants, from the environmental changes and pollution levels to the microbiological disease potential of mankind. Our techniques also enable us to record and analyse thought patterns and therefore anticipate man's course of action before he embarks on it. There is nothing about your world and its people that we are not aware of.'

Another message goes some way to explaining why certain people, including me, have been chosen to receive these communications:

'Our presence has been in your skies for hundreds of earth years but through our cloaking devices you have been unable to observe us. As your cosmic evolution has developed, the time has arrived for you to understand the existence and presence of other life in your universe, thus resulting in us making our presence known to you. Our choice of contacts has been governed by the ability of their spiritual minds to comprehend this contact without anxiety or aggression.

'The movement of our vehicles in the air which you find so strange is because we have overcome the force you call inertia and can fly in any direction instantly without experiencing any form of pressure change. Fields of force are sometimes deployed around our craft but only in the interests of protecting the craft from high-velocity impact from meteorites or missiles. Our propulsion systems work on the principle of electro-magnetism where gravity is of no significance. The three spheres sometimes seen below our craft are our drive systems, but can be detached individually to function as surveillance poles. The magnetic pole within the axis of our craft has many functions. It contains periscopic lenses for high-magnitude observation and assists in the observation of static power for recharging purposes.'

The messages have also made clear what many other experts have already suggested: that, although we have had reports of UFOs since history began, the sudden increase in their presence in our skies in the past fifty years may have something to do with the proliferation of nuclear weapons and the acute pollution and global-warming problems we now face. We have reached a position of being able to inflict irrevocable damage on our own planet, and the aliens are, possibly for their own reasons or possibly altruistically, keen to prevent this.

One message claimed: 'The problems facing your race are many, and are largely due to the focus of your technology being turned towards the hostile aspects of humanity. You have the ability to turn your world into a place of harmony and plenty if you direct your ability and enterprise towards sharing with not only your people, but the natural laws of the universe. You can advance technology, but only for the good of all, otherwise it will destroy you.'

Another said: 'The evolution of your civilisation has reached a critical stage. With the discovery of the matter reaction known as nuclear fusion you have acquired a source of great destructive potential. Such power must be controlled by wisdom and foresight. Your inventive ability has advanced beyond your fundamental power of reason. This syndrome existed on certain other worlds, resulting in their destruction. This guidance is given to you in order that you may realise that energy must be your friend and under control, otherwise it will be your enemy.'

Yet another message delivered hope, stressing that it was possible to avert a catastrophe: 'The evolvement of our race took the same course as yours, many aeons before the dawn of your civilisation. We suffered feudal wars and destructive destabilisation, but evolved through this: as you will. We are by no means superior to you, only older in wisdom because the evolution of our kind preceded yours.

'We are here with the hand of brotherly friendship, to teach you as you evolve. Each one of your kind has the ability to grow in cosmic consciousness. The answer lies within the fabric of you all. We hold great love for you and know that your direction is now turning towards the path of cosmic understanding. We will give all the love, advice and understanding to help you in accordance with cosmic law and the spirit of brotherly affection. But we can only advise: the future of your race must be determined by your own free will. Our view of you shows great hope and expectation and we await with anticipation the day when you will aspire to the federation of cosmic brotherhood.'

Receiving the messages has given me a tremendous feeling of peace. It has convinced me that everything on this planet – soil, trees, grass, as well as insects and animals – is alive, and that the earth itself is a living organism, a whole of which we are only very small parts. None of us can exist without the other parts that make up the whole. Mutual respect for each other and for the natural world around us is the key: when we learn this we will be able to co-exist harmoniously. This is, I believe, the essence of the teaching, and the essence of what I must pass on.

But, as I have been told, there is a great deal more for me to learn. For example, there is a wealth of information now available from the testimonies of abductees across the world that the aliens are involved in a programme of genetic manipulation of our species, and may even be responsible for our very existence. We may be their own pet 'guinea pigs', being manipulated for their own ends. They may be using our genetic material to re-stock their own race; they may be creating hybrids; they may even have deliberately 'seeded' our planet for their own ends.

I frame the questions in my mind, but I do not get an answer to order: the messages of reply happen at different times, usually when I am least expecting them, when my mind is on something as mundane as my garden or the football results. It is as though they make it clear that they tell me what they want me to know, when they want me to know it: and there are still a great many of my questions that are unanswered.

Whenever I ask a question they do not want to answer, I get the reply: 'Too much will make you cry.'

But even as I wrestle with the huge philosophical questions raised by the existence of other living entities, I am investigating more down-to-earth, tangible proof of alien involvement with our planet. One of the most staggering is the phenomenon of animal mutilation.

CHAPTER SIX

ANIMAL VICTIMS

Being in charge of a huge patch of North Yorkshire, my police work brought me plenty of opportunities to see animals which had been attacked by predators. Dogs chasing, worrying and killing sheep was not uncommon, and farmers usually kept the evidence – the dead carcasses – for us to see, especially if they had caught or shot the offending dog. A farmer's livestock is his stock in trade, his living, and he has the right to defend it. Farmers know from bitter experience what the results of a dog attack look like; they also know how other predators – foxes, large birds, etc. – will feed off the dead animal after the dog has killed it. In some circumstances, the deaths appear to be the result of larger beasts preying on the stock: I think there are probably many wild animals, pumas and other large cats, living wild in some of the remoter parts of Britain.

But although there may occasionally be a mystery about whether the killer is a domesticated dog or a wild big cat, death at the hands of a predator animal is instantly recognisable. And the photographs which started to land on my desk from the late eighties onwards were clearly not illustrating the work of such predators. They showed animals – cows, horses, pigs, cats, deer, badgers, foxes and others – which had been systematically mutilated, with a similarity between the corpses which might have suggested a ritual element, had it not been for the fact that the means of carrying out the mutilation appeared to be way

129

ahead of any technology known to man. Instead of the messy, gory, savaged remains of a dog kill, these animal corpses had a neat, clinically tidy appearance, with no blood loss at all, yet an astonishing catalogue of surgical procedures had been carried out on them.

The photographs were arriving in a steady stream because I had, as with abductions, expressed in public my interest in the subject. I had both mentioned it in lectures and written about it for *UFO* magazine, drawing on the research done in America. Once again, as soon as it became known that I wanted information about mutilations, it began to come in. It soon became apparent that the fact that most of the research to that date was American simply meant that investigators there had collected data on the subject: it was not a matter of mutilations only happening in the USA. They were happening here in Britain in large numbers too, and the evidence was piling up on my desk.

The history of mutilations is probably as long and varied as the history of contact between aliens and this planet, but much of the evidence has simply been dismissed and never recorded. A dead cow is not as exciting as strange lights in the sky, UFOs seen on the ground, missing-time episodes or memories of abductions. A dead cow, and the peculiar method of its death, may puzzle a farmer, but farmers are essentially practical men with demanding physical schedules: they do not, as a rule, have time to ponder too deeply about why or how their animal died. Besides, as with all other aspects of ufology, there's a risk of being laughed at and pronounced a crank: it is easier to put the death down to vandals or dogs, regardless of the evidence.

So it was not until the late sixties, when a series of reports about strange deaths in Colorado, USA, were made public, that the phenomenon of animal mutilation was recognised. There had been plenty of earlier reports, dating back as far as the eighteenth century, but they had remained as isolated, and generally ignored, incidents. Then along came a horse called Lady, a three-year-old Appaloosa mare belonging to Berle and Nellie Lewis. Lady was pastured with Nellie's brother, Harry King, a rancher whose land was near Alamosa, in the San Luis Valley of southern Colorado. The horse was healthy, the pastureland was good, Harry King had no knowledge of any predators on the loose. It was a shock, therefore, when, on 9 September 1967, he discovered the body of Lady not far from his home. The head of the mare had been stripped of flesh and muscle, there was no sign of its brain, spinal cord or heart, lungs or thyroid. Equally baffling was the lack of blood around the corpse, and the absence of tyre marks at the scene. The skull was bleached white and clean, as if it had lain under the harsh Colorado sun for days, yet the rest of the flesh had not rotted: and besides, Harry King had seen Lady alive and well less than two days earlier.

What was remarkable to the rancher, and to his sister and her husband when they arrived the following day, was the cleanness of the cut down Lady's neck and chest. Nellie Lewis also remarked upon a strange 'medicinal smell' which she likened to incense.

The park rangers called to the scene by Harry King were baffled. They found fifteen circular marks, which looked like exhaust burns, close to the body; a three-foot circle of eight holes in the soil, each four inches in diameter and four inches deep, forty feet away from the dead horse; and evidence of radiation around the exhaust marks, detected with a Geiger counter. Lady's tracks appeared to stop about one hundred feet from where her body was found.

Dr John Altshuler, a pathologist from Denver, was in the area because he had read reports of strange lights in the sky, and wanted to see them for himself. The lights had been seen all summer, darting across the nearby hills at speed. On the night of Lady's death, a neighbour of Harry King's saw several small high-speed objects which he called 'jets' zooming across the pastureland where the horse died, and Harry's eighty-seven-year-old mother also reported a large object passing over the ranch that same night.

Dr Altshuler met the rangers involved in the investigation, and when they discovered he was a pathologist they invited him to have a look at the body. The pathologist was already shocked by what he had seen in his visit to the area: he had been out at night and clearly saw three bright lights moving just below the tops of the Sangre de Cristo mountains, in an area where there were no roads, thus ruling out the possibility of car lights. The lights seemed to get bigger and be approaching him, and then suddenly shot vertically up into the air.

What he now saw when he examined Lady, ten days after her death, made an even more profound impression on him, but it was not until many years later, when television documentary-maker Linda Moulton Howe was researching the growing number of animal mutilation stories, that he agreed to talk about it. Linda is now a very good friend of mine. She became involved in the subject quite dispassionately, purely as a work project, never expecting to find anything with alien connections. Her previous award-winning work had been about environmental issues. She had heard about the mutilations, and how there were often strange lights in the sky at the time, and unmarked aircraft or helicopters near the scene soon afterwards. She surmised that the mutilations might be part of a secret government research programme, possibly monitoring pollution and contamination caused by a radiation leak or an accidental poison release that the authorities were keeping secret. At best, she hoped to unmask a government cover-up.

The more she investigated, the more she realised that something much more dramatic was happening, although it did involve a top-level cover-up. Her documentary, *A Strange Harvest*, was broadcast across the USA in 1980 and won her an Emmy, the prestigious American TV award. It also fascinated the public at large, and more and more reports of mutilations piled in.

As part of her research, she looked at the case of Lady, which had attracted a huge wave of media interest at the time. She tracked down Dr Altshuler, who by then was Assistant Clinical Professor of Medicine (Haematology) and Pathology at the University of Colorado Health Sciences Centre. He told Linda, for her book, *An Alien Harvest*:

'When I got close to the horse I could see that it was cut from the neck down to the base of the chest in a vertical, clean incision. At the edge of the cut there was a darkened colour, as if the flesh had been opened and cauterised with a surgical cauterising blade. The outer edges of the cut skin were firm, almost as if they had been cauterised with a modern-day laser.

'I cut tissue samples from the hard, darker edge. Later, I viewed the tissue under a microscope. At the cell level, there was discoloration and destruction consistent with changes caused by burning.

'Most amazing was the lack of blood. I have done hundreds of autopsies. You can't cut into a body without getting some blood. But there was no blood on the skin or the ground. No blood anywhere. That impressed me the most.

'Then, inside the horse's chest, I remember the lack of organs. Whoever did the cutting took the horse's heart, lungs and thyroid. The mediasternum was completely empty and dry. How do you get a heart out without blood?'

At the time of Lady's death, laser technology was highly experimental, and the first recorded instance of lasers being used in veterinary surgery – without the precision apparently used on Lady – did not come until the early seventies.

Throughout the remaining years of the sixties and the seventies, more and more cases of animal mutilations were reported, and they all seemed to have several factors in common:

1. An absence of blood. Sometimes a small puncture hole was found in the jugular vein, through which the blood appeared to have been drained, possibly with the animal still conscious while this procedure took place. Under normal circumstances, this would lead to the collapse of the cardiovascular system, but in these cases it remained intact.
2. Sophisticated anatomical knowledge. The cuts on the body, through which organs were removed, were made neatly and in precisely the right places.
3. The use of advanced surgical instruments. The cuts were clean, the wounds appeared to be sealed or cauterised, there was no blood, and where bones were severed, no evidence of bone splinters or dust.
4. The removal of certain internal organs, most often the brain, the rectum and the sex and reproductive organs.
5. Sometimes, evidence that the animal had been sedated.

6. Occasionally, evidence of radiation around the scene of the mutilation.
7. Usually, no sign of disturbance, not even the animal's own hoofprints, near the corpse.
8. Sometimes, the animals would have broken legs and backs, as if they had been dropped to the ground from a great height.
9. Often, the mutilations happened on nights when UFOs were spotted in the vicinity.
10. Blacked-out helicopters or unmarked planes would be seen after the mutilation, and there were often large white vans spotted in the area, perhaps used for transporting the helicopters.

Despite the efforts of the authorities to pass off all the mutilations as the work of animal predators, a feeling of growing alarm was spreading among cattle ranchers across the States. Their instinct was to believe that organised, sophisticated and weirdly motivated vandals were on the loose, and they formed posses to stake out their herds at night to protect them from these unidentified attackers.

In a bid to calm the situation, the head of the Colorado Bureau of Investigation issued a statement in 1975 claiming that ninety-five per cent of the dead cattle had been killed by natural predators. A small sample of carcasses were sent for laboratory analysis, more than half of which were shown to have been cut by a sharp instrument, but the Bureau of Investigation interpreted this as only a small percentage of the overall deaths, rather than as a large percentage of those analysed.

Farmers and ranchers scoffed at the report. Experienced cattlemen expect to lose the odd cow to a predator, and they recognise the damage when they see it. They were not fobbed off. One Kansas sheriff commented: 'You couldn't cut up an animal like that without it getting nasty.' Another sheriff, from Colorado, where the Bureau of Investigation was trying to downplay the epidemic of mutilations, was annoyed when samples taken from mutilated animals were persistently reported by the laboratory to be the work of predators. He used a sharp knife to cut a piece of flesh from a cow, and, true to his expectations, the lab assessed it as damage caused by an animal predator. When confronted with evidence of what he had done, they lamely claimed to have made a mistake.

In the two years between 1975 and 1977, more than 1,500 cases of animal mutilation were reported across twenty-two states of America. Even allowing that some were natural predators' work (and those that were obviously in this category were not included in the figures), and that some were the work of vandals, Satanic cult worshippers and other assorted weirdos who were inspired by all the publicity surrounding the mutilations, this was still an alarmingly high number. Eventually, in 1979, a conference was arranged, organised by Senator Harrison Schmitt from New Mexico, the last American astronaut to have walked on the moon. He called together ranchers who had lost cattle, veterinary experts, and law enforcement agencies, including the FBI.

The conference was not an unqualified success – it only lasted for one day and there was a great deal of shouting between the two sides, with the ranchers opposing the government officials, who were still maintaining there was nothing sinister going on. At least one law enforcement officer, who had gathered a large file of data on mutilations, did not give evidence to the conference, and admitted later that this was not his own choice: in other words, he had been silenced by those above him. But the conference did force the FBI to take control of the investigation, and computerise national records. A report was commissioned from a former FBI agent, who had already come out at the conference as a sceptic, so there was little surprise when, a year later, he issued his finding that 'there is simply no concrete evidence to support the theory that mutilations are being conducted as experiments by highly skilled individuals using precision instruments'.

His damning report was little more than an irrelevance. As more and more people heard about the mutilations, details of incidents flooded in. Linda made her seminal documentary, and other serious researchers became involved. She, and they, went on to uncover plenty of evidence that the mutilations were being carried out by intelligences with technical medical skills far outstripping our own. Dr John Altshuler, the pathologist who first examined Lady, has examined tissues from several mutilated animals, at Linda's request. In many cases he found the incisions in the animal's flesh had been made with high heat, which 'cooked' the haemoglobin at the edge of the cut. But he also reported that in some of the cases, the lines of the cut had a 'plasticised', hardened edge, not consistent with the type of laser technology we can use today (and, if lasers were being used, the amount of power needed to run them would mean small generators being taken to the scenes of the mutilations). In a number of cases, although the incisions were very precise, there was no evidence of heat being used.

There is also plenty of evidence that the American government is monitoring what is going on, which is why the helicopters, planes and vans are spotted with such regularity near the scenes of mutilations. Linda was told forthrightly by an Air Force Office of Special Investigations agent that her documentary had upset 'some people in Washington. They don't want animal mutilations and UFOs connected together in the public's mind.'

It was with a knowledge of this background that I became involved in animal mutilation research. There was obviously a definite link with UFO and alien activity, so naturally I wanted to find out more. I knew there had been a few reports from Britain, but nothing on the scale of what was happening across America and Canada. But I also suspected that this was because the mutilations were not being reported – or, if they were, they were vanishing into local police files and never being collated into a national picture. A report of a mutilated horse or cow would naturally never be a top priority for the police: it is only as part of the overall picture that each one becomes significant.

I was quickly proved right. Some cases had come in to me without prompting, but as soon as it became known that I was interested in animal mutilation, a steady stream of reports began that has never abated. Although there are a number which have to be discounted because they can be seen to have other causes, it is not more than about ten per cent: the farmers, vets and wildlife experts who send me photographs and reports are well able to recognise the tearing and teeth marks which are evidence of an attack by a natural predator. And although some mutilations are undoubtedly caused by sick vandals who enjoy inflicting pain on animals, again, their handiwork is easy to eliminate. For a start, mindless vandals rarely have the skills of a highly trained veterinary surgeon, and whoever or whatever is mutilating these animals has skills which have made vets and pathologists draw their breath in admiration.

The similarities with American cases are enormous. Some aspects have also been reported from the States and other countries: for example, I have collected a huge file of photographs of wild animals which have been found with mysterious holes in the front of their skulls. The bodies of dead badgers, foxes, deer, hedgehogs, etc. are not normally sent for post-mortem examination, so the extent of the mutilation is rarely realised – most people encountering a wild animal with a hole in its head would assume it had been shot. But these marks are not consistent with a bullet hole, and when they have been forensically examined we have found no evidence of bullets. Remarkably, what we have discovered is that through the small hole the brain, and often the spinal column, has been removed.

I also realised, fairly soon after I started to collect evidence, that as well as the sexual organs and the major internal organs being a prime target for removal, the rectum of the mutilated animals is also taken. It is usually 'cored out', as if with a special instrument that can neatly and cleanly take the whole length of the rectal passage. Why this particular part of an animal's anatomy should be of interest, I do not know, especially as the digestive system in general does not seem to be an area that the alien predators are interested in. My findings have again been confirmed from international evidence.

Although, from the hundreds of cases I have heard about, it is not possible to arrive at any statistical conclusions (the reports come in to me from researchers who are interested, so they tend to be from areas where people are aware of their significance, and aware of my interest), there are some clear general conclusions I can draw:

1. The female of any species is mutilated more often than the male, in a ratio of about three to one.
2. There are differences between the mutilations of large and small animals. Large animals, like cows and horses, have attracted the most notice, and therefore the mutilation they suffer is regarded as the classic: the rectum is cored; large areas of flesh are cleanly removed; the head, or part of it, is stripped to the bone; there is total blood loss.

   Smaller animals, any creature from a deer down to a mouse, will have a small hole in the front of its head, above the eyes, through which the brain will have been removed. Removal of organs such as genitalia, tongues, ears and feet can be found in both large and small animals.
3. The mutilations come in clusters, either with individual cases in the same area over a matter of a few weeks, or, more spectacularly, with several animal corpses being found together. Often these are a group of animals which would never be together in nature: e.g. badgers, sheep and foxes all dead in the same field. This makes the possibility of natural predators even more unlikely, and also means, for this reason alone, that the idea of human vandals becomes implausible.

One of the aspects of the mutilation phenomenon that particularly interests me is these multiple mutilations, when the carcasses of several animals are found together, all with mysterious and unnatural injuries. Sometimes these deaths all occur on the same night in the same place; sometimes there is a cluster of mutilations in the same area, happening across a few days or weeks.

One such case that I heard about happened in March 1991, in the small Scottish village of Kinlochewe, Wester Ross. Sheep were dying in strange ways, and rumours were rife among the traditionally superstitious villagers. There was talk of vampires, and of a strange wild beast roaming the area. The case came to my attention when one of my researchers sent me a copy of the *Sunday Mail* which included a story, with the headline 'Vampire Beast on the Loose', claiming that a 'killer beast' was terrorising the remote Highland village: 'The beast, which attacks at night, has killed nine sheep, leaving a puncture wound under each ear. When the bodies were found the crofters called in a vet from fifty miles away.'

The vet was reported as saying that he had never previously seen anything like this, and confirmed the puncture holes which he had, apparently, originally thought were bullet holes. Two local residents reported seeing a large cat-like footprint, measuring two and a half inches across, in the snow, and one of the crofters suggested that the puncture holes could have been caused by a fox which had lost its teeth through age and needed to suck blood to survive because it could not chew meat. But the vets who had been called in were quoted in the newspaper as saying: 'We cannot suggest any animal which could have been responsible for wounds of this nature, and the total loss of blood.'

The researchers who alerted me questioned the vets at length, and again the vets confirmed that they were baffled by what could have caused such distinctive injuries, and how the blood could have been drained so expertly from the body without leaving any marks on the ground. There was no sign of a struggle at the scene of the killing and no tracks in the fields (although the terrain was hard and tracks may not have shown).

The Scottish Society for the Prevention of Cruelty to Animals was equally puzzled. 'We have no idea what caused the death of the sheep, or what kind of animal could have inflicted these wounds,' said a spokesman.

Although it was not suggested in this case, I have heard of mink being made the scapegoat for other killings where puncture wounds are found on sheep. Mink were introduced into Britain in 1929, to be farmed for their highly prized pelts. Some escaped, and were able to breed and become well established along river banks, living off moles, rabbits and fish. The respected naturalist Sir David Attenborough related a television wildlife special in which puncture wounds in dozens of dead sheep were alleged to be the work of the mink. The programme did not explain why the sheep also had holes bored in the top of their skulls, nor how a mink, no bigger than a rat, could fell and hold still a sheep while it drank away the animal's life blood. The film also claimed that the mink were able to swim to a small island three miles away, where they killed 129 terns in one night, the bodies being discovered minus heads. Why the mink only took the heads was not explained. But decapitated birds have been found in large numbers since, notably 180 gulls which were found without heads in a bird sanctuary on the Scilly Isles, on land owned by Prince Charles: again, no sensible natural explanation has been given. Natural predators gore and tear their victims; they do not neatly remove and dispose of the heads, leaving the rest of the body behind.

A few months after the mysterious sheep killings in Scotland, forty-five sheep died in one night in a field at Kettlewell, north Yorkshire. The animals were not mutilated, but their bodies were found in a pile next to a dry-stone wall. One theory was that they had suffocated after jumping over the wall in terror and landing on top of one another. A dog was blamed for causing their panic-stricken leap across the wall.

The report did not make sense to me. If the sheep had been injured and unable to disentangle themselves, I can understand that the ones at the bottom of the heap could have suffocated. But the top ones? That did not add up. Neither did the theory of a dog chase. Dogs single out and attack individual sheep, two at the most. They chase the sheep, persistently biting its rear end, causing tearing wounds until the sheep falls to the ground, at which point the dog tears at other areas of flesh. Dogs do not chase a whole herd of sheep. Nor was there any evidence of any of the sheep being bitten by the dog. Why did it not sustain its attack when it had the sheep cornered and in a pile?

Local farmers I spoke to agreed with me. They had never heard of a dog attack causing death on this scale, and they, too, were puzzled by the lack of wounds on any of the sheep. Unfortunately, no post-mortems were carried out, as it was assumed that there was no other possible explanation. A few years earlier, in the same area of the dales, 400 sheep disappeared from a field one night. The disappearance was ascribed to rustlers, despite the fact that such a large-scale operation would have required a sizeable animal transporter and several men, and would have been noisy and almost impossible to carry out without arousing some local interest. There were no vehicle tracks in the field, nor were any of the sheep ever traced.

During the winter months of 1991–2 I heard reports of strange mutilations taking place in the Orkney Isles. The victims were seals. In a short space of time, the headless bodies of over thirty were found on the local beaches. Animal welfare officers, police and local vets were baffled. Mike Lynch, an inspector with the Scottish Society for the Prevention of Cruelty to Animals, said:

'We're at a loss. I've never seen anything like this before. A post-mortem examination of one of the dead animals revealed that the head had been removed almost surgically. Whoever did this must have used a very sharp knife. The heads have not been hacked off, yet there is no sign of serrations, which rules out normal predators like sharks or killer whales.

'There is no evidence of how the animals have died, and the seals' bodies show every sign of them being in good health. I may be wrong, but the evidence points to there having been a massacre. Without a clue as to who is killing the seals, there is nothing we can do.'

Orkney Seal Rescue, a charity set up to protect the seals of the islands, could throw no light on the strange deaths. A spokesman said:

'What is baffling is that in a small community, where people usually know what is going on, nobody has come forward with a clue . . . It is possible that these deaths have been caused by fishermen protecting their fish stocks. But why remove the heads? It does not make sense.'

When I contacted the local police chief he told me that the police would not normally be involved in this type of case, but due to the strange circumstances they had been called in to assist. He explained that there was a disagreement between the conservationists, vets and police, with some believing that the seals had been killed on the beaches where they were found, while others were of the opinion that they had been killed at sea and washed ashore.

There was no evidence to support either theory. If they had been killed on the beaches, why was there no sign of blood, and no marks in the sand around the bodies? If they were killed at sea, how had they all washed ashore together – and what kind of predator only took heads?

I spoke to the veterinary surgeon who performed the post-mortem on the seals, and she said:

'We cannot guess what killed these animals, but whatever it was had a knowledge of seal anatomy. The cuts were clean and precise and had gone between the vertebrae without actually damaging the bones. There was a total blood loss commensurate with them having been killed at sea, but if they were killed on the beaches where they were found there was no blood to be seen.'

Within weeks of the seals' deaths, large numbers of sea birds were found dead on the shores of the Orkney and Shetland Islands: again, their heads had been removed. Again, we are left wondering if there is an unknown, but natural, predator which has a taste only for the head of its victim: in which case it is displaying a discrimination rarely found in the animal kingdom. Or is there another predator, one not killing for food but because certain parts of the anatomies of certain animals hold a fascination for it? If this is the case, we are dealing with a predator who is not human. At the time of the seal deaths, residents in the Orkneys were reporting strange lights in the skies, just as has happened at the scenes of so many of the American mutilations.

I am not claiming, and never have, that all mutilations are the work of aliens. As the subject has received publicity, so there have been plenty of horrific attacks on animals by vandals. There was a spate of attacks on horses, but the nature of the mutilations made it clear that they were the work of ham-fisted amateurs, and would never be confused with the surgical exper-tise of the alien mutilations. You do not have to be medically trained to see the difference.

In the summer of 1990 there had been massive publicity

surrounding crop circles, those strange, precise and frequently very complex shapes made in fields of corn, with no damage to the surrounding crop. Not only were genuine mysterious circles appearing, but also, because of the controversy, hoaxers were out in force creating their own versions, and journalists and television camera crews were following the story in droves. On Saturday 30 July 1990, the activity was centred on Wiltshire, and two crop circle researchers were out early, hoping to find a new circle. At 7.15 a.m. they were horrified to come across the body of a dead and mutilated horse near the famous White Horse earth monument.

They described the horse as a large white male, lying on its left side. There was a wound where its sexual organs had been removed, and another where the left ear had been removed, but there was only one spot of blood on the ground, no bigger than a ten-pence piece, four feet away from the corpse. The horse's feet were caught up in a large-link fence, there was foam at the corners of its mouth and its eyes were bulging: the crop researchers described to me their horror at the 'lonely, agonising death' it must have suffered. Yet, although the obvious conclusion was that it had wounded itself on the partially collapsed fence, there was not a sign of blood or torn flesh on the fence.

The horse had died within the previous two hours, as rigor mortis had not set in, and the foam on the mouth was still wet, so there should have been plenty of signs of wet or coagulating blood. Another crop circle researcher, out even earlier, had heard cries, like those of a child, coming from the valley where the body was found about an hour before the horse was discovered. Within a short space of time, the body of the horse had been removed.

There were elements of this story which were not typical of an animal mutilation: for example, if the sound of crying had been the horse's death throes and the bulging eyes were indicative of, as the researchers guessed, an 'agonising' death, this does not fit the general pattern, where no sound is ever heard, and the animals appear to have been tranquillised or anaesthetised before death. Also, although there was little sign of blood, the body had not been drained, nor were the wounds as surgically precise as in other mutilations. Questions were asked about the horse, and though the police originally denied that anything had happened, they later admitted that a horse had died 'of natural causes'. Rumours took off, and before long there were stories of UFOs being seen on the ground, and alien figures disembarking and carrying out the killing. It was then laughed off as preposterous.

My own feeling – and I have in my files a first-hand report from one of the researchers who discovered the body – is that this was a case of brutal vandalism, done to mimic a mutilation: the location, so close to the White Horse monument, and the presence of TV crews in the area, make it all very suspicious. Yet whoever did it was well prepared and well equipped. It is possible that the police made as little of it as possible because they did not want to trigger copycat mutilations carried out by mindless idiots: they were already coping with university undergraduates and army cadets going out in the night to ruin farmers' crops by creating phoney circles.

Although I do not support the crop circle hoaxers – their handiwork confuses the genuine and important research going on into this phenomenon – I can understand how a group of bored young men can amuse themselves by sneaking out at night to try to fool the experts with their amazing mathematical symbols in flattened corn: what I cannot begin to understand is how anyone can hoax an animal mutilation, killing a beautiful horse simply to achieve two minutes of anonymous fame. Whoever carried out this mutilation, and others which I know are human in origin, must have a very sick personality indeed.

But, hoaxes aside, there are plenty of genuine cases to investigate. Throughout 1993 and 1994, my phone rang many times with reports of animals being found with strange mutilations in an area stretching from the south-east coast of Scotland down to Whitby, Scarborough, Bridlington and Grimsby, on the north-east coast of England. The animals involved included cattle, sheep, deer, foxes and badgers. In the case of the cattle, the rectums were cored out and various parts removed from their bodies, including the udder, tongue, brain and internal organs. In the case of the small animals, the rectum was again removed, and each animal had a neat hole bored in the forehead, through which the brain and spinal column were completely removed. In every case, there was no spillage of blood at the scene, and the removal of the brain and spinal column through a hole no bigger than a ten-pence piece again required a surgical skill far in advance of anything known to man.

The information came to me from a contact of mine in the area. I have to protect his anonymity, because he works on local farms from time to time, has links with the Forestry Commission, and knows many landowners. One of the code names I have used for him in the past is Cedar, and that is what I shall call him here.

Some of the farmers in the area who lost stock reported these unnatural deaths to the Ministry of Agriculture, Fisheries and Food, and they were visited by inspectors from the government agency. But at no time were they given an explanation for what was happening, nor did they find their official visitors helpful or communicative about a problem that was affecting their livelihoods. In fact, they found these shadowy figures so obstructive that they simply do not report the mysterious deaths any more. Cedar heard from one of his contacts that small mutilated animals were being taken to a MAFF depot, where they were sealed in plastic containers and sent abroad: unfortunately, he does not know where they went.

Determined to get to the bottom of what was going on – and protect their stock – the farmers arranged a vigil at one field between Scarborough and Whitby where a spate of mutilations had occurred. They hired infrared cameras, which would be triggered by movement in the field. The sensors were rigged so that they would record any movement above the height of a sheep, so that they would not be fired by the sheep moving around the field in the night. Armed with shotguns, a group of farmers spent the night in the open, next to the field. The cameras flashed three times, but the farmers neither saw nor heard anything. The following morning, however, they found another mutilated lamb, only yards from their observation point, and two more at the other side of the field. There had been no sound of disturbance in the flock during the night, and again the mutilations were surgically precise and bloodless, each animal having a small, neat hole in the forehead and its rectum cored out. When the films were developed they showed only a black background with a small white cloud in the centre.

The farmer whose sheep had been killed arranged for a private autopsy of one of the bodies, which was carried out at a university department of veterinary studies. The report stated that a one-inch hole had been made in the lamb's skull, through which the brain and spinal cord had been expertly removed. There was, according to the forty-page pathology report, a high level of radiation in the animal's body, and the DNA structure of the blood was abnormal.

At the time that these mutilations were being reported from the north-east, I was also hearing independently of sightings of strange lights in the sky over the same area, and in November 1993 two young women out walking on land close to the Fylingdales early-warning station saw what they described as three UFOs flying low, close to them. The middle one was cigar-shaped, and the other two were disc-shaped. The women claim they saw the larger, cigar-shaped object lose height rapidly and crash on to Ministry of Defence land inside the Fylingdales perimeter. Meanwhile the two smaller objects travelled very fast towards them and stopped abruptly, hovering just above the ground. The women saw what they believed was a small figure, the size of a child, climb out of one of the hovering objects. They were very frightened and ran away, reporting what they had seen to a National Parks warden they encountered and, later, to my contact, Cedar.

The two young women have since become very frightened, and have moved house because they believed they were being watched. One of them claims to have narrowly escaped being kidnapped by three men in a large black car, being saved only because some friends were waiting to meet her nearby. The other one disappeared completely, but was later found in France, suffering from memory loss. Her friends brought her home and looked after her. The park warden, whom Cedar had met before, also disappeared: when Cedar called at his home he was told he was away.

Cedar, acting promptly after he heard the girls' report of the crashed UFO, went with others to the point nearest to the site of the crash, but found, unusually, the perimeter fence at Fylingdales under guard by what appeared to be military personnel, wearing camouflage clothing. Using binoculars, the group could see signs of activity in the distance, where the women estimated the cigar-shaped object had hit the ground. There was a large metallic object partly in view, and around it were several people dressed in one-piece suits with head visors. They appeared to be holding hosepipes and spraying the object with a vapour.

After Cedar had reported the crash to me, I drove over to meet him, and together we went to see the site. We were in the Dolby Forest when we were stopped by two men in an unmarked four-wheel-drive vehicle. They were in their late thirties, with short military-style haircuts, but wearing the sort of casual outdoor clothing you would expect a park warden to wear. They challenged us brusquely, asking where we were going and what we were doing. We told them we were lost. I noticed one of them noting down our registration number. We were directed back to the nearest road, and told we should not be in the forest. I did not want to make an issue of it in the circumstances, but the forest is open to the public and we had every right to be there.

Shortly afterwards, Cedar's home was twice broken into, and photographs and documents about the crash were taken. On one occasion he was actually talking to me on the phone when there was a loud banging at the door, which I could hear quite distinctly. I heard him being ordered to open up, but refusing because the men outside did not have a search warrant. They replied that they did not need one, as he was in breach of the Official Secrets Act by being in possession of documents. As they began to attack his door more violently he told me he was ringing off, in order to quickly phone his solicitor.

His home has been burgled again, despite having an alarm system, and he lost more files and photographs. The thieves ignored their usual haul of TV, videos and cameras, confirming that not only were they looking for specific information, but that they were making no attempt to disguise their actions as an opportunistic theft. It was, as well as a burglary, a warning to him.

Mysterious mutilations have continued to happen in the area. In February 1997 in a clearing in the Dolby Forest the dead bodies of seven rabbits, one fox, one badger, one sheep and one deer were discovered in an area no bigger than the average family sitting room. They each had a hole in their head, their rectum cored and square patches of their skin neatly removed.

The following month, Cedar became embroiled again in a curious sequence of events. A friend of his who is a scrap-metal dealer was driving home in the dark from Ravensthorpe along the isolated Whitby road when he became aware of some blinding headlights approaching him. They were coming at such speed, and there was something so scary about them, that the scrap dealer pulled his car to the side of the road until they had passed. They went by so fast that he could not make out what type of vehicle they belonged to. Driving on, he suddenly came across several dead animals. Their corpses, still warm as if they had died very recently, were blocking the road. There was a donkey, two deer and a fox, and he later reported that they all had a neat hole in their forehead.

The scrap dealer was baffled, but, typically for a country dweller, he loaded one of the deer into his van, to eat the venison. He had to pull the donkey off the road to be able to drive on. Knowing that Cedar had an interest in the welfare of animals, he drove straight to his friend's home, where he poured out his story. Cedar took photographs of the deer in the van, after recognising the injury. He told me later that there was a trace of blood at the edge of the hole in the animal's forehead, but that it dried up almost visibly: between taking the first and third pictures it had vanished completely and the white bone of the skull was showing.

Cedar then gave his camera to his friend and asked him to go back to take photographs of the animals in the road, as he himself had a prior engagement that evening. When the scrap dealer had not returned with the camera by midnight, Cedar was worried, and went round to his house. The dealer was in bed. He had taken the photographs, but said that by the time he had returned to the scene the body of the fox had been stripped to the bone, although the other animals were intact. He agreed to get up and return to the scene with Cedar. They were inspecting the corpses when a taxi pulled up alongside them, and the driver told them to be careful because earlier in the evening he had seen several men wearing one-piece suits grouped around the dead beasts. They had told him the animals were contaminated, and to drive on.

Cedar and the dealer took more pictures and drove on across the moors. There was nothing else to see, so they turned to go back the way they had come, but when they reached the dead animals they found the road blocked by two soldiers. They were not allowed through, and were sent home by a circuitous route. Cedar warned his friend not to eat the venison, but the scrap dealer was not prepared to waste a gift like that, and took no notice. He appears, to date, to have suffered no ill effects.

Nine months later, in December 1997, five cows were found dead and mutilated, with their udders sliced off, in a field near Fylingdales. MAFF men arrived at the scene within a couple of hours of the deaths being reported, and ordered the disposal of the bodies.

There is a constant flow of reports, not all as detailed as this, arriving on my desk: here are a few samples from my files.

In October 1994, a dead and mutilated cow was found near a forest at Newry, Northern Ireland. The rectum of the animal had been cored out and the udder removed in a precise and surgical way. The flesh of the jaw and face had been totally removed, leaving the exposed skull bones. There was no sign of any blood whatsoever, no marks on the ground of a struggle, or any tracks left by either an animal or a human predator.

In October 1995, a pedigree Jersey cow was found on a farm in Jersey with the rectum cored out, the right eye missing, and the tail removed. There were severe injuries to the face, and the animal appeared to have lost all its blood. But again there was no blood on the ground and no marks left by the killers. The carcass was removed within thirty minutes of the herdsman finding it. The herdsman, a casual labourer, was given another job to do, away from the scene of the death, and was ordered not to talk to anybody about what he had seen. He was told the cow had been attacked by dogs, but that if he mentioned this to anyone, he would not be given more casual work on the farm. From his own experience he knows that what he had witnessed was not the result of a dog attack. And if it was, why the secrecy? Farmers usually band together to protect their stock from a rogue dog on the loose, and the first thing they do is let their neighbours know of the risk. The herdsman saw the animal being removed by a four-wheel-drive vehicle towing a horsebox; neither of the vehicles belonged to the farm. My researcher in Jersey tried, in vain, to track down the vehicles.

As I have seen before, there appears to be a swift and set procedure when mutilations are officially notified. This cow was moved in much greater secrecy and haste than would have been the case had it fallen victim to dogs, or to disease.

In May 1995, local hikers crossing fields in north-east England came across a scene of carnage, with bodies of sheep, lambs and, curiously, badgers littered around the place. The farmer was called, and when he had finished sorting out the mess he had counted seventeen dead sheep and five dead badgers, each with a hole in its forehead and the rectum cored out.

In April 1996, I read an item in a daily newspaper about a Vietnamese pot-bellied pig which had been found with its head cut off, and one front leg missing. It had happened at riding stables at Lanescott Mines, in Cornwall. Reading the article reminded me of a similar case, in the seventies, when a wallaby and several exotic birds at Newquay Zoo were beheaded; in each case there was no blood at the scene of the killing. In the case of the wallaby, the carcass had been transported over several fences too high for it to have jumped, into a paddock fifty yards away, eliminating the possibility of any known natural predators. Remembering this, I asked a contact of mine in Cornwall to find out more about the headless pig.

He contacted the owner of the stables and she told him that the whole family was distraught over the loss of the family pet. The pig normally slept in the stables with its mother, and on the night of its death the doors were closed, but not locked. During the night, the husband of the stable owner went out to investigate a mysterious light on the hillside behind the stables, at the site of an old engine house. He distinctly felt he had been tapped on the shoulder as he made his way there, but when he swung around there was nothing to see, and no bushes or trees which could have brushed against him. The light had also disappeared. The next morning the whole door of the stable, approximately seven feet by four feet in size, had been wrenched off its hinges and the piglet was missing. Later, the stables were examined but there was no sign of blood or a struggle. The torso of the animal was found half a mile away: the head and missing leg have never been found. Again, there was no blood at the scene, leaving the local police to conclude that the killing had occurred elsewhere and the body had been dumped there. The police suggested a dog could have done it, but the stable owner told my researcher that the head and leg were severed 'as cleanly as the butcher would do it'.

The RSPCA was called, and an autopsy arranged. The pig's remains were passed to a government veterinary establishment near Truro, but requests from both my researcher and the owner of the pig for the results of the autopsy have been turned down, and a member of staff working at the centre has repeated that the mutilation must have been the work of a dog. If it is so simple and straightforward, why will they not release the autopsy report? And why have an autopsy at all: they certainly do not do this routinely for an attack by dogs.

The family who lost the pig were devastated, especially as they had three years earlier had a horse killed and mutilated. The mare was in foal, and her vagina had been slit open and the foal removed. The hair of the tail and mane was missing. Even more puzzling, although far less tragic, a brown horse in the field with the mare had turned white overnight. At that time, July 1992, there had been a spate of other animals in the area being killed or going missing: these included chicken, sheep and domestic pets. Again, foxes or dogs were blamed. In the same month, a horse was found dead and mutilated in Wiltshire, again near a crop circle.

At the time the pig was killed, I was receiving a steady flow of

UFO reports from Cornwall. On the same date as the pig's death, the night of 18 April, a man was sitting in his car, parked on a hill in Plymouth, when he saw a silver ball flash overhead, travelling across the sky at phenomenal speed.

After a subsequent run of UFO reports from the south-west of England, I heard from witnesses who saw a UFO on the ground: the following day all the sheep in the field where the strange craft had been seen had aborted their lambs.

In the summer of 1996, residents of a remote Dartmoor village were dismayed to lose eighteen cats in three months. It was, apparently, not the first time that large numbers of domestic cats had gone missing at the same time. There were theories that the cats had been kidnapped for vivisection or for their fur, or even to be turned into animal food. It was clear they had not been taken by an animal predator, because there were no trails of blood, nor were any bones discovered. But at least one corpse was found: decapitated and with several ribs neatly and expertly cut out.

I have in my files several other reports of cats disappearing in large numbers. In one spate of missing cats, in Cornwall in 1994, an owner reported that one of her surviving cats had been sick, and had turned 'a strange blue/green colour'. In 1998, in London, another eighteen cases of missing cats were reported to the police: one body was found, and it had been decapitated. The police enquiries ruled out the usual catnapping gangs.

Interestingly, in Canada a few years ago, a schoolgirl reported an abduction experience. Aboard the craft she said that everything she saw was translucent, as if not fully materialised, with the exception of a domestic cat. When she asked what the cat was doing there she was told by the aliens that they were 'growing' it, and that it would ultimately be returned. It is not unknown for domestic-looking cats to occasionally achieve the size and build of a big-cat cub, approximately three times the size of the normal moggy.

In 1997, a farmer in Wales reported several classic mutilations to cows from his herd. One night, alert and vigilant because of the damage to his stock, he went outside when he thought he heard a noise, and saw a pair of bright-red eyes in a bush about thirty yards away, at a height of around three feet. He was terrified: the eyes stared at him unblinkingly and he knew, although he is not sure how, that this was the creature responsible for the damage to his cattle. Yet the eyes did not belong to any recognisable animal. After a few seconds they disappeared, but it was some time before the farmer had the courage to go to his animals. Predictably, during this time another mutilation had occurred.

I have, in my files, a picture of this cow. Its teeth are still connected to its bottom jaw, and all its legs are badly broken, as if it has been dropped from a height. There is a small hole in the carcass, less than three inches in diameter, through which several huge internal organs have been removed. The eyes, ears and tongue have been expertly removed, and there is, barely discernible in the photograph, a white powder around the body. Those who saw it said this powder had a phosphorescent glow. A sample was analysed, and from the combination of chemicals found in it the scientist who did the analysis said that the best description he could give, in layman's terms, was that it was the sort of compound that would result if a human body was burned. The analysis was carried out in a university laboratory, and I have the full details, but have promised not to reveal the name of the scientist who helped us.

The farmer in question has, like others I have talked to, refused to report the mutilation of his cattle to the authorities. He says his main priority is to make a living, and the prospect of having government scientists and military investigators crawling all over his property is unpalatable. He, in his own mind, has no doubt that what has happened to his cows is not the work of a natural predator, nor that of a human vandal. Like most farmers, he's a pragmatist, and as he cannot do anything about it, and feels sure that the authorities can do no more, he simply wants to be allowed to get on with earning his livelihood. He happily co-operates with my researchers, but wants no publicity or interference with his work.

From Wales I have also received several reports of the dead bodies of sheep being found, with their thyroid glands cut out.

In April 1997, forty pigs mysteriously died in one night on a farm near the east coast of England. Every one had a neat hole on the forehead, but there were no other obvious signs of injury. The vet who was called ordered their immediate burial, although the farmer was not told that he had an infectious disease problem. The animals were buried that same day.

Obviously, most attention is focused on animals with a value to humans – expensive farm stock or much-loved domestic pets. But there are plenty of examples in my files of wildlife mutilations, and there must be many thousands more which go unrecorded, because the bodies are taken by other animals or decompose before they are discovered. Nor is the phenomenon confined to large or medium-sized animals. I have heard of two examples where mice were the victims. In Barnoldswick, in Lancashire, in 1994, a woman found several dead mice on her lawn, with neat holes in their foreheads: hardly the work of the village cats.

Jason Andrews, the teenage abduction victim whose family's smallholding in Kent has been the scene of a great deal of strange activity, also found four dead mice, laid out in an unnatural straight line, by the gate to the farm. Each one had a neat round hole in the forehead, the left eye missing and the rectum cored out, as well as other mutilations: one had lost part of its stomach, another had the flesh stripped from its jawbone, one had a paw cut off. The Andrews family have also found the farm cat dead, with a hole in its forehead, and wild animals like foxes and badgers with similar injuries, as well as three magpies drowned in a water butt and ten rats floating in a water tank. But they have also suffered more serious problems with their animals. They have had cows which died mysteriously, others which, although clearly pregnant, became inexplicably barren; horses too which died unexpectedly. One of their horses was found one morning, very calm and obviously not in pain, with a neat flap of skin cut with surgical precision, from under which a scoop of flesh had been removed. There was no bleeding around the wound, and the vet they called was baffled both by the expertise which had gone into cutting the skin away, and by the lack of blood. The calmness of the horse led him to say that it appeared to have

154

been both tranquillised and given a powerful local anaesthetic.

Although my own investigations of animal mutilations centre on Britain, I receive reports from all over the world from fellow researchers. Jan-Ove Sundberg, from Sweden, has been studying the phenomenon and collating data as assiduously as I have been, and a report of his work was published in *UFO* magazine. He has researched cases of animal mutilation going back to 1977, when a large number of cows and horses were found mutilated in remote pastureland in a sparsely inhabited part of the country. Throughout the seventies and eighties, more and more cases were reported, and vets again agreed that the mutilations, which as usual involved the removal of the rectum and sexual organs, had been carried out with unprecedented surgical skill. Jan-Ove has studied in depth more than 132 cases which took place between 1988 and 1991, including the killing and mutilation of pet rabbits. Vandalism was ruled out, because the animals had been drained of blood.

One of the cases he investigated involved fifty pigs out of a herd of 100. The dead pigs had been typically mutilated, but also had unusual triangular-shaped marks on their bodies (similar marks had been seen on mutilated horses in the 1970s). Remarkably, the pigs which were wounded and killed had apparently made no noise, and the rest of the animals, which squeal and panic at any intrusion into their yard, were calm and quiet.

One of the most puzzling cases in Jan-Ove's file is that of a dead moose, found in the famous Hunneberg wilderness region of Sweden, the traditional hunting ground of the Swedish royal family. Today, the Hunneberg provides a natural sanctuary for many types of wild animal. On the night the moose died, in August 1988, there were more than a dozen reports of strange lights being spotted over the area. The moose, which was not mutilated, had all four legs broken, just as the cow in Wales had, yet there was no trace of bullet wounds or even any puncturing of the skin. The legs were broken identically, and a veterinary report said it appeared as if the bones had been blown up from inside, at hip level. The moose was found lying on its back, with its legs splayed around it. The only sensible conclusion seems to be that it had been picked up and then dropped, the impact

155

breaking all four legs at the same point and the same time. There were hoofprints leading to close to where it was found, but it could not possibly have walked there if it had broken its legs accidentally. It seems likely that the unexplained lights hovering over the area were an alien craft, and that having picked up the moose, either they realised it was not the animal they wanted, and dropped it, or they carried out whatever examination of it they needed to do, and then disposed of it.

In Puerto Rico, a great deal of hysteria has been whipped up about a strange beast, the Chupacabra, which goes around killing and mutilating animals. In a country rife with superstition, the story could have been nothing more than the latest colourful rumour. But one thing about the reports that found their way on to my desk fascinated me. Chupacabra means 'goat sucker' in Spanish, and the dominant feature of all the Chupacabra killings is that the victim is drained completely of blood. The beast is held responsible for killing a whole range of different animals, domestic and wild, ranging in size from horses and cattle down to cats and chickens. Because word has spread through South America into the large Spanish-speaking population of North America, the existence of the Chupacabra has come in for a great deal of mockery. It could well be that the beast is mythical: but the mutilation it leaves behind is definitely not, as serious investigators have found.

A recent case I have been monitoring has been sent to me by a researcher based in France. In February 1998 more than twenty dolphins were found, in less than three weeks, on the Languedoc-Roussillon beaches, between the seaside town of Agde and the Spanish border. They all had a six-inch wound, in exactly the same place on their throat, cut with a precision which ruled out a natural predator, or disease. There was no sign of them having been entangled in nets, so accidental death from encountering a trawler, or death at the hands of fishermen, was also ruled out. One theory is that they had been trained by the US Navy to carry out surveillance, and when they outlived their usefulness their signal collars were exploded by radio control. I am still waiting to receive a full autopsy report on one of these dolphins.

Every time I have come across a case of animal mutilation where there is enough evidence to take things to the authorities, I do. Often, farmers have agreed to allow photographs to be taken and have given statements on the understanding that the matter is not reported to MAFF. They have been happy to put the death down officially to the work of a natural predator, simply because they do not want to find themselves in the middle of either an official investigation or a storm of publicity. But many farmers are willing to report the truth, especially if it is their first experience of a mutilation. They naturally assume that the men from the ministry or from the Royal College of Veterinary Surgeons or the National Farmers' Union will be able to give them answers about the puzzlingly unnatural mutilation of their stock.

Yet whenever I approach these experts, I am told that they have no record of strange mutilations to domestic or wild animals. The replies to letters I have sent to MAFF, the NFU and the Royal College all have the same refrain: 'We are unaware of any cases of this nature.' Yet I personally have reported some, and know of many others of which they have been notified. The NFU insurance scheme has paid out thousands of pounds to claimants who have lost cattle, horses, sheep and pigs to these unnatural predators.

In America, when the FBI and the CIA both became involved in the investigation of animal mutilations, a surprising number of 'official' witnesses – law enforcement officers, representatives of government departments – either changed their evidence or suddenly found that they had no evidence to give. Some of them admitted privately that they were leaned on: it was suggested to them that in the interests of their job and salary they should cease to be involved in this whole subject. There is, in other words, a cover-up going on orchestrated from above.

Could this also be the case in Britain? I am sure that it is. If not, then there is an appalling level of apathy among experts who are choosing to ignore a steady stream of unexplained deaths. Mutilations are happening in such numbers and with such regularity that there ought to be a full-scale national enquiry. There would be for any other cause of death among

157

livestock running at this level: that there has not been suggests forcibly that the authorities have a good idea what is going on, but do not want to share their knowledge with the general public.

Linda Moulton Howe, the American documentary-maker and author whose assiduous research sparked a great deal of the initial international interest in animal mutilations, visited me in August 1997, and we compared notes. She saw many of the photographs in my files, and we agreed on most of our conclusions.

Whenever the subject of animal mutilations is aired in the press, two culprits are routinely offered: vandals, or weird Satanic cults. As neither group is likely to have teams of expertly qualified surgeons with state-of-the-art laser technology at their disposal, they are, to me, non-starters. But even more damning is the fact that these cultists and vandals never get caught. If they are carrying out mutilations, why are they not being arrested – or shot by angry farmers? Not only are they precision surgeons, but they are also expert at arriving and disappearing without leaving a trace. Although I have dealt with many cases of animal mutilation, I have never heard of the prosecution of anyone who has carried out anything other than brutal, mindless cruelty. The 'night surgeons' have never been caught.

However horrified we may feel about animal mutilations, there are even more sinister possibilities to be considered.

CHAPTER SEVEN

DEATH FROM THE SKIES

Every year 250,000 people in Britain are reported missing. The vast majority have left home of their own choice, to get away from husbands, wives, parents or other family situations they find unbearable. The sadness of the families left behind is something that I, as a police officer, became familiar with. But like most other officers working directly with the public, I developed an instinct about these cases. It was sometimes clear to me that the missing person was acting completely out of character and that there were no signs of any friction in the family which would have precipitated such a disappearance. In all missing persons cases the police would make enquiries, but in these, where things simply did not add up, we'd be working even harder, checking out bank balances and appealing for information of sightings. Sadly, what we were looking for was evidence of a crime having been committed, and quite a few times in my twenty-five years' service that was what we found. These were the very worst murder cases to deal with, where the victim had been taken for no other reason than that they happened to be in the wrong place at the wrong time.

Sometimes, too, we would fail to find anything: no body, no evidence of a crime, nothing to convince us that the person had left voluntarily, just a big black hole into which a human being had vanished. Eventually, the police enquiry would be put on a back burner while more pressing cases were dealt with, and the family would be left to come to terms with the totally baffling disappearance. My heart went out to them: it is much harder to grieve for the unknown than it is when the case is resolved, however sadly.

There were other cases, too, where a body would be found, perhaps seriously decomposed, and we would be unable to identify it. Despite all the amazing modern techniques used to identify corpses – DNA samples, dental records, etc. – unless there is a missing persons report to match up to the body, the police are at a loss to know who it is. We live in a world where some families allow their youngsters to drift away from them, to live hand-to-mouth existences on the streets of big cities, to become involved in drugs and prostitution, and to be truly known by nobody: these unfortunates are able to disappear without anyone noting or lamenting their loss.

These unsolved missing persons cases and unidentified bodies form only a small residue of all police enquiries, but they do exist. Some of them will be the results of undetected human crime. But the more I have seen of animal mutilations and deaths, the more I have wondered whether these alien predators are carrying out their macabre experiments only on lower animals. Might they not, also, be using humans? We know that the purpose of abductions is almost always medical, as if the abductors are monitoring certain aspects of human physical development. We also know that they take tissue samples: we regularly see strange scoop marks in the flesh of abductees. Yet abductions, despite being by their nature terrifying, are benign: the victims are returned, unhurt, to the place they were taken from. I use this fact as a mainstay to comfort abductees and their families: I can, I tell them, guarantee that they will be unhurt and will wake up back at the spot where the whole experience began. Despite one or two small problems – clothes inside out, being left outside the house instead of inside – I am able to reassure them with confidence.

But the more I know about alien interaction with earth, the more I am convinced that we are not simply dealing with one race of intruders. If the 'greys', the archetypal small figures with large heads and huge black almond-shaped eyes, and their companions the 'Nordics', the tall humanoids, are all we have to worry about, I think we will eventually be able to make a comfortable accommodation with them. We are a long way from fully understanding their role in our lives and our existence, but we know enough to realise that their interest is not malevolent.

However, just as it is foolish to think, with all the billions of stars in our galaxy and billions of galaxies in this universe, and possibly billions of universes beyond this, that we humans are the only intelligent life form, so it is naive to think that there is only one alien life form with the technological capability to reach earth. I have been told, in my telepathic communications, that there are many races of aliens; I have other evidence of my own; and I have my common sense: all of these things tell me that the aliens who abduct humans to their spacecraft are not the only ones with an interest in life on earth. The abductors, should they wish to find out about the physical make-up of animals, would surely simply take them to the craft in the same way that they take humans. I have no doubt that they do this: we simply do not hear from cows or horses or dogs about the strange lights they see in the night and their missing-time episodes!

So the mutilations are being carried out by another, more hostile race, and if they are mutilating animals as medical experiments, it is highly likely that they are doing the same things to humans. I am not the only researcher to have come to this conclusion: there are others, principally in America but also in other countries across the world, who have realised what is going on.

At present, the hard evidence for human mutilations is nowhere near as great as we have for animal mutilations, but there are good reasons for this, the most obvious being an even greater reluctance to ascribe a human death to something super-natural than we have seen with animals. Secondly, if there is a cover-up surrounding the mysterious animal deaths, how much more of a cover-up there must be around the subject of human mutilations. If the point of the high-level international agree-ment is to keep all information about UFOs and aliens outside the knowledge of ordinary people, it becomes essential that any deaths caused by aliens be kept strictly secret, at least until they can be disguised as something more acceptable.

Nevertheless, there is some evidence. In the early 1950s Sergeant Jonathan Louette of the US Air Force was serving at the White Sands Proving Ground in New Mexico, a vast, remote base where the latest US technology is tested. There are many stories linking White Sands to alien contact: captured alien craft have been tested there; and 'back engineering' programmes, by which human scientists have been able to work backwards to find out how some of this advanced technology works, have been carried out too. As with all secret bases, there are regular reports of UFO activity in the sky above White Sands.

The sergeant and a senior officer were detailed to travel several miles down the missile range in a military vehicle, looking for debris from spent missiles. At one point they left the vehicle to scout the desert. They separated, in order to cover a wider area of the sand dunes more quickly. Suddenly the officer heard screams from the area of the dunes where the sergeant was searching. He ran towards the noise, and as he reached the top of a dune he saw a disc-shaped craft hovering low above the ground. A long tentacle from the underside of the craft was wrapped around the sergeant. It dragged the screaming man into the craft, which then shot away at great speed.

The officer returned to base in a state of shock. When he reported what he had seen he was not believed, and was arrested on suspicion of murder. Three days later, Sergeant Louette's mutilated body was found, twenty miles down the range. The mutilations were clinical and precise, and involved the removal of the genitals, the rectum and the eyes. Typically, there was no blood in the body, but the cardiovascular organs had not collapsed. The officer was released without charge.

Although many strange stories have come out of the Vietnam conflict, there can be none stranger than that reported at a UFO conference in Las Vegas in 1989 by an ex-USAF man who was serving as a photographer in Vietnam in the late sixties. He was involved in a mission to investigate the mysterious crash of a B-52 bomber, and was air-lifted by helicopter into the jungle where the plane had gone down. The first surprise was to find the plane intact, and no sign of a crash-landing: it was as if the plane had been air-lifted and gently placed into position. Inside the cabin, though, was a much greater shock. The four-man crew were still strapped into their seats, but all had been mutilated, with the typical clean, non-bleeding wounds that we see in animal mutilations. After inspecting the plane and photographing both it and its occupants, the investigation team was ordered to burn the bodies and the aircraft.

I have also had reported to me, although without a hundred per cent corroboration, the story of two hunters who in 1979 discovered the body of a naked man in an isolated area of Idaho. The genitalia had been removed, the lips had been sliced off, and there were several other surgical cuts to the body. Although the body was barefoot, there were no cuts or scratches to the feet or legs as there would have been had he walked through the wilderness terrain, nor were there any tracks of humans or animals, and it would have been impossible to get to the spot by vehicle. The police subsequently found the man's possessions several miles away.

At least a couple of American researchers, good friends of mine, have started serious investigations into unidentified and mutilated bodies which are reported to the police, and also into the complete and baffling disappearance of what, when taken over the whole country, is quite a substantial number of people.

Don Ecker is an American researcher with whom I get on very well: we are both ex-cops, and we both approach our investigations in the same way, using all the tricks of our old trade. Don used a contact of his, a serving police officer, to access the national crime database held by the FBI in Washington. He asked for information on all unexplained human deaths involving mutilation in one area of the USA, the north-west, covering five states, and stretching back over nearly twenty years. He expected to receive reams of information. Instead, his friend phoned him to say that there were no deaths at all that met the criteria. What was more, his contact had been warned off: told that he would have to get proper authorisation for any further requests – even though, as a serving law enforcement officer, he was entitled to access this data bank at any time. The reply that

163

there were no unexplained deaths involving mutilations was obviously meant to fob Don off: at the time, in that area of the States, there had been a serial killer preying on young women and mutilating their bodies. There is no suggestion that his victims were killed by anything other than a sadistic human hand, but nonetheless, the deaths fitted the requested criteria and their details should have been thrown up by the computer. In other words, the whole file had been suppressed.

Don tried several other avenues to get the same information, and was even offered help by a Drugs Enforcement agent stationed in Florida, who also ran up against a brick wall. The DEA agent telephoned Don and advised him to stay away from this whole area 'if you know what's good for you'. Don is still chipping away at the whole subject, but has found that the cover-up is even tighter than that over animal mutilations.

Here in Britain, one of the most puzzling cases is that of Zygmunt Adamski, a miner who came to England from his native Poland after being held as a prisoner of war during the Second World War. He and his wife settled in Tingley, near Leeds, where they led a quiet, happy life with no problems apart from Mrs Adamski's poor health. On 7 June 1980, the couple had been shopping in Leeds, and when they got home Mrs Adamski remembered there were no potatoes for their meal, so fifty-seven-year-old Mr Adamski set off to the corner shop 200 yards down the road to buy some. Four days later his body was discovered in a hollow on the top of a coal tip in Todmorden, Lancashire, thirty miles away. He had no known connections with Todmorden, nor had anyone seen him in the four days he was missing.

Even more mysteriously, there were burns on the back of his head, scalp and neck round to his breastbone, caused by a corrosive substance that forensic scientists were unable to identify. The back of his head also appeared to have been shaved, and there was an open horizontal cut at the base of the back of his neck. This wound was deep, but not considered to be the cause of death. Although he was on the top of the tip, there was no sign of him having climbed up it. There were some small scratches on his hands and knees, but there was no apparent

164

reason for his death, apart from an existing chest condition which contributed to heart failure. According to the consultant pathologist, Dr Alan Edwards, from the expression on Mr Adamski's face, he appeared to have died from shock or fright.

Although he was wearing his jacket, his shirt was missing. His wallet was also missing, but if theft was the motive it is surprising that the thief left the £5 note that was found in his pocket – probably, according to his widow, all the money that he had on him. The coal tip had not been disturbed, nor had the body, which was found lying on its back, not dirty apart from where it was touching the coal.

A local man who had been walking his dog around the area of the tip earlier that day was sure there had been no sign of the body then.

The West Yorkshire coroner, James Turnbull, a sensible man whose inquests I attended many times during my police service, made every attempt to clear up the mystery of Mr Adamski's death. He delayed the inquest for over a year to allow the police to carry out extensive investigations, and appealed for witnesses who had seen Mr Adamski during the missing four days to come forward. Nobody did.

'It is quite the most mysterious death I have investigated in twelve years as a coroner,' said Mr Turnbull.

The first policeman on the scene when the body was discovered was PC Alan Godfrey, whom I knew well. PC Godfrey and a colleague were in their car in the Todmorden area when they were called to the coal yard where the body was discovered: and for several hours previously they had been watching strange lights in the sky. There were other reports of UFO activity in the area at the time.

The coroner said at the inquest: 'As a trained lawyer, I have to rely on facts. Unfortunately we have not been able to uncover any facts which may have contributed to this death. I tend to believe that there may be some simple explanation.

'However, I do admit that the failure of the forensic scientists to identify the corrosive substance which caused Mr Adamski's burns could lend some weight to the UFO theory.'

Mr Adamski's body was taken back to Poland for burial. I

was still serving in the police at the time of the death, but in my own time I investigated the matter as thoroughly as I would have done had it been a case I was dealing with professionally. I talked at length to PC Godfrey, and to others involved in the case. Alan Godfrey reported that, shortly after the enquiry began into how the body got on to the tip, he was visited at the police station by two men who told him not to talk about it. All he knew about them was that they had authority: they were not simply members of the public.

My own conclusion has to be that if there is a simple explanation, after all the public appeals someone would have come forward who saw Zygmunt Adamski in those missing four days. A person does not simply disappear on a walk to the shop to get potatoes. I believe the story of Mr Adamski is that of an alien abduction that went wrong, a medical experiment that resulted in a death, and a body that had to be disposed of.

One curious but irrelevant coincidence is that Mr Adamski shared his name with perhaps the first of the modern abduction victims, George Adamski, who in 1953 published a book about his meetings with aliens. There is nothing significant about this: Adamski is a fairly common Polish name, not on a par with Smith, but certainly more common than Dodd!

As with animal mutilations, human mutilations are happening globally. The best evidence to date has come from Brazil, with some convincing, if gruesome, photographs of a human mutilation which have been obtained from police files. Although authorities the world over appear to be united in their desire to keep the whole subject covered up, not all are as sophisticated as the Americans and the British, and fortunately for the whole field of research into UFO-related deaths and mutilations, these Brazilian pictures have found their way into the public domain.

The mutilated body, of a man, was found near the Guara-piranga Reservoir in Brazil on 29 September 1988, and as a matter of course photographs were taken of the corpse. A police technician, Sergio Rubens, later gave copies of these photographs to his cousin, Dr Goes Rubens, who he thought would be interested, medically, in the way the corpse had been mutilated. Appreciating at least partly the significance of the pictures, Dr Rubens showed them to a friend, Encarnacion Zapata Garcia, who he knew was interested in ufology. She immediately recognised the similarity of the wounds to those she had seen in animal mutilations.

When the police were approached for more information, the head of the investigation, Dr Cuenca, surprisingly opened his files: an incredible stroke of luck not just for the original investigators, but for all of us battling to get this subject into the open. Among the papers in the file was the original autopsy report, written by forensic pathologists who had no previous knowledge of mutilations.

There were many striking observations:

1. Although the victim had been dead for forty-eight to seventy-two hours, there was no sign of it being eaten by animals or starting to rot, as would be expected.
2. There was no smell.
3. Bleeding from the wounds had been minimal.
4. The lips and flesh from the face had been cut away.
5. The eyes, ears and tongue had been removed.
6. Neat round holes, one to one and a half inches in diameter, had been made on the shoulders and arms, head, stomach and anus, and tissue and muscle had been extracted. The holes had not been made by bullets.
7. The major organs within the chest cavity had been removed.
8. The navel and intestines had been removed, a perfect small hole having been made through which extensive digestive organs were extracted.
9. The scrotum, but not the penis, had been removed, and all pubic hair had disappeared.
10. The rectum had been cored out.
11. Despite the devastating mutilations, there was no sign that the victim had been bound or had struggled in any way.

Encarnacion Garcia had copies of seven of the photographs which were in the file. Although the victim has been identified, in deference to his family, details of his identity have never been published.

When the photographs were first published, they caused a great stir among serious UFO researchers. It will, of course, take more than a set of seven horrific photographs from Brazil to make the authorities open up about the extent to which human bodies are being discovered in a mutilated state, but for those of us who already know a great deal of what is going on, the photographs are important confirmation. If only there were government employees here, and in America, who were prepared to risk their jobs by leaking similar material, my work would be much easier.

However, some professionals who came into contact with the UFO phenomenon are prepared to speak out, despite a risk to their careers, as we shall see in the next chapter.

CHAPTER EIGHT

FATAL CONTACTS

A very high proportion of UFO sightings and reports come from pilots and aircrew: hardly surprising, when you consider that they spend a much greater percentage of their time than the average man or woman staring at the heavens. If strange objects are moving about out there, you find them by looking for them – as I know from personal experience. What is so useful for serious UFO researchers like me is that reports from experienced pilots and crew are highly reliable: these men and women are trained observers, unlikely to make some of the common – though genuine – mistakes which I deal with all the time from members of the public.

For example, a meteor trail, a shooting star, a low and very bright planet, a satellite, a weather balloon, lenticular clouds, a vapour trail, aeroplane lights, the reflected lights from a laser show: these are all things which have been reported to me, in good faith, as UFOs. It can take me a couple of hours of research, ringing the meteorological office, local airports, etc., just to discover that the 'UFO' has a very prosaic explanation. But when I get a report from a pilot or a member of aircrew, I am confident that I am dealing with people who are familiar with the tricks that can be played by lights and weather in the sky, and I know that before they pick up the phone to speak to me, they have eliminated these obvious causes.

Most of them, when passing information on to me, wish to

remain anonymous, especially if they are employed by one of the major airlines, or are serving in the RAF. There is a tacit understanding in most airlines that reporting UFOs attracts ridicule, and that anyone who does it also attracts the disapproval of their bosses. In confidence, many pilots admit to me that they have seen unusual and unidentifiable objects in the sky, and they are happy to accept these are extra-terrestrial in origin; in public, however, they deny it.

Pilots flying with the RAF, or any other country's air force, may also possibly have found themselves scrambled to chase strange craft through the sky. Naturally, any unexplained object which shows up on radar has to be treated with suspicion, as it could be unfriendly in origin. Over the years, many stories have leaked out from behind the official cover-ups, showing that planes have been mobilised on a very regular basis to investigate unidentified craft in the skies. Often the chases have come to nothing, with the object disappearing at phenomenal speed from the radar screens. Frequently pilots have returned with their own incredible stories to tell, but no proof.

One reliable contact of mine, a pilot in the RAF, recently brought a friend of his, a Belgian pilot, to see me to report an encounter the Belgian had in 1992 near the town of Liège. The Belgian authorities had been receiving a string of reports about large black triangular objects, with lights at each corner, appearing in the skies at dusk. Several times, F-16s were scrambled to intercept, and the pilot I talked to was one of those ordered into the air. He and another F-16 pilot were able to pick up the UFO clearly on their radar: it was almost stationary, travelling at between fifty and 100 m.p.h., at about 5,000 feet altitude. The pilot described it as 'almost hovering, very at ease'.

But when he and his colleague got to within twenty miles of it, it suddenly accelerated from idling speed 'straight to mach 8, mach 9, mach 10, and straight up to 60–70,000 feet altitude just in a split second. We saw it on radar and we just could not follow it. That was it, we came back.'

The pilot said he had the distinct impression that it was under intelligent control: 'It really knew what was going on. It sits there, waits till we approach then says OK that's enough. I had the feeling that night that we were chasing after something that was playing with us.'

His report is typical of so many that I receive: inconclusive in itself, but seared on the memory of an experienced pilot who knows what he is talking about. Occasionally, sadly, a plane gets so close to one of these objects that its occupants are threatened, and then the superior technology of the uninvited visitors means that the plane, and its pilot, have to be disposed of. When planes crash, or mysteriously disappear completely, 'pilot error' is the standard excuse. But although, of course, tragic accidents can happen, experienced professional flyers do not make the sort of basic mistakes that cause their planes to simply drop out of the skies, and those around them – family, colleagues and friends – are sometimes hurt by the suggestion that the death was caused by a silly and avoidable error. It is unjust, especially when the pilot died courageously in pursuit of an unknown enemy – on, if you like, active service on behalf of his country.

In this chapter I shall deal with two very significant cases, where highly trained, expert pilots have died inexplicably when they have been sent in pursuit of UFOs.

The phone call came out of the blue. The voice on the other end had an American accent, and sounded elderly. He wanted to tell me something, he said, which related to an old, classic UFO story, one that is famous in the annals of UFO research: the mysterious death in 1948 of American air force pilot Thomas Mantell.

Although I am fascinated by old cases, I generally assume that they have been thoroughly researched, and that my own time is better spent investigating the mass of new information that is coming forward all the time. I knew about the Mantell case, and like everyone who has ever read anything about it, I knew that Captain Mantell's death was the result of something extremely strange which had been covered up by the American military authorities. But now, on the phone to me, I had someone who could not only confirm the cover-up, but was there on the day of Mantell's death, went to the scene of the crash, and talked to the mysterious investigators who turned up immediately afterwards.

171

The caller was Jim Duesler, an ex-USAF major who had been serving at a small air force base near the scene of the crash, and was responsible for putting Captain Mantell on the trail of a strange unidentified object. Jim was well into his seventies when he contacted me in the spring of 1993. He had read something I had written, and he had a strong urge to set a few records straight before the end of his life. Sadly, he died in October 1996, but in the three and a half years I knew him we spent many hours in conversation, going over his memories of the Mantell case. He was as straightforward and honest a man as I have ever encountered. He had no particular interest in ufology: probably, if he had, he would have become embroiled in the controversy over the case many years before. He simply realised that he was nearing the end of his life and that the evidence he possessed would die with him, and he felt he had a duty to share it. He had lived in England ever since leaving the American forces, because he had met and married an Englishwoman, and it was only after her death that he began to think of putting his house in order by making sure the truth of this strange event was known.

The story Jim had to tell confirmed a great deal of what we already knew – and what we suspected – about the death of Thomas Mantell. Most importantly, perhaps, when I told Jim that his signature was on the bottom of an official statement made at the time of the incident and contained in Project Blue Book, the top-secret file kept by the US Government on UFO reports, he categorically denied ever making the statement. Project Blue Book, with its headquarters at Wright Patterson Air Base, collated all reports of mysterious objects in the skies, with the purpose of determining whether they were a threat to the USA, or whether they contained advanced technology from which American scientists could benefit. There was a third and vital purpose: to publicly dismiss UFOs as weather balloons, stars, satellites, fireballs, etc., in order to obfuscate the whole issue for the general public. Their determination to keep UFO researchers in the dark apparently permitted them to fake statements from serving officers like Jim Duesler.

The official version of the death of Thomas Mantell goes like this: on 7 January 1948, Mantell was leading a flight of four P51

172

Mustang aircraft belonging to the National Guard, flying between Marietta, Georgia, and Standiford Field Air Base, Kentucky, when Godman Field Air Base, near Fort Knox, radioed them and asked them to investigate a sighting of an unidentified object near the base. One of the pilots, Hendricks, was low on fuel, and radioed back for permission to carry on to their destination, Standiford Field. He peeled off from the other three, who pursued the unknown object. Then one of the others also asked for permission to go on to Standiford: some of the original reports state that he, too, was short of fuel, or that he had lost his bearings, or that he realised he was short of oxygen at the height they had reached. The third pilot was told to accompany him, and these two, Hammond and Clements, arrived at Standiford forty minutes after the first Mustang landed.

This left Captain Mantell alone in pursuit of the object. The declassification in 1985 of a joint air force and navy intelligence analysis of UFO sightings, made in 1948 and classified top secret, shows that his last reported message to the radio control tower was: 'It appears to be a metallic object, tremendous in size, directly ahead and slightly above. I am trying to close for a better look.'

A few minutes later his plane crashed to earth, 130 miles from Godman base and two miles south-west of Franklyn, Kentucky. The official report said that he died of anoxia – oxygen depriva-tion – because of climbing too high (the planes were not equipped with oxygen) while 'chasing' the planet Venus. Later this was changed to a weather balloon.

This never added up: an experienced pilot like Mantell would certainly have been able to recognise a planet or a weather balloon. Besides, on the day in question, the planet Venus was only thirty-three degrees above the horizon, and could therefore never have appeared to be above Mantell's plane. It is important to remember that it was the control tower at Godman that spotted the UFO: they, too, were experienced enough to be familiar with weather balloons and the normal disposition of the planets in the sky. There had been reports to the Kentucky State Police throughout that day of a large circular object in the sky: Mansville, Irvington and Owensboro were just three of the places from where civilians reported sightings, and although it is arguable that a rogue weather balloon or a low planet could have fooled these people more readily than the USAF personnel, it is unlikely that they all got it wrong. For the rest of the day, after Mantell's death, people further south were reporting sightings of the strange round object.

So UFO investigators had long believed that Mantell's death was significant, and that the authorities covered it up. Nearly fifty years later, with the evidence of Jim Duesler, I was able to confirm that what happened on that day in January 1948 was nothing to do with the planets or balloons: Mantell died chasing an alien craft.

Jim Duesler joined the US Army Air Corps in 1941, just after the Japanese bombing of Pearl Harbor. He believed it was his duty to help out the war effort. By the end of the war and at the time of the death of Thomas Mantell he was ranked a captain. He left the Air Corps later that year, finished a law degree he had started before joining up, then rejoined in 1961, by which time the Air Corps had become the US Air Force. Serving in England, he met and married his British wife, and in 1970, after spells based in Turkey and back in the States, he retired with the rank of major, and settled in Norfolk.

Godman Field Air Base was, he told me, nothing more than a landing strip serving Fort Knox, famous now for containing the Federal gold reserves, but also, at that time, the American Army armoured division base. The airfield saw many distinguished politicians and military commanders pass through on the way to Fort Knox. Just after lunch on 7 January, Jim was standing on the parking apron talking to Captain Warren Carter, the base operations officer, when one of the operations clerks, a sergeant, came to tell Captain Carter he was wanted in the control tower.

The two captains, Carter and Duesler, could not work out why Captain Carter was needed in the tower, as the operations staff were seasoned members of the Air Corps, all of them sergeants or lieutenants with many flying hours behind them, and an excellent training in operations. Jim Duesler teased his friend, who was rather large and did not relish the long climb up several flights of stairs to the top of the tower. But after talking to the tower on his intercom, or the 'squawk box' as it was nicknamed, Captain Carter went up.

Shortly afterwards Jim got a message that he, too, was required in the tower. His immediate reaction was that it was a joke, that Carter was getting even by making him climb up all the stairs too. But again, over the intercom, he was told it was serious, so he went.

The tower was roughly twenty feet square. In the centre was a console housing the radio equipment. The console was about five to six feet square and about four feet tall. On the console was a broom handle pointing generally in a southerly direction with one end propped up with books. Jim was told to sight down the broom handle. The tower operators had stuck a small scrap of paper on the window and he was told to line up his sighting down the broom handle to the piece of white paper.

'There was something there. I did see it, it took me several minutes to find it, but eventually I did, and it was the shape of an inverted ice-cream cone,' he told me. 'You couldn't tell the size because of the distance and the altitude, and the day was a bit hazy so I'm unsure about the colour. But it appeared to be a light grey or white and the wide bottom was red. It was rotating; at least there was a black stripe from top to bottom which seemed to move across our vision and go around and come back. We didn't time the length of rotation but it was a matter of a few minutes.'

While Jim was looking at the object, the flight of four Mustangs from Kentucky Air National Guard, a civilian reserve group, led by Captain Mantell, flew over on their way back to their Standiford base.

'One of us in the tower asked them if they would turn around and examine or explore what we had been watching,' said Jim. 'One man had to go home, he was late for work, so he carried on. These guys, although they were paid, were volunteers with other jobs. So three agreed to go back to find out what this object was. They were flying from the south almost due north, so they turned, and a little while later one of the three said he had to return to base, but he was lost, he didn't have his bearings. The second of the three offered to take him home, leaving the flight leader, Captain Mantell, on his own. Mantell flew for a few minutes until he notified us that he could see something but he didn't say what. A few more minutes passed, and Mantell radioed in that he was at 15,000 feet and closing in for a better look. That was the last we heard from him.'

Eventually the object was obscured or faded out due to the sunset and thickening clouds, but not before Jim and the other officers in the control tower had persuaded the weather officer to unlock his theodolite, which had a three-power magnification. The magnification did not really improve their visual assessment of the strange object, but they did determine that it was about 185–195 degrees above the horizon, around six times higher than the planet Venus.

Jim reckoned that he and his colleagues were watching the UFO over a period of about four hours, and it was only obscured for approximately twenty minutes, by a very small scatter of clouds. But towards the end of the afternoon the clouds were thickening and the light was failing, and they lost sight of it. They were surprised to hear no more from Mantell, but assumed he had gone back to his base. Jim returned to his quarters at about 5 or 6 p.m. and later had dinner and went to bed. Although the events of the afternoon had been unusual, he expected that the following day he would hear a rational and plausible explanation.

At around 11 p.m., when he was already in bed, the control tower rang him to say they had spotted something else in the sky. They described it. Jim went outside his quarters and saw what he assumed they meant: it was the North Star. He confirmed this with a navigator who was stationed at Godman, a Captain Lou Dumky. Amused by this mistake, Jim went back to bed. He reckoned that because this was a different shift of operators, and because everyone on the base had by this time heard about the afternoon's excitement, they simply wanted to get in on the act.

Between midnight and 1 a.m., the tower called him again: this time, naturally, Jim was reluctant to leave his warm bed to give them lessons in astronomy. But the control tower operators were insistent that they could see something unusual, which they could not identify, in the sky. Whatever it was, it was so low to the horizon that Jim could not see it from outside his quarters, nor from the landing field, so he made his way up the tower.

'There was definitely something there. Again you couldn't tell how large it was, as there was nothing to compare it with, and I couldn't tell how far it was as it was a rather dark night. There were stars out, but it was pretty black. This object, which the tower guys had watched for a while, was circling from, when they first saw it, a little south-east of Godman, around to the north. When I saw it, it was to the west of the object we saw during the day, and it was a dull orange colour, shaped a little like a cigar. It was a steady light, it didn't flicker and it continued moving in an arc heading round to the north. It disappeared behind some hills which were about 2,000 feet high to the west of Godman, and as it did so we could see the silhouette of the trees on the hilltop.

'It looked different from the object we had seen during the day, a different shape and colour. But that could have been accounted for by the lighting and the visibility. I don't know.'

Meanwhile the tower was talking to Wright Patterson Air Base, which was about 100 miles from Godman, and the conversation was picked up by another control tower at an air base in St Louis, Missouri, about 200 miles west of Godman. The St Louis base informed the Godman tower that they had been contacted by a squadron of B-25 Mitchell bombers who had reported a similar object. The B-25s were flying in solid cloud, and consequently had no view of the ground or sky above them: they had nonetheless all seen an object which they described as orange, travelling rather slowly, although this was hard to calculate because, without any idea of its size, assessing its distance was impossible. The B-25s had contacted St Louis control to ask if they knew of any aircraft in the area which could, possibly, explain what they had seen. There were none.

Soon after Jim started to observe the UFO, it suddenly disappeared. Although he was fascinated, he was also relieved, as he was very tired. He had been woken twice, and all he could think about was getting back to bed for the rest of the night. Unfortunately, that was not to be. The next call, at 3 a.m., shocked him wide awake within seconds: Captain Mantell's plane had been found, crashed, 130 miles to the south. As Jim was a member of the aircraft accident investigation board, he had to go: and what he saw at the scene of the crash amazed him.

'I drove down with a couple of men. The crash wasn't far from the highway. It was most unusual: the plane had gone straight into the ground, not nose first, but on its side. It was lying on its left side, with the right wing and tail assembly within 100 feet of the rest of the plane.

'The plane had hit flat on its side, with one wing crushed beneath it. I guessed that the up wing, the right wing, had broken off on impact. It may still have been partially connected because it was close to the body of the plane. The rudder elevators were just 100 feet away, and I guess impact would have thrown them that far: I don't think they broke away until it hit the ground. The most staggering thing was that there was no indication that the plane was moving forward: it appeared to have come straight down, sideways, not a nose dive. Fighter planes were nose-heavy, which always caused a nose dive in my previous experience of many crashes.

'The other unusual aspect of the crash, which really got those of us who saw it, was that there wasn't that much damage to the plane itself. Usually they are going forward and you've got wreckage scattered for a mile or so: but this plane was perfectly all right except for the wings and the tail section, and it was narrower than it should have been. It was crushed, but this seemed to have happened evenly. The Mustang was about two and a half feet wide in the cockpit and this one was down to nine to twelve inches wide, yet remarkably undamaged. It looked as if it had been made that way. When the wreckage was lifted, we could see the prop blade was not bent, it had been driven straight into the ground: marks and scratches from the rocks and earth went straight along the length of the blade, which was not bent. With any forward motion it would have been ruptured and misshapen.

'I don't remember seeing the canopy of the plane. I guess it would have been smashed. We didn't see accidents like that normally. Dropping from 20,000 feet or so, I wouldn't expect it to look like that. It didn't make much sense. It should have rolled, spiralled, and then hit the ground nose first, spreading debris over a wide area, and then caught fire: I never saw such a serious crash where there was no fire. Instead, it just seemed to have fallen straight out of the sky.'

The plane was in a clearing inside a semi-circle of tall, straight trees, and this, too, puzzled Jim. He did not see one broken branch; again it looked as if the plane had dropped vertically into its position. Even if it had managed to glide in, it would have cut a swath through the trees and gouged a groove into the ground.

By the time Jim arrived at the scene, the body of Captain Mantell had been removed. The crash, it was estimated, had taken place at 3 p.m. the previous day, just after the Godman control tower lost radio contact with the Mustang: it had taken twelve hours for the news to reach Jim because the local sheriff had initially not known who to contact, and the news had been passed via the National Guard to Fort Knox and then on to Godman. There had been no eye-witnesses to the actual crash, so there was no confirmation of the plane's unusual descent.

Jim was astonished to find that there was no sign of blood inside the cockpit, and his amazement was compounded when the state police on the scene told him that the pilot's skin was not punctured anywhere, and yet every bone in his body appeared to be broken, crushed and pulverised to a powder. In years to come, UFO researchers would use the fact that Captain Mantell was buried in a closed and lead-lined coffin – not the normal practice in this part of the States – as evidence that something very odd had happened: but Jim was at pains to point out to me that this was a red herring, as most victims of air crashes are not in a fit state to be put on show to the grieving relatives. What was surprising about Captain Mantell, according to what Jim heard, was not how badly he was disfigured but how oddly intact the corpse was.

The following day Jim and his team were joined by another investigator, a Dr Loading from Wright Patterson Air Base. Jim was not surprised: it was a National Guard plane that had crashed so it was not technically his job to run the investigation;

and he had seen enough that was abnormal for him to assume there would be a high-level enquiry. Dr Loading, who told Jim his doctorate was in aeronautical engineering, said that he was in charge of what he called 'the Saucer Project'. Although it was not known widely at the time – or for years to come – the US Government had very recently (in the final months of 1947) established an investigation team from air force intelligence to look at reports of extra-terrestrial activity. Officially it was called Project Sign, but it was often known, to both those working on it and those who subsequently found out about it, as Project Saucer. Jim had never heard of it, nor did he have any idea that there was an official body looking into such things.

(Project Sign stayed in business until 1949, and although it publicly explained away most of the incidents it investigated as non-paranormal, secretly it concluded that there were some UFOs which defied rational explanation, and which could not possibly be functioning with the technology available to man: therefore they had to be extra-terrestrial in origin. Dr J. Allen Hynek, who joined Sign in early 1948, was a complete sceptic until he had spent several years looking at the data: he too came to see that there were too many reliable reports that could not be rationalised away. But when the Pentagon realised that Sign was finding something worth investigating, the project was closed down and replaced with Project Grudge, which rejected all of Sign's conclusions, and eventually with Project Blue Book, which also repudiated the existence of UFOs.)

Jim worked with Dr Loading for a couple of days, during which time the scientist told him about the research that was going on. He said that at the time, the whole of the investigation into UFOs was being done by him, with two pilots assigned to help him: one based in Pittsburgh and one in Birmingham, Alabama, because these were both areas of high UFO activity. Loading said he would like to expand the operation, and have someone like Jim working for him.

'He told me that sightings occurred generally around areas of high industrial or military activity,' said Jim. 'It so happened

180

that about fifty miles from where Mantell's plane was found was Camp Campbell, an infantry base which was having a very large training exercise at that time.

'He said that he had many files on UFO activity at his office at Wright Patterson Air Base, even going right back to the reports found in Christopher Columbus's log books. I clearly remember him saying, "Thank God these things are not hostile, otherwise we wouldn't stand a chance." '

Shortly after Loading arrived, two plain-clothes investigators from either the Criminal Investigation Division or the Counter Intelligence Corps turned up: Jim was not sure exactly who they were, but he was not impressed by them, regarding them as hampering rather than helping the crash investigation. They were dispatched to interview two witnesses, two women who had, separately, reported seeing a strange object in the sky on the day of Mantell's death. It was established that the women had no connection with each other, and lived about sixty miles apart. Their descriptions of the object tallied in many ways with the one given by Jim and his colleagues in the Godman control tower, and they both confirmed that it was travelling from east to west.

The official statement put out after the enquiry into the crash was that Thomas Mantell had died from lack of oxygen. Jim was surprised at this conclusion.

'Of course, it's possible: pilots did go unconscious from too little oxygen and it could have caused a crash. But it just wasn't talked about when we were investigating, like it would have been if it had been a real possibility. If Mantell died from lack of oxygen, I'd have probably heard from the police guys who saw the body: you get a bluish colour with lack of oxygen. That wasn't mentioned.

'Also, why would an experienced pilot like Mantell let that happen to him? We knew, flying those planes, just how high we could go, and we knew to come down when we recognised that we were short of oxygen. And it just doesn't explain the crash, how the plane came down the way it did. I'm sure there was no malfunction on the plane, because Mantell would have told us when he was in radio contact.

'No, in the end they put it down to pilot error, going too high. I don't buy that, but it is a possibility. I don't believe that Mantell was chasing a planet or a balloon either, but again they're possibilities. Convenient possibilities.'

The official report by the Department of Defense contained a statement signed by Jim Duesler: this is the statement that Jim told me, in no uncertain terms, was a fake. It concluded with the words 'Certified a True Copy – James F. Duesler, USAF'. At the time, Jim was still serving in the US Army Air Corps: although the US Air Force had been constituted four months previously from the Air Corps, the transfer of personnel had not been concluded, and to the end of his service later in 1948 Jim was technically with the Air Corps.

Although Jim was always intrigued by what had happened that night, his own life was busy at the time: he was arranging his discharge and looking forward to getting back to his law degree. Besides, he had no idea how controversial the death of Thomas Mantell would become. He was not ordered to keep quiet about what he had seen, but his senior officer, a colonel, made it clear to him that if he talked publicly about flying saucers he would be laughed at, and would bring discredit to the base.

Jim's version of events is supported by others who were around at the time. The Godman Field Air Base commander, Guy F. Hix, also saw the UFO, and watched it through binoculars for an hour. He, like Jim and the others working in the control tower, would have been unlikely to confuse it with a planet. Richard T. Miller, who was serving in the operations room of Scott Air Base in Belleville, Illinois, heard the radio transmissions between the Godman tower and Mantell, and also reported that a local farmer had seen the plane enveloped in a blinding flash of light as it fell from the sky, after which its descent was unnaturally slow.

Jim, who suffered from chronic bronchitis, died on 30 October 1996. He had lived a good, interesting life, and I am glad that in his final few years I was able to help him set the record straight about what, at the time it happened, had seemed only a curious and mysterious event, but which he had thought about more and

Newspaper headlines describing animal mutilations which have baffled the police and animal welfare officers.

Driving through the Dolby Forest in the north east, shortly before we were turned back by two men in an unmarked car.

Two deer (left) and fox (below) with typical round holes in their skulls, found near Fylingdales, North Yorkshire, 1996. (*Mr Cedar*)

Cow found mutilated in Caldwell, Kansas, USA, in 1992. (*Linda Moulton Howe*)

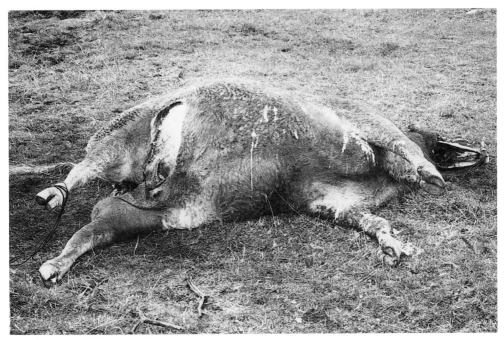

Mutilated cow found in Newry, Northern Ireland, March 1995.

Human mutilation found on the banks of the Guaraparinga Reservoir, Brazil, September 1988. (*A.J. Gevaerd*)

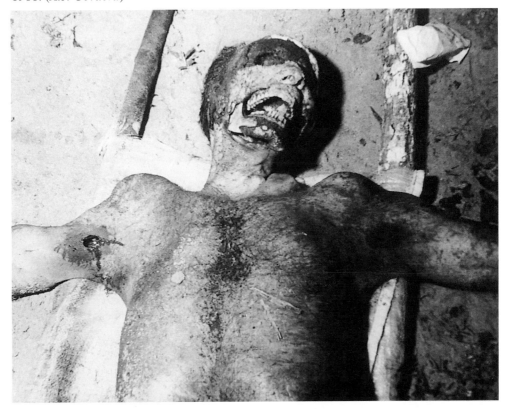

Investigating alien activity in Iceland in 1993, with Major Virgil Armstrong (*right*), a former CIA officer.

In the area of the Snæfellsjökull glacier in Iceland. I believe this is the scene of much clandestine alien activity – a fact that major world governments are trying to conceal.

more as the years went on. His death, at the natural end of a long, full life, was sad: how much sadder, though, was the death of that young pilot, Thomas Mantell, who had survived active service in World War II only to perish in an inexplicable accident which was put down, by the authorities, to pilot error.

In an interesting postscript, in 1993 I received a number of reports on the UFO Hotline from the Manchester area. Two people, on the same night but quite independently, described to me a UFO which looked like 'an ice-cream cornet standing upright'. It was described as metallic grey with a rusty red or orange band at the widest part of the cone – exactly like the object seen by Jim Duesler and others over Godman Air Base.

Pilot error was also said to be the reason American pilot Captain William Schaffner disappeared when his plane ditched in the North Sea off the coast of Grimsby on 8 September 1970. Journalist Pat Otter has researched the affair in great detail, and with the help of a contact we have agreed not to name, we believe we have come up with a more truthful account of what happened.

The fatal flight of Foxtrot 94 was, we believe, part of a massive operation being conducted along the whole of the east coast of the country, to investigate an epidemic of UFO reports. A covert operation, code name Operation Aeneid, was set up to try to track down the strange objects which were being reported almost nightly by pilots and members of the public. Sufficient strange blips had appeared crossing the radar screens at great speed for the Ministry of Defence to be on alert: they wanted to know what was happening.

The disappearance of Captain Schaffner was always a mystery, but a great deal of fresh and important evidence came to light when Pat Otter, assistant editor of the *Grimsby Evening Telegraph*, decided to look at the case again in 1986. He had been contacted by aviation expert and author Barry Halpenny, who was researching aviation mysteries, and suggested Pat should dig out the old newspaper cuttings of the crash. There was more to it, Barry said, than initially appeared. Pat naturally anticipated some problems digging out a story which was, at the time, sixteen years old. But as soon as he started asking questions, he discovered that it was even more difficult than he had expected: the Ministry of Defence, the USAF and the United States Embassy were all evasive and unhelpful. He realised that Barry was right: there was more to this than a simple case of pilot error, and he concluded that a blanket of secrecy had been thrown over the whole case.

Two years later, Barry published an abridged version of events in a book, and Pat wrote about his own researches in the *Grimsby Evening Telegraph*, reconstructing what was known about the last flight of Captain Schaffner. But they were not the only two people who were fascinated enough to be trying to unearth the truth: Pat was contacted by a man who was on the original crash investigation team, and who had been so surprised by the way the team were treated that he had, over the years, been carrying out his own research into the background. By coincidence, when Pat's articles appeared, this man was in Cleethorpes, following up lines of enquiry in and around RAF Binbrook, where Schaffner had been based, and he rang the journalist. He had already found out quite a lot, and was eventually prepared to share it.

With this man's evidence, Pat's invaluable research and my own contacts, we have been able to piece together a great deal of what happened during the autumn, winter and spring of 1970–1. Much of what our source has told us remains uncorroborated and has, in parts, been challenged by serving RAF officers and ex-RAF pilots. Neither Pat nor I was able to get anybody in authority to confirm it. But that hardly surprises us: to paraphrase Mandy Rice-Davies, they wouldn't, would they? And although we do not doubt the testimony of the former RAF officers who have presented a different picture, we believe that they were also kept in the dark about the nature of the operation. What we have managed to get are sufficient leads, sufficient quiet nods, to give us confidence in the picture we have built up of the events of those six months.

Between March and June 1970 the MoD, civilian airports and RAF establishments were all dealing with a spate of phone calls from the general public reporting sightings of unidentified lights and shapes over the North Sea, close to the east coast of Britain. The authorities were concerned enough to feel that something had to be done, and a joint US and British operation, with support from Norway and Iceland, was launched. Named Operation Aeneid (perhaps by a commanding officer with a classical education), it was to run from September 1970 until March the following year: there were never any plans for it to be a long-term commitment. The brief was to find out what was happening in the air over the east coast and south-west of Britain, both areas with vital military bases which would be vulnerable to air attack.

Only a handful of British civilians were involved in Aeneid: the rest of the British personnel were from the RAF, Royal Navy, Royal Observer Corps, Royal Corps of Signals, Royal Engineers and Royal Corps of Transport. Thirty-seven special observation sites were set up around the country, most on military bases, with four in Lincolnshire (the area about which we have been able to glean the most information). Other posts in the east-coast link were in Yorkshire, Norfolk and Suffolk.

The posts were manned by about half a dozen men, and were connected to command centres at RAF High Wycombe in Buckinghamshire, and RAF Rudloe Manor in Wiltshire. Information collected was transmitted to an American command centre at Wright Patterson Air Base in Ohio. Every post was equipped with a generator, communications equipment, state-of-the-art cameras and special night sights.

On 2 September, the second operational day of Aeneid, there were two notable incidents. The first involved two USAF Phantoms being scrambled from their base at Keflavik, in Iceland, to intercept an object travelling at high speed from the north-west towards the Icelandic coast. When they got within seven miles of the object, they were warned by ground control that the UFO had been joined by three others, all travelling at the same speed and in the same direction.

Within seconds the Phantom crews were radioing in that they were surrounded by the strange craft, three of which were conical in shape, with two of them having what appeared to be a glass ball trailing in their wake. The third had five of these glass

185

balls. The fourth object was different: it was described as a large slab with tapered ends. All four were surrounded by a bluish haze.

For two whole minutes, communication between the planes and ground control was lost. Even the pilot and navigator were unable to make contact with each other, and all on-board instrumentation ceased to function. Then, precipitately, two of the conical-shaped objects and the large slab-shaped craft accelerated away at phenomenal speed. The fourth object, still accompanied by its glass balls, went north at a more sedate speed. The Phantoms returned to Keflavik and reports were filed.

Later the same day two RAF Lightnings were scrambled from Binbrook Air Base, near Grimsby, Lincolnshire, to intercept a UFO over the North Sea. It withdrew at high speed before the aircraft could get within visual range. The following day, the pilot of an RAF Gnat – probably flying out of RAF Valley, Anglesey, in North Wales – reported being buzzed by a conical-shaped object while flying over the Irish Sea. The pilot stated that the object appeared to be accompanied by a single glass sphere.

Five days later, one of the observation posts in Wiltshire reported seeing a glowing rectangular object up to thirty feet long moving slowly across Salisbury Plain. The sighting was preceded by a complete power cut. One of the men in the post, Corporal Dan Perry, recalled seeing a colleague bathed in a brilliant blue light as the object moved past. Apart from a faint crackling sound, the craft moved in silence, dropping in height to within fifty feet of the observation post, and momentarily stopping. Two of the men shot off a series of photographs before the object passed out of vision. As it disappeared, their electricity came on again, but the radio link with their parent station at Hullavington was still down.

Twenty-four hours on, and the tragedy of Foxtrot 94 began to unfold. It was at 8.17 p.m. on the night of 8 September when a radar operator at Saxa Ford, on the Shetland Isles, one of the chain of British radar stations scanning the skies over the North Sea, picked up an unidentified object. It was travelling at 630 m.p.h. at 37,000 feet, heading south-west across the North Sea between the Shetlands and Norway. Its speed suddenly increased to 900 m.p.h. as it turned thirty degrees and headed due south, increasing altitude to 44,000 feet. Following normal procedures, two Lightning interceptors were scrambled from the nearest NATO airfield, RAF Leuchars, near Dundee. They assumed they were on the tail of a Russian long-range reconnaissance plane, as these were the Cold War years, and there was a well-established game of cat and mouse between the Eastern Bloc countries and the West.

But before the Lightnings could make contact, the object confounded the radar operators by executing a 180-degree turn and disappearing from their screens in seconds, at a speed later calculated at 17,400 m.p.h. It certainly was not a Russian war plane. The Lightnings were ordered to remain airborne and on patrol. During the next hour the mystery blip on the radar screens reappeared several times, from the north, but before the Lightnings could get within range it shot away at incredible speed. Two USAF F-4 Phantoms were scrambled from Keflavik, and with their more sophisticated radar were able to lock on to the object; but again, before they could get close, the UFO vanished.

NATO commanders were now so concerned that an alert was issued to the Ballistic Missile Early Warning System at RAF Fylingdales, Thule BMEWS base in Greenland, NORAD headquarters at Cheyenne Mountain, Colorado, and the US Detection and Tracking Center at Colorado Springs.

At 9.05 p.m. the object disappeared from the radar again, only to be picked up once more at 9.39 p.m., heading south-west off the northern tip of Denmark, with its speed reduced to 1,300 m.p.h., and an altitude of 18,000 feet. The first two Lightnings had been ordered back to Leuchars, but had been replaced with four others: two from Leuchars and two from RAF Coltishall, Norfolk. At the same time, Fylingdales heard that the USAF Strategic Air Command HQ in Omaha, Nebraska, was ordering its B-52 bombers into the air, an order which can only have been taken at the highest level, the White House. At this point, it seems almost certain that President Richard Nixon was involved and informed, and making decisions.

At this time, the USAF informed NORAD that there was a USAF pilot of great experience, with many hours of flying time in Vietnam to his credit, stationed at RAF Binbrook in an exchange arrangement between the two air forces. Captain William Schaffner was on his second tour in England, and had been at Binbrook long enough for his wife to have joined him: he was well liked and immensely respected for his proven flying skill and courage.

Schaffner was ordered to join the search, despite the fact that at this stage Binbrook's QRA (quick reaction alert) fighter planes were being held in reserve. Schaffner was sitting in the crew room of 5 Squadron when the call from High Wycombe came through. Still in his flying suit, having returned from a training sortie, he ran out to the runway where two Lightnings were being prepared for flight. One, XS894, was having its fuel tanks topped up, but was otherwise ready. Schaffner climbed in, waved aside the ground crew who were supposed to carry out pre-flight checks, ordered the refuelling to stop and failed to sign the regulation form stating that he was happy with the aircraft.

One of the ground crew was Brian Mann, from Grimsby, who was driving one of the fuel bowsers. He remembers the urgency of the take-off vividly: he was in the process of filling the Lightning's fuel tanks when the plane's engines started, nearly blowing in the windows of his tanker. He also remembers Captain Schaffner disregarding the ground marshal as he swung the Lightning, call sign Foxtrot 94, round for take-off at 10.06 p.m.

'His actions were unorthodox, to say the least,' Mr Mann said, when he recalled the incident years later. The last he, and the other ground staff at Binbrook, saw of the Lightning was its navigation lights, heading out over the North Sea.

By now the mystery object, which had led to five Lightnings, two Phantoms, three tankers and a Shackleton being scrambled, with B-52 bombers on alert, was being tracked by the radar station at Staxton Wold, near Scarborough. It was travelling parallel to the east coast, ninety miles east of Whitby, at a speed of 530 m.p.h. and an altitude of 6,100 feet.

Just a few minutes later, the Lightning of Captain William Schaffner ditched in the North Sea. The body of the pilot was never found. What happened in those few minutes is told vividly in a transcript of a conversation between Captain Schaffner and the Staxton Wold radar station. We have not been able to officially authenticate this transcript, but we believe it comes from a reliable source.

Schaffner: I have visual contact, repeat visual contact. Over.
Staxton: Can you identify aircraft type?
Schaffner: Negative, nothing recognisable, no clear outlines. There's a bluish light. Hell, that's bright . . . very bright.
Staxton: Are your instruments functioning, 94? Check compass. Over.
Schaffner: Affirmative, GCI, I'm alongside of it now, maybe 600 feet off my . . . it's a conical shape, Jeez that's bright, it hurts my eyes to look at it for more than a few seconds.
Staxton: How close are you?
Schaffner: About 400 feet, he's still in my three o'clock. Hey, wait . . . there's something else. It's like a large soccer ball. It's like it's made of glass.
Staxton: Is it part of the object or independent? Over.
Schaffner: Negative, nothing.
Staxton: Can you assess the rate . . .?
Schaffner: Contact in descent, gentle. Am going with it . . . fifty, no, about seventy . . . it's levelled out again.
Staxton: Is the ball object still with it? Over.
Schaffner: Affirmative. It's not actually connected . . . maybe a magnetic attraction to the conical shape. There's a haze of light. Yee'ow . . . it's within that haze. Wait a second, it's turning . . . coming straight for me . . . shit . . . am taking evasive action . . . a few . . . I can hardly . . .
Staxton: Come in, 94. Foxtrot 94, are you receiving? Over, come in.

As the controller lost contact with Captain Schaffner, a radar operator who had been tracking the Lightning and the mystery object watched his screen in amazement. The two blips,

189

representing the aircraft and the UFO, slowly merged into one, decelerating rapidly until they became stationary 6,000 feet above the North Sea. Two and a half minutes after the blip came to a halt, it started accelerating rapidly to 600 m.p.h., and climbing to 9,000 feet, heading south towards Staxton. Seconds later, the single blip separated into two, one maintaining its southerly direction, somewhat erratically, at about 600 m.p.h. and gradually dropping altitude; the other turning through 180 degrees to head north-west and vanishing at a speed later calculated to be 20,400 m.p.h.

At this time the Shackleton, which had been on patrol off the Firth of Forth, was ordered to Flamborough Head, near Bridlington. Then Staxton Wold re-established contact with Schaffner's Lightning.

Schaffner: GCI . . . are you receiving? Over.
Staxton: Affirmative, 94, loud and clear. What is your condition?
Schaffner: Not too good. I can't think what happened . . . I feel like kind of dizzy . . . I can see shooting stars.
Staxton: Can you see instruments? Over.
Schaffner: Affirmative. But, er . . . the compass is u/s [useless].
Staxton: Foxtrot 94, turn 043 degrees. Over.
Schaffner: Er . . . all directional instruments are out. Repeat u/s. Over.
Staxton: Roger, 94. Execute right turn, estimate quarter turn. Over.
Schaffner: Turning now.
Staxton: Come further, 94. That's good, is your altimeter functioning? Over.
Schaffner: Affirmative, GCI.
Staxton: Descend to 3,500 feet. Over.
Schaffner: Roger, GCI.
Staxton: What's your fuel state, 94? Over.
Schaffner: About thirty per cent, GCI.
Staxton: That's what we calculated. Can you tell us what happened, 94?

Schaffner: I don't know, it came in close . . . I shut my eyes . . . I figure I must have blacked out for a few seconds.
Staxton: OK, 94. Stand by.

At this time the Shackleton arrived over Flamborough, the area into which Foxtrot 94 was being guided by the Staxton controllers.

Schaffner: Can you bring me in, GCI?
Staxton: Er . . . Hold station, 94. Over . . . Foxtrot 94, can you ditch the aircraft? Over.
Schaffner: She's handling fine. I can bring her in. Over.
Staxton: Negative, 94. I repeat, can you ditch the aircraft? Over.
Schaffner: Yeah . . . I guess.
Staxton: Stand by, 94. Over. Oscar 77. Over.
Shackleton: Receiving. Over.
Staxton: 94 is ditching. Can you maintain a wide circuit? Over.
Shackleton: Affirmative, GCI. Over.
Staxton: Thanks, 77. Stand by, 94, to execute ditching procedure at your discretion. Over.
Schaffner: Descending now, GCI. Over.

A period of six or seven minutes elapsed without any contact.

Shackleton: He's down, GCI. Hell of a splash . . . he's down in one piece though. Over.
Staxton: Can you see the pilot yet? Over.
Shackleton: Negative, going round again, pulling a tight one. Over. [Two minutes later.] The canopy's up . . . she's floating OK . . . can't see the pilot, we need a chopper out here GCI. No sign of the pilot. Where the hell is he?
Staxton: You sure he's not in the water? Check your SABRE receptions. Over. [SABRE was the search-and-rescue beacon carried by all RAF aircrew.]
Shackleton: No SABRE yet, no flares either. Hang on, we're going round again. [Two minutes later.] GCI. Over.

191

Staxton: Receiving you, 77. Over.

Shackleton: This is odd, GCI, she's sinking fast but the canopy's closed again.

Staxton: Can you confirm the pilot clear of the aircraft?

Shackleton: He's not in it. We can confirm that. He must be in the water somewhere.

Staxton: Any distress signals or flares? Over.

Shackleton: Negative, GCI. We're going round again. Over. [A short time later, contact resumed.] She's sunk, GCI. There's a slight wake where she was. Still no sign of the pilot. I say again, GCI, we need a chopper fast. Over.

Staxton: A Whirlwind's on its way from Leconfield. Are you positive you saw no sign of the pilot? Over.

Shackleton: Nothing, GCI. The first pass we assumed he was unstrapping. He must have got out as we went round for the second pass, but why shut the canopy? Over.

Staxton: That's what we were thinking. Maintain patrol, 77, he must be out there somewhere.

Shortly afterwards, the search-and-rescue helicopter arrived and a systematic search of the area began. Lifeboats from Bridlington, Filey and Flamborough joined in as the weather began to deteriorate. The search continued overnight and into the next day, without success and without receiving any transmissions from the beacons carried by the pilot. The following day, there was a report of flares being seen ten miles offshore, and the Grimsby trawler *Ross Kestrel*, which was in the area, went to investigate but found nothing.

A month after the crash, divers from HMS *Kiddleston* inspected the wreckage of the Lightning on the seabed and reported that Captain Schaffner's body was still in the plane. But when it was brought to the surface two months after the crash, there was no trace of the pilot. The plane was remarkably undamaged, the cockpit canopy was closed, and from the position of the air brakes it was obvious that the pilot had been flying as slowly as possible when he hit the water.

The wreckage was taken to RAF Binbrook, where it was stored under armed guard: normal procedure would have dictated that the remains of Foxtrot 94 were taken to the MoD Crash Investigation Branch at Farnborough. Instead, a crash investigation team from Farnborough went to Binbrook. The informant who has done so much invaluable research into the case of Foxtrot 94 was one of this team, and it was the reception he and his colleagues received that sparked his lifelong interest in the mystery. They expected that they were about to mount the usual detailed investigation into a crash, which would culminate in a report to an MoD board of enquiry.

But they found they were only allowed to examine the plane for a few hours, and were constantly supervised by five civilians, two of whom had American accents. What they discovered surprised them: many of the cockpit instruments were missing, including the compass, voltmeter, standby direction indicator, standby inverter indicator and the complete auxiliary warning panel from the starboard side of the cockpit. This was a serious breach of procedure: the team were assured the instruments would be returned for their inspection, but they were not.

The plane smelled fusty and felt slimy: not surprising after two months beneath the North Sea. The ejector seat was there, but seemed to be 'wrong', and the team suspected that it was not the original one fitted to the Lightning. They were given assurances by the commanding officer of 5 Squadron that it had not been tampered with, but some of the investigators were not convinced. After their cursory few hours inspecting Foxtrot 94, the team from Farnborough were told their job was over and dispatched back to their base where, the following day, they were summoned to the main office and instructed never to discuss any aspect of the ditching of the Lightning, not even with members of their own families, for reasons of national security.

When I made enquiries with the MoD about Captain Schaffner, I was told that the file on the case is still classified, but that it was an accident and there was no UFO involvement. I have heard, from contacts, that the wreckage of Foxtrot 94 was taken to Kirkland Air Base in America. While the MoD will not confirm this, a spokesman said it is quite possible, because the crash involved an American airman.

After publishing his research, including the transcript of the contact between Captain Schaffner and Staxton, Pat Otter heard from two pilots who had been flying Lightnings on the night of the crash, both of whom reject any suggestion that the crash was anything other than a tragic accident. Mike Streten, a former 5 Squadron CO, says he was told that Foxtrot 94 was on an exercise shadowing a Shackleton. He believes that Captain Schaffner was disorientated, with stars above and the lights of fishing boats below, and hit the sea while trying to recover from a slow-speed situation.

He acknowledges that the missing body, with the ejector seat and seat dinghy still inside the aircraft, and the canopy closed, was a mystery, but completely rejects the idea that anything extra-terrestrial was involved. Furz Lloyd, another former Lightning pilot, also believes that the ditching of Foxtrot 94 was an accident. The plane, he says, was flying as slowly as possible to weave behind the target it was shadowing, and the pilot miscalculated and hit the sea, with no time to extricate his life raft.

We cannot prove that these versions of events are not correct, but there remain so many anomalies that it is hard to accept the disappearance of Captain Schaffner as so easily explicable. He was a very experienced pilot, and while I accept that even the best pilots occasionally suffer disorientation, it seems unlikely that he would have allowed this to happen. Why did he take off in such a hurry, without proper clearance? Why, if the crew of the Shackleton saw the Lightning floating for some time, was he unable to get his life raft clear? What happened to his emergency beacon? Why was the wreckage not taken to Farnborough? Why was the investigation team thwarted, and then ordered to remain silent? Why is the file on this incident still classified, after so many years?

Although, as I said, we have been unable to find cast-iron corroboration for the information supplied by the member of that team, who wishes to remain anonymous, there are other, completely independent witnesses to the UFO activity over the North Sea on that night. I have interviewed a housewife from Bridlington who watched six strange shapes in the sky, and a couple and their daughter who were walking their dog along a coastal path at Almouth Bay, Northumberland, almost at the nearest point on land to the place where Captain Schaffner had his encounter with the blip on the radar screen. They heard a loud humming noise, and witnessed several very bright flashes of light, which they reported to the local police.

The mystery of Foxtrot 94 has also got to be viewed in the context of what we have now unearthed about Operation Aeneid. Although it was, without doubt, the most dramatic event of the whole six-month operation, it was not an isolated incident. Conical-shaped UFOs were sighted by an RAF Argosy transport plane over the Bristol Channel, by a USAF Phantom off Goose Bay in Canada, and off the Yorkshire coast, where eleven objects with 'glass balls' in attendance were reported by observation points at Carnaby and Lisset. Similar sightings were made off the Lincolnshire and Suffolk coasts.

A six-man team, headed by Captain Bob Miller of the USAF, were manning an observation post at the RAF bombing range at Donna Nook on the Lincolnshire coast on 28 October 1970 when they saw a bright light, which they first took to be a plane, approaching from the North Sea. Captain Miller saw it first, as he had left the wooden shack where the team were based, about fifty yards from the range centre, to collect stores. The light was about 2,000 feet up and heading down and in, as if going to land.

Captain Miller's report, of which Pat Otter obtained a copy, said:

'My initial thought was that it was an aircraft, but then I remembered that the next plane was not due in for three-quarters of an hour. I watched the light for about a full minute, during which time it descended sharply before disappearing. I sprinted back to the hut and alerted the guys. "I think we've got visitors," I said.'

Captain Miller and the five RAF airmen piled out of the hut with their equipment. They saw the UFO coming towards them over the foreshore. His report went on:

'It was surrounded by blue haze, which would occasionally flare out with brilliant intensity. I shouted to the guys to get the

195

cameras rolling as they stood there gawping. The air was filled with electricity, which crackled loudly against anything metallic, including all cameras, and a strong metallic smell, like after rainfall, permeated the air. The object was silent.

'I realised that I was well within the blue haze, yet we could see clearly. All the hairs on my body were standing on end. There was also a feeling of weightlessness, of being top-heavy.'

The UFO turned slowly until it was sideways on to the airmen. It was then that they noticed five 'glass balls', each about two feet in diameter.

Captain Miller's report continued:

'As the object turned, its metallic surface, far from being smooth like in sci-fi movies, appeared weathered and worn. There were no portholes, no sign of organic life that I could see. As we stood there, one of the glass balls came slowly towards us until it was no more than four feet above our heads. You could see straight through it with only minimum distortion. For one crazy moment I thought of throwing my camera at it. As if it could read my thoughts, it gracefully withdrew towards the main object. At no time was I frightened. For some reason I kept thinking about my wife, and how she would never believe me.'

Miller said that as the UFO and the glass balls moved away from them over the sea, they were again conscious of the blue haze which surrounded it. It picked up speed and rapidly accelerated away to the north-east, disappearing in thirty seconds.

Miller's report went on:

'Within a minute all hell broke loose, in the form of wild chatter and excitement. I was in the process of shouting the guys down when the guys from the range control came running over. Apparently they too had been visited: a glass ball had flown right up to their window and hovered there for a full minute. So there must have been six of them.'

The sightings continued. Early in 1971 there was another dramatic incident, when a Fleet Air Arm Sea Vixen flying over South Wales was approached at high speed by a UFO. All controls on the plane ceased to function, and the pilot and navigator later estimated that they were 'held' stationary over the

Severn Estuary for two minutes, before some of the aircraft systems came back to life and, unable to make radio contact with the ground, they made an unscheduled landing at RAF Kemble, in Gloucestershire.

Two weeks later, on 25 January 1971, radar stations along the east coast picked up several unidentified objects on their screens, travelling at between 400 and 600 m.p.h. and at 80,000 feet. USAF Phantoms were scrambled from Iceland and RAF Leuchars in Scotland, Binbrook in Lincolnshire and Wattisham in Norfolk, with support from Victor tankers and Shackleton search-and-rescue aircraft. Up to forty 'contacts' were initially reported, eighteen of these increasing to a speed estimated at 4,700 m.p.h. and an altitude of 87,000 feet, and flying across the United Kingdom east to west, before turning 180 degrees and heading back at an estimated speed of 1,400 m.p.h.

The Lightnings were sandwiched between two groups of UFOs, eight in all, and again the pilots reported seeing glass balls. The UFOs pulled away at enormous speed after a few minutes pacing the fighter planes. Other planes were scrambled to intercept, but we have been unable to get hold of any more details about this sortie.

Soon after this encounter, Operation Aeneid was wound up. Many of the observation posts had already been shut down, before the end of 1970. It is difficult to understand why, when such dramatic results were being obtained: perhaps it was felt that too many 'ordinary' people, air force personnel, were finding out too much and that inevitably information would leak. Eventually it has done, but the whole operation has remained remarkably watertight for many years: the government files on it are covered by the 100-year security rules, and, much as I would love to get my hands on them, I accept that it is highly unlikely that I ever will.

What would be good, though, is if some of the airmen involved in Aeneid would now come forward. At the time, they would have been told they were taking part in 'tactical evaluation exercises', and for many of them that is all it will have seemed like: but for some there was real contact with UFOs, which I am certain they will remember vividly, because it was so out of the ordinary. Of course, they will have been instructed not to talk, and neither Pat Otter nor I would ever want to compromise them by revealing their identities. But we would like to find out more about what went on during those six months of 1970 and 1971.

Again, we have had some corroboration from totally disinterested parties. Two people holidaying in a caravan in Scarborough in November 1970 saw an encounter between two fighter planes and a strange object capable of travelling at astonishing speed. One of the holidaymakers, unable to sleep, went for a walk on the beach at 6 a.m. and was astonished to see a large disc-shaped object hovering over the North Sea. He rushed back to the caravan to wake his sleeping friend. They saw two planes approach the object, which then hurtled away at incredible speed, disappearing in seconds.

These two sane, sensible, normal people believe the evidence of their own eyes. They do not believe the official version: that nothing happened.

There are many others who are unhappy with the way important events are covered up. Some are prepared to risk a great deal to help me, as we shall see in the next chapter.

CHAPTER NINE

THE MILITARY RESPONSE

As well as getting information from pilots and aircrew, I also receive help from other sources whose identities I have to protect, because of their careers – and because many of them have signed the Official Secrets Act, and are putting a great deal on the line by contacting me. These are men who have seen things which they know are important, and which they believe should not be kept under wraps. Sometimes I do not even myself know their real identities: usually, though, they are happy to let me know exactly who they are because they want me to take their information seriously. Of course, I never compromise their need to have complete secrecy and protection. For this reason, some of the details I would have liked to include in this chapter have been left out.

The vast majority of reports I have received on the UFO Hotline are from ordinary members of the public who have seen mysterious objects and lights in the sky. Their information is very valuable, especially when I get several independent sightings of the same UFO, or of a spate of UFO activity in one particular area of the country. But although these reports help build up an overall picture of the extent of alien contact with earth (and I have had many thousands of sightings notified to me over the years), I am particularly interested in the leaks which come to me from military personnel and government officials. To get on the phone to me at all, risking their careers and pensions, means that what they have to say is of great significance. These are people who are aware of the presence not just of alien craft in the heavens, but of the contact that exists between governments and the intelligence piloting the craft.

Let me give you a simple example. I had a call in February 1995 from a man who gave me enough details about himself for me to be able to check out that he was genuine in his claim that he was serving as a communications officer in the British Army in the eighties.

He told me that he was one of a group of soldiers put on seventy-two-hour alert. They were not told what for, but because he was receiving and relaying messages, he knew, in advance, that an important arrival at the base was expected. He had no idea what, although from the nature of the messages he encrypted he knew it was airborne. When it arrived, 'it was nothing like I've ever seen before', he told me.

'It was a reddish-blue glow that seemed to come slowly across the sky, but when it got close we could see it was actually travelling very fast, faster than anything I've seen. We've got military aircraft that go faster than Concorde, up to 4.5 mach, but this was much faster.'

He described how it hovered and then came down in what was obviously a controlled landing, on the anti-tank ranges.

'It was a controlled putdown but something was obviously wrong with it. It collapsed on one side as it touched down, just crumpled up. It was about the size of a Phantom jet, but smooth and slightly boomerang-shaped. Screens were put up around it immediately. About forty of us watched from outside the screens as the occupants of the craft were transferred to the waiting vehicles. They were driven away for decontamination.'

I asked him how he knew the occupants were not human, and he replied, 'Because I received the incoming messages.'

My informant was reluctant to tell me any more over the phone. He promised he would come to see me to pass on the details he knew from the messages, but he has not been in contact since. It could, of course, be a hoax, but I have an instinct for these things, and when I listen to the recording I made of the phone conversation, I am sure that he was genuine. The small, unimportant details that nobody ever makes up are there. It is also obvious that he is very nervous about speaking to me, and particularly concerned that if he does release the content of the messages he will be breaching the terms of his contract with the army in a much more serious way than simply telling me about the craft landing. I would dearly love to contact him for more information, but I respect his right to secrecy. I hope he will one day tell me more, and that he will, as he promised, find other soldiers who witnessed the same event.

Another nervous ex-serviceman who contacted one of my researchers was a member of one of Britain's élite highly trained forces who had been taking part in an exercise which involved him being dropped in a remote and fairly barren area of the British Isles. His mission was to evade capture and make his way to a certain check-in point by the next morning. In the middle of the night he was walking along the edge of a rough track when he heard the sound of a vehicle approaching. Assuming it was his colleagues, who were 'the enemy', he dived over a fence. He had seen signs along this fence warning the public to keep off because of unexploded bombs, so he knew it was military territory. To his great surprise, as he looked up from the position he had rolled to under a hedge, he found himself staring along the barrel of a rifle.

At first he felt bitter disappointment: he had obviously been shadowed and captured by his colleagues. But he quickly realised that this was not part of the exercise. The guard who arrested him was American. He was taken across country to a hillside, in which there was a very well-disguised door. Once inside, another American, who was sitting behind a desk, ordered the soldier who had arrested him to take him to a lift. To his astonishment, the lift took him down several floors, into the heart of what can only have been a huge subterranean base. He was taken into a room, where he was questioned for several hours by an American and a well-spoken Englishman. Because of his training, he would only give his name, rank and number. After a few hours had elapsed, the Englishman came into the room and told him that he had been checked out, and that they knew he was part of a training exercise. He was going to be released, but before that could happen he would have to sign two sets of documents, one from the British Government and the other from the American forces, compelling him never to reveal what had happened.

As he was taken out, he saw another of the many doors along the corridor open, and a man in a white coat emerged. The room, or what little of it he glimpsed, looked like an operating theatre. He was driven away from the underground establishment and dropped close to the point where he was supposed to check in. Despite his obvious physical bravery and his tough training, this man was nervous when he gave his account of events. He was overwhelmed by what he had seen, because he had no idea that secret bases like this one existed, and he was worried that whatever was happening there was not accountable, in the way that most military activities are open to at least a certain amount of public scrutiny.

Another trusted contact, with whom I have had several conversations, has given me details of a quick-response team set up during Margaret Thatcher's government, and as a result of her co-operation with President Reagan. This team, again made up of élite forces, was on permanent stand-by to attend the sites of any UFO landing or crash, carrying bleepers which would summon them any time they were needed. Helicopters were permanently ready to ferry them to the scene of the crash. Their role was to seal the site from the public, if necessary evacuating any civilians living within the sealed perimeter. They set up two cordons, a tight one around the actual UFO and a wider one to isolate the whole area within several hundred yards.

They also attended sites of animal and human mutilations, which shocked and horrified them: as my contact said, they could accept the horrors of war, but they were not accustomed to seeing such brutal wounds to animals and humans in peacetime.

It was the secrecy surrounding the whole of their operation that made him feel it was his duty to alert the public to what was going on. Unfortunately, the first contact he made was with an inexperienced young UFO enthusiast, who secretly recorded their conversation. This young man played the tape to other UFO researchers, and talked about it at their meetings: he was very naive, because within days a mysterious fire broke out in his office at home, and all his files were burned. He realised he was in over his head and contacted me – he sounded terrified. His wife was so frightened she moved out and left him: luckily, they are now back together again. But he made it clear that he wanted nothing more to do with this investigation, and passed it over to me.

The soldier had also decided it was a mistake to talk, and he was very wary of me when I first contacted him. I had to send him photostats of my driving licence and proof that I had been in the police before he would agree to talk to me. He told me he had discussed me with his colleagues from the quick-response team, and they had agreed to him helping me, as long as it was very discreet. They all shared his feeling that the public were being kept in the dark.

They attended crash scenes across Europe, including Spain and Germany. They were not supposed to make any recording of what they saw, but he has photographs of some of the mutilations, and also a piece of debris he picked up at the scene of a crash. At one site in Spain there were several human bodies spread around the site of the crash, all naked and without body hair, and all mutilated by having limbs, etc. cut off.

They also saw dead aliens, of more than one type. The most terrifying was large and reptilian, looking like a seven-foot-tall lizard only with arms and legs. It appeared to be attached to a box which was connected by a thick cord to its back. The box had flashing lights. This type of alien has been reported before, not just to me but to other researchers. Although a lot less common than the 'grey', it is obviously around earth in sufficient numbers to be consistently seen, and we have plenty of reasons to believe that it is, unlike other types, not friendly towards the human race. Another, much smaller, alien seen at another site was a typical 'grey', except that instead of hands and feet it had small round stubs, which my contact described as like 'little cherries'.

At each scene they attended they were aware of Americans,

203

and possibly Canadians, who did not fraternise with them or even talk to them. My contact remembers, particularly, the brusque way they were treated by these people: typically, for British forces, one of the first things they established at each scene was a field kitchen to serve tea, and when they offered cups to these men they were ignored. On one occasion, though, one of the Americans did speak. A local policeman had turned up at the site of the crash, and was ordered away. He refused to go, saying that this was not military land and he was within his rights, as an officer of the law, to know what was going on. After a brief exchange, in which the policeman stood his ground, one of the Americans turned to the British troops and said, 'Shoot him.' The instruction was repeated forcibly enough for the soldiers – and the policeman – to realise it was serious, at which point the policeman hastily withdrew.

I asked if they had ever needed to use their firearms, and my contact told me they would shoot at bushes and large clumps of grass within the containment area, to make sure there was nobody there. They carried Geiger counters as part of their issued kit. On one occasion my contact was within five feet of a crashed object, and he and several others ended up in hospital being treated for severe blistering, so bad that he still has some scars.

At one site they saw a shiny tube, about four feet long, which looked as though it was made of chrome, but it was glowing all over. Nothing was ever explained to them, which they feel resentful about, especially as the job they were doing was obviously potentially dangerous. My contact saw enough to make him take the whole UFO phenomenon very seriously indeed. He said to me:

'I tell you this, Mr Dodd, there is no way I will let my children out on country lanes after dark.'

I am still researching the work of this quick-response team, which has since been disbanded, by John Major's government, on the grounds of cost. Again, all those who were part of it are bound by secrecy, and stand to lose a lot of protection and pension if they are found to have leaked information. The one who came forward did so out of an overwhelming feeling that they had been involved in something so big that it should not be kept secret. Officially, of course, no such team ever existed . . .

With ordinary UFO reports, I tend to hear about them soon after they happen. When I was running the UFO Hotline I would have the answering machine on all night, and would often wake to hear it buzzing into life in the early hours of the morning, as someone rang in to report a strange shape in the sky more or less simultaneously with seeing it. Monday mornings were always very busy, as I would be deluged with sightings from over the weekend, when many people tend to stay out later at night.

The military reports, on the other hand, often take many years to surface, as the people who have seen mysterious things wrestle with their conscience as to whether or not it is right to report them. They also realise, as time wears on, that the astonishing thing they witnessed is not going to come out into the open through official sources. It took more than twenty years for one soldier to come forward, to talk of events which made headlines back in 1974.

It was on a cold, dark January night that residents of Llandrillo and Llandderfel in North Wales were startled by a huge explosion, which shook the ground and their homes. Many residents rushed out into the street, and later told of seeing a large, pulsating orange glow high up on a remote mountainside of the Berwyn range. The local police switchboards were jammed as reports were made of a ball of light which appeared to fall to earth just before the bang. The impact was great enough to have registered on seismology recording equipment of the British Geological Survey in Edinburgh, who confirmed that the centre of the explosion was Bala (very close to the spot reported by locals) and that it registered on the Richter scale as the size of a small earthquake.

There were many witnesses, including a nurse who lived in Llandderfel. When she contacted the police she said she thought it must be a plane crash. They asked her to go to the scene in order to help out with any casualties. Accompanied by her two teenage daughters, she drove along the B4391 road to a point where they could clearly see the object which had landed on the mountainside. They watched the glowing, pulsing UFO for twenty minutes, during which time they saw little flecks of white light zigzagging up the hillside towards it.

As it was obviously not a plane crash, and because her daughters were becoming frightened, the nurse returned home. On the way, they met a military vehicle and were ordered to leave the area. Another witness, a member of the staff of a nearby hotel, said that the place shook as if it had been hit by an earthquake. She said that in the following days, talk in the bar was dominated by reports of military police sealing off the area, and local farmers being prevented from going on to their own land for over a week. Other local residents reported driving up to the mountainside in the hours immediately after the crash, and finding the road sealed by soldiers and air force personnel. Because so many cars went up there, it took time to get them all to do a difficult turn on a narrow road, so their occupants had time to look across at the object. All the descriptions were consistent: it was large, pulsating, and giving off an orange-pink glow. Large numbers of military vehicles were seen in the area for several weeks after the incident.

Margaret Fry, a UFO researcher who lived in the area, started an immediate investigation, and collected witness statements from many of the people who saw the object. Several said that after a few hours on the ground, the pulsating glow had taken off into the air and disappeared at enormous speed.

Margaret went with the nurse to the spot on the B4391 from which she had observed it, and in daylight both women realised that the small flecks of light which the nurse had assumed were the torches of military personnel going to the scene were a long way across desolate, treacherous terrain. There was no way that anyone could have reached the place where she saw the flickers of light in the time since the explosion – unless they had already been on the mountainside, waiting for the crash. There was no sign of the object, but there was a patch of lighter ground underneath the peak of Cader Berwyn, which the nurse said was the place where the landing had happened.

Within days of this incident, there were two other unusual

happenings reported from North Wales. A family who lived within the boundaries of the Snowdonia National Park, just twenty-five miles north of the Berwyn mountains, were returning home in two cars from a social outing. They were travelling along a narrow road through a Forestry Commission plantation, with no houses or buildings in the vicinity, when they heard a purring noise, loud enough for both cars to halt. Then a saucer-shaped craft with a dome on top of it came gliding across the tops of the trees, hovering in the road in front of the cars. It had cobalt-blue lights around it, and coloured beams, also in the same blue, shone from beneath it to the ground. The family members later agreed that they felt no fear, and that it was a very attractive object. Some of them climbed out of the cars to see it better. Slowly, the UFO set off again, skimming the treetops, until it dropped out of view towards a clearing. The family continued their journey home.

Another case, just days before the mountain crash, involved two long-distance lorry drivers who were travelling from Lincoln to their home area of Maentwrog, the other side of Lake Bala. They were hoping to get home in time for a pint at their local. When they were about an hour away from Bala they suddenly saw an enormous black cigar-shaped object with lights down one side. They carried on driving, while watching the object, which disappeared rapidly into the night.

When they reached their local they were puzzled to find it locked up and the lights out: it was only when they looked at their watches that they realised it was 1 a.m., and they were three hours later than they had expected to be.

The initial research on all these cases was carried out by Margaret. At the same time, Gary Rowe, another UFO researcher, was investigating a very similar case to the Berwyn mountain incident. A farmer with land just outside Aberystwyth, fifty miles south on the coast of mid-Wales, heard an explosion. When he investigated, he found a swath of pine forest had been destroyed, but by the time he arrived at the scene there were military vehicles and soldiers refusing him access to his own land. For a week the area was cordoned off, and during that time a JCB earth-mover was brought to the site and all the topsoil removed and taken away. Gary later heard, from good contacts, that no craft had been found, but that army personnel did remove small fragments from the crash.

All these cases happened a long time ago, and I would never have become involved with them had I not received information from a man who was serving as a military officer at the time of the Berwyn mountain incident. Again, he had been loath to come forward while on the army payroll, and was still reluctant because he had to overcome his natural instinct to obey orders and say nothing. He gave sufficient information about himself to confirm his background, and although I cannot reveal it here, I can confirm that he was a serving officer at the time.

This is the statement he gave:

'On 18 January 1974 I was stationed at a barracks in the south of England. I cannot name my unit or barracks as they are still operational. We, that is my unit, were put on standby to move north at short notice. On the night of 19 January we had moved up to Birmingham. We then received orders to proceed with speed to North Wales. We were halted at Chester in readiness for a military exercise we believed was about to take place. On 20 January we received orders to proceed to Llangollen and to wait at that point.

'On arrival our unit was split into four groups, and at that point we noticed a great deal of ground and aircraft activity. At approximately 11.30 a.m. we, that is myself and four others, were ordered to go to Llandderfel, and were under strict orders not to stop for any civilians. When we reached our objective we were ordered to load some cargo into our vehicles. The cargo comprised two large, oblong boxes. We were at this time ordered not to open the boxes, but to proceed to the Porton Down facility and deliver the boxes. [Porton Down is a government research centre in Wiltshire, the Chemical and Biological Defence Establishment, where top-secret research into chemical and biological warfare is carried out. The work done there includes research into decontamination and protection from radiation.]

'We set off south with our cargo, and during the journey we stopped off to get a drink and were immediately approached by a man in civilian clothes who produced an ID card and ordered us to keep moving and not stop until we reached our destination. We eventually reached Porton Down and moved the boxes inside the facility. Once inside, the boxes were opened by staff in our presence and we were shocked to see two creatures, which had been placed inside decontamination suits. When the suits were opened it was obvious the creatures were not of this world, and when examined were found to be dead. What I saw that day made me change my whole concept of life.

'The bodies were about five feet six inches tall, humanoid in shape, but so thin that they looked almost skeletal, covered in skin. Although I did not see a craft at the scene of recovery I was informed that a large craft had crashed and was recovered by other military units. Some time later we joined up with the other three elements of our unit, who informed us that they had also transported bodies of alien beings to Porton Down, but said that their cargo was still alive.

'This was the only time I was ever involved in something of this nature. This event took place many years ago, and I am now retired from the armed forces. This is a true account of the events which occurred in January 1974. I am not certain of the accuracy of the dates and times given.'

Although I have no doubt about the sincerity of this officer, or the general accuracy of the report he gave (he was elderly, and admitted that he might have confused the actual dates), it is obvious that some of it is hearsay. For example, he only heard it from other soldiers that some of the aliens were alive; he also only heard rumours that the craft was captured. From the eye-witness evidence of the night – when several people saw a craft take off again – I feel sure that there were probably two alien landings, one to rescue the survivors of the crash. The small lights seen on the hillside were so close to the crashed UFO that they cannot possibly have been humans travelling from the nearest access roads, and there was definitely other UFO activity in the area, as we know from various reports. My own personal guess is that a second UFO came down, and this is what was seen departing. If this is so, it is highly unlikely that it left living aliens behind.

I wrote an account of these developments in the Welsh case

209

for *UFO* magazine in the autumn of 1996, including Margaret Fry's telephone number for anyone who wishes to contact her. She received quite a bit of feedback from other military sources, confirming the main elements of the case as detailed by the retired officer.

It is not only military personnel who approach me with reports of events like these. A civilian employee at a nuclear submarine base in Scotland rang me on 25 January 1995. He would not give me his name or address, because he was concerned about jeopardising his job, but he wanted me to know about an event that happened in July 1989, when he was working the night shift at the Holy Loch base. He and approximately fifty other workers were working on the maintenance of a nuclear submarine which was suspended in the Los Alamos dry dock when, at about 3 a.m., the shipyard klaxons started up, causing all the workers to stop what they were doing and look up.

As they watched, they saw a brightly glowing airborne object, green in colour, approaching their position across the bay. The object was triangular in shape, moving slowly and soundlessly at a height of about thirty feet above the water. When it got to within thirty to forty feet of the watching men, it stopped and just hung in the air, as if it, in turn, was watching them. Suddenly a second object appeared, from the same direction as the first, veering away from the first UFO, passing silently under the suspended nuclear submarine and reappearing at the other side. It then moved around the sub and positioned itself next to the hovering UFO.

For about fifteen minutes the two triangular glowing UFOs stayed there, silent and motionless, while all around the base was confusion and panic, as vehicles containing armed guards dashed about the place and men shouted to each other. Then both craft started to move, executing a slow turn in the air before disappearing at great speed in the direction whence they came.

All the witnesses were debriefed before leaving the base the next morning. They gave individual statements about what they had seen, and they were then interviewed and warned that they must not speak of it to anyone, not even their wives or closest family.

The caller explained that in a high unemployment area, jobs like his were highly prized, and he had no wish to do or say anything that would compromise his regular wage packet. Nonetheless, he had been unable, in the ensuing five and a half years, to put what he had seen out of his head. By telling me, he felt he was placing it on record, and that he might be able to get some peace from it in the future. I hope he has: I have never heard from him since.

That our alien visitors are particularly interested in military establishments is a recurring thread running through all the reports I receive. I estimate that approximately one in ten genuine UFO sightings takes place above or near military land. For example, one investigator I know took video footage of a strange object which appeared over an MoD base in Brecon, South Wales, on 22 June 1995. The object initially appeared as an orange ball of light which hovered above the ground, while a series of red lights moved up from the ground towards it, then reversed direction and travelled back to earth. On the film, the UFO is clearly a large circular object with segments missing round the edge: a curious shape, but one familiar to UFO watchers, because it has appeared before in film taken over England, Scotland, New Zealand and the controversial Area 51 secret base in the USA.

Even when the UFO does not appear above military territory, there is frequently a military presence in the area. An example is an incident which was witnessed by several local residents on 31 October 1994, when a barrel-shaped object fell from the sky on to a field at Hipton Hill, between Church Lench and Norton, Worcestershire. The residents reported that the field was instantly cordoned off, and the object taken away by a Royal Navy vehicle, accompanied by a police escort. Police and fire-fighting equipment were seen entering the field, but the local police, the RAF and the Royal Navy later all denied any knowledge of the incident. The local fire brigade claimed they were called out to a burning bale of hay – a story which did not wash with the locals who watched the whole event.

211

There are frequent reports of military aircraft and Chinook helicopters at the scene of UFO activity, but their presence is almost always officially denied. I am completely used to official denials, but I continue to ask the right questions, not because I am ever hopeful that some co-operative bureaucrat will suddenly reveal all, but simply because I feel it is my duty to keep on, perhaps picking a tiny hole in the blanket the authorities choose to throw over this whole subject.

Although I ought to be inured to it, I still feel outraged by the way the authorities insult the intelligence of the general public who report these sightings to me. In November 1995 several residents of the small Yorkshire town of Sowerby Bridge were amazed to see a very large UFO hovering over Scammonden reservoir, to the south of the town. It was described as disc-shaped, glowing bright white, with coloured flashing lights around the bottom. As they watched, the observers saw seven fighter aircraft and three helicopters flying in circles around the object, which was hovering several hundred feet above the reservoir.

One of the local people rang me while watching this activity, which lasted for about ten minutes before the UFO shot away at phenomenal speed. I in turn immediately telephoned West Drayton, a joint RAF and civilian radar station, and asked for their comments on what was being observed. After holding on for a few minutes I was told there were no aircraft in the area and nothing was appearing on radar. They also told me they had checked with Manchester Airport, whose radar system covered this area, and they were also reporting nothing. I asked how it was possible for several witnesses to see this activity from the ground, yet it was apparently nonexistent: the reply was simply that the operator did not know.

Fifteen minutes later, to my surprise, the West Drayton operator to whom I had been speaking phoned me back. I had not given him my name or phone number, and this was before the general public had access to British Telecom's 1471 system. He told me that they now felt they could explain the UFO sighting: large floodlights had been installed at the reservoir by Yorkshire Water who, in drought conditions, were ferrying water by tanker

212

to this stricken supply centre. The floodlights helped the round-the-clock tanker service. Low-flying military planes, he said, were probably exploding the floodlights, which had confused the witnesses.

I was amused: only quarter of an hour earlier he had been telling me categorically that there were no planes in the area; now he was blaming military aircraft for the sighting. I telephoned Yorkshire Water, who were helpful: they checked with their electrical department, and no floodlights had exploded. When I told the witnesses that the official line was that they had been fooled into seeing a UFO by popping floodlights, they were, understandably, insulted.

For me, it was just another example of the official cover-up and denial which hampers all investigation into this subject. I am used to it, but I do not accept it. Nor do I underestimate it. It comes, as the next chapter shows, from the highest sources.

CHAPTER TEN

UNDER THE OCEANS

For some years I have believed that world governments, headed by the Americans, not only have contact with alien races, but have reciprocal agreements with them, allowing them to come and go around our planet without hindrance. I have collected a substantial file of evidence to suggest that there are alien bases under the sea in the North Atlantic, and that these are protected by a high-level international conspiracy. Since I brought it out into the open, other researchers have found evidence to support this: I also now believe that there are underground bases on land and in other areas of the ocean, although I maintain that the North Atlantic seems to be the most significant, possibly the largest, sea base in European waters. Other reported underwater bases are in South American waters – in the areas of Puerto Rico and Brazil – in Antarctica, and in other deep and unobserved areas of ocean.

From the alien point of view, it is a logical choice. Three-quarters of the surface of the earth is covered in water, and, assuming that their technology is so superior to anything we know about that they can cope easily with the transition from water to air, the North Atlantic is relatively unobserved. To us it is a difficult, dangerous stretch of water; to them it is good camouflage, and a mineral-rich seabed (which I believe is a major part of the attraction).

Iceland has long been the centre of many stories about UFO

incidents and alien sightings, but it was a sequence of events in the winter of 1992 that alerted me to the scale of activity in the Arctic Circle.

Iceland played a crucial role during the Cold War years, with huge radar bases built around its coast to monitor the activities of the Soviet fleet, slipping out into the Atlantic from their Barents Sea bases. On many occasions, fighter planes were scrambled to pursue blips on the radar that turned into encounters with UFOs. Iceland is a land rich in legend and folklore, and its people have many strange tales to tell of small creatures seen out on the glaciers, particularly the Snæfellsjökull glacier, where local residents leave food out for 'the little grey people who live under the glacier'.

In the winter of 1992, there were dozens of UFO sightings in the north of Scotland, causing a flurry of media interest as literally hundreds of witnesses reported strange shapes and lights in the sky. But there was one incident that did not get reported in the national press. On 20 December, near the Orkney Islands, a UFO was tracked on radar and a fighter plane ordered up to intercept it. I heard, from a reliable source, that the plane and the UFO merged on the radar screen, just as had happened with Foxtrot 94, and that again radio contact was lost. A search-and-rescue plane took off, and hours later made a mysterious discovery. In a remote and inhospitable stretch of the Orkneys the plane was found, intact, in an area where it would have been impossible to carry out a controlled landing. The pilot was missing.

While I was making enquiries about this incident, which I never managed to verify, I stumbled across my biggest and most important investigation ever: the Icelandic affair. On the same date, 20 December, an Icelandic naval source of mine telephoned to say that three large UFOs had been tracked coming down and entering the sea off the east coast of Iceland, close to Langeness. Other witnesses confirmed seeing these UFOs, and they were also tracked on radar. The following day, Icelandic fishermen reported seeing large, fast-moving underwater craft, with flashing coloured lights. They appeared to be tracked by (or be tracking) a glowing object in the sky which was travelling

216

south in the general direction of Scotland. The underwater craft caused a great deal of damage to the trawl nets of the fishing boats.

The fishermen, a hardy bunch used to pitting their strength and endurance against the huge seas and bitter cold of the Arctic Circle, were disturbed and alarmed by the strange underwater craft. They knew they were not submarines: they travelled far too fast, and they had never seen submarines with flashing lights. After reports from the crews of the fishing boats, patrol boats from the National Icelandic Coast Guard were dispatched to the area.

On 23 December, two gun boats from the Icelandic navy and a coastguard vessel were sent 'on observation' to Langeness. The crews were given no information about why they were there, but I heard later from one of the seamen that a sense of unease pervaded the atmosphere on board the naval vessel. They were joined in the area by a fleet of NATO warships (including British vessels) who were officially on 'a naval exercise' – despite the fact that it was Christmas. Newspaper stories reported the fleet as tracking large underwater craft, thought to be a new breed of Russian super-submarine. On Christmas Eve, the crew of two British hunter-killer submarines were suddenly recalled from leave and sent to rendezvous with the fleet. If this was only an exercise, it was done at the worst possible time for morale, as these men had just settled down with their families for the Christmas break when they were told to return to their ships instantly. The only justification they were given was that they were taking part in something important.

From my sources, I know that four more UFOs were tracked coming down into the sea, in the same quadrant as the first three, and again the fast-moving underwater craft were seen. Shortly afterwards an American ship was reported missing. All the NATO ships joined in the search, during which one of the British submarines mysteriously lost power and struck the seabed. Fortunately, power was restored and the submarine resumed action.

On 12 January 1993 the weather closed in hard, and the smaller Icelandic vessels had to run for the cover of Langeness

Fjord, where they were forced to remain for three weeks, before taking up their original positions.

While this was happening at sea, Icelandic radio was broadcasting reports of large UFOs seen over the mountains in the eastern part of the country, and residents living in the area of Langeness Fjord, where the Icelandic naval vessel and gunboats were enduring appalling weather conditions, reported seeing small figures on the ice around the fjord.

By 25 February 1993, there was an American flotilla of three destroyers within the Arctic Circle, and all other vessels were warned not to approach within three nautical miles. From outside this exclusion zone, radar on the other ships picked up sixteen airborne contacts with the American fleet, and these contacts could be seen as bright yellow/amber lights descending from the sky – the distance involved means they must have been much bigger than helicopters, and the atrocious weather conditions meant that no helicopters would have been able to fly anyway. The lights appeared to hover above the US vessels for a short time, and then sped away in formation at great speed.

The following month, crew and passengers of an Icelandic Airlines plane travelling from London to Reykjavik reported that they were tailed by two large balls of white light from the north of Scotland until they were over Iceland. Then, in April, two Icelandic fishing boats went missing, and the search crews reported white tubular-shaped lights hovering over their vessels. At the same time, the radios on their ships refused to function, but worked normally again when the lights moved away. All the seamen involved in the search were warned not to divulge any information about what they had seen – my contact reported back to me in the greatest of secrecy.

By 15 April, only two American destroyers remained in the area, and the other vessels were again ordered to search for a missing warship. The names of the remaining US ships had been blacked out, and their crew were seen to be wearing full battle dress. All civilian ships, including fishing boats, were again ordered to stay three nautical miles away from them, probably because the US authorities already knew that information about their activities was being leaked: I had been making enquiries in

America about what was going on.

The colleague I spoke to in the USA approached the Office of Naval Intelligence to ask what was happening off the coast of Iceland, outlining to the woman intelligence officer some of the reports we had been receiving about underwater craft and a missing US ship. The officer jokingly dismissed it all as rubbish and rumour, saying that she would have been aware of anything like that. She promised to make a couple of phone calls to check it out. Some time later, my American friend received a call from ONI: this time, the friendly, amused tone had changed and the same officer demanded to know where the information had come from. Her attitude was threatening and aggressive.

Immediately after this, my direct ship-to-shore contact with the flotilla ceased: my contact next rang me when he was on shore. There had, he said, been a huge clampdown on calls after it was reported that information that could only have come from one of the vessels taking part in the exercise was being leaked.

Also in the middle of April, Russian naval vessels joined the party in the North Atlantic: they appeared to be co-operating with the NATO ships, covering the mouth of the Barents Sea. At one stage a message between two Russian vessels was intercepted by one of the others, and I was later told that the message said: 'We are engaging unknown underwater craft.'

The unusual activities in the area did not completely escape the attention of the rest of the world. On 16 April a British newspaper carried the headline 'Joint American and Russian Military Exercises About To Take Place'. The report said that for the first time since World War II, American and Russian troops were working together. The exercise was said to be taking place in Siberia, with US troops being shipped in to Tiksi. Interestingly, Tiksi is the nearest Russian port to the area where the naval operations were taking place.

I later learned from a highly placed American source that at this time a team of 'remote viewers', working for the US Defense Department, were asked to assist in trying to find the missing warship. Remote viewing involves using gifted psychics, who can travel in their minds to distant locations and describe what they see. The use of psychics by the US Government is highly controversial, and was kept secret for a long time. But it is now well known that they were used during the Gulf War, and at other times. When asked to find the warship the psychics said that it was a Sea Shadow, a newly developed 'stealth ship', and had been towing a barge loaded with advanced surveillance equipment, to monitor underwater mining operations carried out by aliens. It had suddenly disappeared, but they could shed no light on how. The idea that the aliens could be mining the area makes sense: there are known deposits of naturally radioactive material in this inhospitable area.

From this sequence of events, it was clear to me that something serious was happening in Icelandic waters, and I began to make more enquiries and collate more reports from other independent sources. A very close and reliable friend, with extensive contacts in Iceland because of his professional links, helped me to establish contact with several of the fishermen, who now report direct the strange things that they see. I only hear from them occasionally nowadays: they are so familiar with large black triangles, as big as football pitches, speeding under the water, with coloured lights around them, that they no longer regard a sighting of one of these as worthy of report. Yet they know that they are observing something very strange: these are seasoned sailors, working in difficult waters, where they have, over the years, become familiar with Russian and UN submarine patrols.

I also have a good source inside Icelandic Airlines, who has continued to feed me information about UFOs sighted in the air. There have, since 1993, been a couple of serious panics when strange circular objects appear to have attached themselves to planes. One pilot apparently nearly ditched in the sea as he tried to shake off two of them, one on each wing. Whatever manoeuvre he attempted, they stuck with him.

I was becoming more and more fascinated by Iceland. Not only was I getting detailed information about activity off the coast of the country, I was also beginning to feel a real telepathic pull towards the place, as if I was meant to go there. My friend with the Icelandic contacts, whom I cannot identify because it would not only prejudice his job, but also his role as a contact for future dealings, was also aware of an instinct to go to Iceland, a country he had visited several times before. He is not a ufologist, but had become interested in the subject after having an encounter with a UFO. He heard me giving a lecture, and recognised that I was talking about things he intuitively understood. I have since realised that he, like me, receives telepathic messages, and we were both being gently nudged in the direction of Iceland as a scene for a possible meeting with the aliens themselves.

So in the spring of 1993 we flew to Reykjavik. We hired a light aircraft and flew low across the glaciers and remote regions, both hoping that we would somehow sense where we should go. There was no blinding flash of realisation, but we both felt that our instinct that Iceland was the right place was confirmed, and there was one particular area, on the edge of the glacier Snæfell-sjökull, that had a good feeling about it. We decided, therefore, to arrange a UFO conference in Reykjavik, and bring in speakers from all over the world.

It is hard for me to describe my feelings about Iceland. It is one of the most uncontaminated and sparsely populated places on earth, and arriving there is like stepping back 10,000 years. The water is crystal clear, the air sharp, the scenery spectacular and yet slightly daunting. I felt, in some curious way that I cannot explain, connected to the place. Because, for so many years, it was in the buffer zone between the Eastern Bloc countries and the West, it has seen its share of modern history being made, when Russian and American leaders have secretly met there, yet there is a sense of timelessness about the place, as if ancient ways are still as current as present-day life.

Unfortunately, because there is no UFO organisation in Iceland, there was only a small attendance at the conference, held in November 1993. But our arrival was trumpeted in the local media, and there were camera crews from America and France as well. I was acting on a strong premonition that one of the alien intelligences wanted to make more substantial contact with me, but because of the media circus I quickly knew that nothing could possibly happen. When the camera crews followed us out on to the glacier, with their huge lights, it was like a scene from *Close*

221

Encounters of the Third Kind. After a couple of days, my friend and I returned to England, disappointed but not disheartened.

Interestingly, within days of our return, I received a report from a member of the Royal Norwegian Air Force, about an incident which had happened at 7.15 a.m. on 9 December, in northern Norway. It was apparently a beautifully clear, cold day, with the temperature at minus twenty degrees Celsius. Suddenly a large horizontal flame appeared in the sky above Bardufoss. It was known that it was not caused by any normal atmospheric phenomenon or meteor activity, nor were there any aircraft in the area. The flame was described as very long and wide, and the only possible explanation was that it had come from some sort of airborne vehicle either accelerating or decelerating into the cold atmosphere. There was no sound to be heard.

Later that day, there was a series of UFO reports from local residents, which were reported in the local press. One witness described the sighting as like 'ten helicopters' bound for Bardufoss Air Station, but they made no sound and had very strong lights which appeared to emanate from their centres, and radiate outwards. The reports were made from a radius of forty miles around Bardufoss, but nothing was picked up on radar and no official explanation was ever given.

I continued to receive information about activity in the North Atlantic. Throughout 1996 and 1997, the crews of the Icelandic fishing boats, who took my telephone number with them to sea, called in to describe mysterious sightings, usually of the large triangular black objects. The reports went in clusters, with a few sightings within days of each other and then nothing for a few weeks: similar to the pattern of sightings in the sky at places from where UFO reports are common.

At 7.30 p.m. on Monday 12 February 1996, I received a ship-to-shore telephone call from a fishing vessel in the Denmark Strait, off the west coast of Iceland. The caller told me that a huge triangular craft had appeared and was hovering low in the sky close to his boat. The transmission cut off as he was talking to me. He rang again, fifteen minutes later, to say that all electronics on the boat had suddenly failed. He said that he and the rest of the crew had seen the triangular object move away from the boat and then suddenly descend into the sea. The moment it had disappeared, electronic power was restored.

Six days later, at 9 p.m., I had another call from a fishing vessel. The caller told me the whole crew were terrified because three large triangular black objects, accompanied by three independent red balls of light, had emerged from the sea and were hovering silently close to their boats. I asked if they were picking the objects up on radar; he replied no, but that radar was irrelevant, in view of the fact that the whole crew was on deck watching them.

He said the objects were close, hovering over the port bow, and completely silent. Although they were black, there were small lights visible at different parts of their outline. Again, the phone line went dead, and when he called me again it was to report that the objects had all vanished beneath the sea.

The following day, another fishing boat crew reported watching a gigantic sphere hovering in the air, not far from the boat. It slowly moved away and then descended into the sea. An hour later, there was another phone call from the same boat:

'There are now six large fluorescent-tube-like objects hovering in the air close to our position. They are a blue colour and not making a sound. All these strange things are making the crew very frightened, we don't like this at all.'

Two months later, at 10.55 p.m. one evening, I was contacted from on board a ship fishing 200 miles south-west of the coast of Iceland. The caller said:

'You are not going to believe what we have just seen. We were fishing fairly close to a group of American warships and suddenly there was a blinding flash of light and one of the warships just disappeared in front of our eyes. I know it sounds crazy, but I can assure you it happened a short time ago. Soon after this an American boat came over and ordered us and other fishing boats to leave the area immediately.

'Our captain was happy to go. He told us to get the boat out of the area as quickly as possible and return to our base in Iceland. We are now underway for Iceland. The incident has upset us all, but particularly the Captain. He is in his cabin with a large bottle of whisky.'

As with the other disappearing ships, the American authorities denied all knowledge. I was puzzled as to how, if not only ships but substantial numbers of naval officers and men were going missing, the whole affair was kept quiet in the States: surely there would be anxious families kicking up a fuss if they were fobbed off without proper explanations? My American contacts, some of whom have high-level contacts in the US military and defence establishments, assure me that silencing families poses no problems to the authorities, who know how dependent they are on pensions and other support systems. On the other hand, I realise that the US Navy could have been testing an amazing high-tech masking device, to effectively conceal a ship from an enemy. I have no knowledge of any such device, but it is the only strictly terrestrial explanation I can come up with.

Throughout that summer of 1996, I received a series of reports of aircrew notifying their ground control of strange lights, and objects near them which could not be picked up by ground radar. A keen researcher who was monitoring the airwaves picked up messages from RAF and commercial planes around the coast of northern England and Scotland which, coupled with the reports I was still receiving from Icelandic aircrew, underlined that something continuous and unusual was going on.

In the autumn, two mysterious incidents happened. The first was a major UFO flap over East Anglia, after a red and green rotating light was seen in the sky over the sea, south-east of Skegness. It was spotted by local policemen, the crew of a ship at sea, passenger aircraft in the area, coastguard officials, and local residents, as well as appearing on RAF and coastguard radar screens. I obtained, from some excellent and reliable researchers, David Dane and Roy and Ann Wilkinson, a transcript of messages which were recorded at Yarmouth Coastguard HQ, starting at 3.14 a.m. with a message from Skegness Police:

03.24 Skegness Police: We can see a strange red and green rotating light in the sky directly south-east from Skegness. It looks as if it is stationary and there is no aircraft sound in the area.

03.26 RAF Kinloss (Scotland): [RAF] Northwood have a radar contact bearing 221 degrees at sixteen miles. It looks to be stationary and there is no way of determining its height, but it must be quite a size if it can be seen from Skegness.

03.46 Conocoast (oil) tanker (at sea): We have these lights on visual. Now they are flashing red, green and white. Cannot identify as an aircraft as it looks stationary and it is approximately one mile high.

Yarmouth Coastguard: Did you see from which direction it appeared?

Conocoast: No, it just appeared and is stationary.

03.53 RAF Kinloss: [RAF] Neatishead say it could be caused by the weather.

Yarmouth Coastguard: I don't think so as we have visual contact.

RAF Kinloss: Well, [RAF] Neatishead and [RAF] Northwood report that there is no transponder on this object and therefore no means of interrogation. It is obvious that whatever it is does not want anyone to know that it is there. Also [RAF] Neatishead report its position directly over Boston [Lincolnshire].

04.08 Conocoast: It is still stationary and flashing red, green, blue and white. It looks very high, north of us, there is no engine noise.

04.17 Yarmouth Coastguard: Skegness, can you get video footage as the RAF are very interested and may require it later.

04.27 RAF Kinloss: [RAF] Neatishead are keeping a log of what looks like clutter on the radar.

04.45 Yarmouth Coastguard: Conocoast, can you give us an update?

Conocoast: We can see two lights flashing, green and red.

05.01 Yarmouth Coastguard: Give us the bearings of the two lights.

Conocoast: There is one stationary light at 345 degrees true and the other is at 160 degrees true. The lights are both visible with the naked eye and both exhibit the same characteristics flashing red, blue, green and white.

05.17 Boston Police: We can still see the light, it is towards south-east and seems about forty to forty-five degrees in the sky. It is just a bright light to us.

05.21 RAF Kinloss: [RAF] Neatishead are running a trace on this and cannot explain it. If they are helicopters they are fast approaching the end of their endurance as it is well over two hours since the first report let alone how long they were up there before they were actually sighted.

05.52 Conocoast: We can still see the lights and they are on the original bearings and flashing the same colours but they seem higher and dimmer.

07.08 Flight-Lieutenant McFarlane, RAF Neatishead: We had a report from [RAF] Northwood that a civil flight had also reported strange lights in the area. They fit exactly what was seen from the ground, multicoloured, flashing, stationary lights.

07.31 Flight-Lieutenant George, RAF Northwood: This echo is still on our screens and we cannot explain this at all apart from it being a meteorological phenomenon but then again we have visual sightings also. The civilian flight that reported these lights as a flare was six miles away at the time. All very strange.

11.09 RAF Neatishead: The object has still not moved, the London Radar and [RAF] Waddington can also see it.

19.20 Anglia Radar: There is nothing there now, we are of the opinion that it was Boston Stump.

Flight-Lieutenant Sweatman of RAF Neatishead later commented to the local press: 'We have not been able to offer an explanation. The number of independent reports we have had suggests there is something to follow up. We will be investigating thoroughly.'

Ministry of Defence spokesman Nigel Sergeant said: 'We are trying to prove that it does not represent any sort of security threat and that it was not an aggressive intrusion into our airspace. This is one of the bigger sightings recently, and has caused quite a bit of interest.'

The police at Skegness confirmed that they had made a video of the UFO, which they described as a red boomerang shape with a green light over the top of it, and sent it to the MoD for analysis.

Despite the RAF and the MoD having no explanation to offer, some were put forward. Boston Stump, as suggested by Anglia Radar, is a church spire, a local landmark but not visible out at sea, where the tanker was. It seems nothing short of astonishing if Britain's local radar stations are unable to distinguish between a church spire and airborne activity. The planet Venus, which is often used as a scapegoat, was suggested by coastguards: but Venus would not have been visible after sunrise, as we confirmed with Jodrell Bank. Yarmouth weather station later suggested a storm at sea, with lightning causing the flashes. But the light reported was coloured, and not consistent with lightning: what's more, the coastguard reported at the time that the sky was clear and visibility twenty miles.

Perhaps the most intriguing piece of evidence that our investigators unearthed was that an order went out from senior military commanders that planes were not to be scrambled to intercept the UFO – yet the official statement said that the MoD were trying to prove it did not represent a threat to national security. How would they know, if they did not send planes to intercept it?

The second strange event that autumn happened north of the Isle of Lewis, in the Outer Hebrides. On 27 October 1996 there were reports of an explosion, followed by burning debris falling to the sea. A huge air and sea rescue operation, estimated as costing as much as £200,000, was launched, and local residents assumed that a plane had gone down. But there was apparently no recovery made.

I was given details of the operation by a contact with access to information from RAF Kinloss, where the first reports were received at 5 p.m. on Sunday 27 October. The RAF station issued an alert to coastguards and other vessels in the area of 'something seen spiralling into the sea, possibly larger than a

227

helicopter'. Two lifeboats were launched. An RAF Nimrod, call sign Rescue II, was airborne, but poor weather and visibility meant the search had to be called off by midnight. It was resumed the next day at 7 a.m.

There were half-hourly SITREPS (situation reports) from the Nimrod to RAF Kinloss. At 8 a.m. a message from the Nimrod picked up by my researcher was unreadable, but Kinloss's reply was clear: 'Confirm . . . six feet long and three feet in diameter.'

Officially, when asked by journalists investigating the incident, the authorities said that nothing was seen or retrieved.

A week later, a NATO naval task force moved into the area north of Lewis, on what was described by a Royal Navy spokesman as a 'routine training exercise' and nothing to do with the explosion. The arrival of the ships was reported in *The Scotsman* newspaper on 4 November. It was, it seemed, a rather large 'routine' exercise: there were thirty-two surface warships, seven submarines and eighty aircraft.

Everything went quiet for a few months, until the beginning of 1997, when a large number of UFO reports came in from Iceland. Civilians, aircrew, fishermen and naval personnel were all reporting a massing of lights in the sky. On Monday 20 January all flights attempting to land or take off from Keflavik Airport were delayed because UFOs were seen in civilian air corridors.

In December 1997 international attention was focused on Greenland, when a giant flash lit up the sky at 5 a.m. on the 9th. It was reported by three fishing crews, and was also picked up on a car park security video at Nuuk, on Greenland's west coast. One of the fishermen, Bjorn Ericksonn, the first mate on the trawler *Regina*, described the flash:

'I have never seen so strong light in the middle of the night. In the strongest part of the light there looked like a circle that was burning.'

According to experts, it was a large meteorite. Danish Air Force planes searched in vain across the huge, icy expanse of Greenland, trying to locate the crater made by the meteor. The only reason given for it not being found was that the ice forms so quickly in that remote territory, and snow was falling so thickly, that the contours can change overnight. The meteorite might even have melted through the ice cap, and newly formed ice and snow, it was said, could have formed over it.

However, I received a different report: a foreign politician contacted me to say that it was an alien spacecraft, and that it came in for a controlled landing, which the Americans were expecting. A further landing apparently took place six days later at Jan Meyern Island, a remote and desolate place between Iceland and Greenland, with another UFO coming down the next day, 17 December, on Eglinton Island, off the north coast of Canada. Throughout these two weeks, there had been a lot of American troop activity at the USAF base at Keflavik.

I received more reports of UFO activity over Canada in February 1998, when over 300 'flying objects' were tracked across the northern territories. Canadian airmen were convinced they had seen a top-secret, highly developed USAF plane, capable of evading radar.

In April 1998 the British press, including the *Daily Telegraph* and *Daily Mail*, reported a giant UFO being chased across the North Sea by both British and Dutch jet fighters. The RAF radar station at Fylingdales reportedly described the UFO as over 900 feet long, or 'as big as a battleship'. Although no date was officially given for the encounter, several witnesses in Ireland saw a large UFO on the night of 28 February. UFO researchers in the Netherlands investigating the involvement of Dutch air force planes have met a stone wall when trying to get official confirmation: they have found hitherto helpful sources within the government have clammed up completely.

Although I am particularly monitoring Iceland and the area of the North Atlantic where much of the activity has been concentrated, I have also received reports of large black triangular objects coming out of the sea in other places. Spanish fishermen have reported them, and, closer to home, I have even had an account of one emerging from the Mersey estuary, and from other points around the coast of Britain, particularly Lincolnshire. My conclusion – and it is only a theory – is that they can take refuge under water anywhere, but that there are tremendous concentrations of sightings around the sites of their bases, and the most well-documented of these, and possibly therefore the biggest and busiest, is the one under the North Atlantic.

That they also appear to have an interest in our domestic water supplies is worrying: I have heard of triangles hovering over canals and reservoirs, and one man even reported seeing one dropping what looked like a tube down into the water. If their intentions are malevolent, interfering with our water supply would be an effective way of hitting the whole population. On the other hand, I am more inclined to believe that they are monitoring the contamination levels, which fits in with the genetic monitoring and hybrid breeding programme of which abductees appear to be part. One thing is certain: they act secretly, and come and go like shadows. We may think we are watching them and gathering information about them, but in fact it is they who are observing us.

They are not only evident near water. I was recently told of a large black triangle which landed near a German military base. German troops opened fire, and it responded by shooting back with a laser-type weapon, blowing a hole in a road. The craft appeared to be deliberately not shooting directly at the soldiers.

UFOs are frequently seen in the vicinity of military bases, nuclear missile sites or areas of military operations. They have been spotted for many years appearing over high-security military establishments, nuclear power stations and even underground military complexes. They appear to have the technology to locate the most sensitive hidden areas. Expert witnesses have reported that their manner of overflying the land is consistent with mapping the territory. They have the ability to neutralise electronic equipment: they have done so on many occasions. They could be assessing our strength, or deliberately flexing their muscles to allow us – or at least, our military and governmental heads – to see that they are here in strength. But I think it is more likely that, for whatever reason of their own, they are watching a primitive culture working towards its own self-destruction. I do not think we are in control: they are here, and they are dictating what we do.

It is a difficult psychological leap for us to make: to accept that we are not, in fact, the highest form of life on this planet; that we are, to them, of no more significance than a troop of monkeys to be studied in our natural habitat.

Alongside all the research I was doing about naval activity in the North Atlantic, and my steadily growing conviction that this area is, indeed, the main centre for alien activity on this planet, my own personal odyssey was progressing dramatically. Although my friend and I had initially been disappointed that our trip to the glacier had received so much media hype, we both had a strong feeling that there was more to come. In 1997 my friend, who lives in Hampstead, north London, received a registered letter. The note inside told him to go to one of London's many foreign embassies, urgently, to meet a named diplomat. He phoned me, and I advised him to go. The diplomat wanted to know why he and I had concluded there was alien activity in the North Atlantic. My colleague was surprised by the question, and the directness of it: he got the impression that the diplomat was a very straightforward person, not prepared to mince words or play games. He explained that we had some evidence, but that we also both had a very strong intuitive feeling about it.

The diplomat seemed satisfied by this, and after a brief hesitation he confirmed that our instincts were right. He said that he had personally attended meetings with alien beings, along with other politicians from several countries, as well as military leaders. He had been present, he said, when a couple of aliens had specifically said that they wanted to meet me and my colleague. This was the only reason, he said, that he was talking to my friend. The meeting, he said, would probably take place in America. He warned that we should be ready to fly at twenty-four hours' notice.

When all this was later relayed to me it sounded preposterous – and yet, with the information I already had, there was no reason for it not to be true. I was sure that organised contact was taking place between alien races and human beings, so why should I be so surprised to find out that I was in line for a first-hand experience? I was excited at the prospect, but aware that I should not get my hopes too high. Sure enough, at a subsequent meeting with the diplomat, my friend was told that the Americans, whom the diplomat described as 'the big boys', had vetoed the inclusion of civilians, unless with top-security clearance, in any of the meetings. Furious, and believing that he had been betrayed, the diplomat then agreed to co-operate with us to provide proof that these meetings take place.

He told us that the only reason he was doing this was because the aliens had, themselves, expressed a wish to meet us. It was easier for him to meet my friend, who lives in London, than me, 300 miles further north. To one of these meetings he brought a package of photographs. One showed one of the 'greys', the grey aliens with the almond-shaped eyes (the ones who are responsible for human abductions), on board a warship in the North Atlantic with US military officers. Yet my friend pointed out that it was not a replica of the 'classic' alien that we see in so many pictures: although the body was the same, the facial features were slightly different. Another photo showed a UFO on the ground at a USAF base, with aircraft in the background and a group of three or four greys in front of the craft, talking to USAF officers.

Yet another showed a different kind of alien, with a reptilian head and a powerful body, two legs and two arms. Its height was estimated at over seven feet. The ambassador said this was an aggressive type of alien, but highly intelligent and dangerous. The word my friend used to describe it was 'fearsome'. It was not the first time I had heard of reptilian aliens: the quick-response soldier also described one, and there have been several other, independent reports. One American expert claims he saw them at Area 51, the top-secret US Government establishment in Nevada. (At a later contact, the diplomat told us about known underground bases in remote desert areas of the USA where these reptiles live, aware that the US authorities are watching them. A surveillance team was attacked by them in the spring of 1998, and twenty soldiers were killed or wounded: surveillance is now organised from a great distance.)

The diplomat told my friend about another type of aliens, with dark skin and an Oriental look, who are apparently the most friendly of all. He spoke of the feeling of calm that pervades a room when they are in it, a feeling so strong that some humans are unable to stay in the room. (Interestingly, I have heard abduction victims describe Oriental-looking beings, and several of them report being met by 'Oriental people', who appear to be human, in the days after an abduction.) The Oriental aliens, he said, are concerned to warn the human race about the attention that the aggressive, predatory reptilians are now showing to us. It is the reptilians, they say, who carry out mutilations on both animals and humans. Like the greys, who abduct people and animals for medical research, the reptilians are interested in the functioning of human and animal bodies: but their methods of obtaining information are much crueller and less subtle. The diplomat said that, although he had seen videos of greys, he had never actually met one.

The diplomat promised that he would get copies of these photographs for us. When I heard about the pictures, I regretted not being in London that day: I would have taken photographs of the photographs, on several rolls of film, and not had them developed until I was back home. Within days of this meeting promising the copies, a knock at my friend's door brought him face to face with a man and a woman who asked him whether he had been given anything by the diplomat. He said no, and asked them what it had to do with them. They said, in a reprise of the warnings I was given in America, that he was being monitored, and that he should be very careful.

Worried because we knew the transfer of the photographs was going to be difficult, my friend and I discussed it at length, using public telephones or phoning from the homes of other friends. We knew that because the ambassador had diplomatic immunity, the pictures would not be taken from him. But the moment they were handed over, they were vulnerable. I devised a plan that involved me and several other of our trusted colleagues all being in London on the day of the handover. Unfortunately, our plans were completely overturned by events: the diplomat was suddenly recalled to his own country. He was given such a brief time to organise his return that he contacted my friend and said that the handover would have to take place that day, 27 October 1997.

They arranged to meet in a quiet street in Hampstead, the area where my friend lives, and which he knows well. It was after the package was handed over that the chase described in the introduction to this book began.

Two days after my friend put the package in the letterbox, the diplomat called. He was devastated to learn that the photographs he had copied had gone astray. He said that the package had contained more pictures than my friend had already seen, plus a video of UFOs landing at a USAF base. The video is irreplaceable, but it is possible that we may yet get hold of copies of the photographs.

I hope so. I already know that there is plenty of hard evidence for the existence of extra-terrestrials; I have seen with my own eyes their vehicles. Now I look forward to the day when there is the kind of proof that nobody can challenge or argue with. I think we nearly had it: we will have it again.

The inevitable question is: who is so determined to stop us having this conclusive evidence? It can only be the intelligence services, with the Americans at their head. The more difficult question is why. It could be for religious reasons, because revelations about the true extent of alien presence on earth would rewrite the history books and overturn organised religion as we know it. I am personally not convinced that the governments of the world – and, remember, there are many colluding in this cover-up – are altruistic enough to have agreed a watertight secrecy pact to preserve religion.

It is, I suspect, far more likely to be because of the risks in making all their information about aliens public: sudden revelations would probably precipitate mass hysteria and panic. Perhaps, by allowing a ground-swell of interest in the subject, and only thwarting investigators like me when we get too close to the enormity of the truth, they are preparing the way for future generations to accept either co-existence with – or domination by – aliens, here on planet earth.

When I first became involved in UFO research, more than twenty years ago, I had no idea where it would lead. At the time it was straightforward: there was a mystery, and I wanted to solve it. Now I know that it is anything but straightforward: it is complex, dangerous and demanding, and I have so far only scratched the surface of the truth. If I compare it to a jigsaw puzzle, there are still many pieces missing, and those I have in my hand do not necessarily slot into the others yet. Eventually, as the work I – and many other dedicated researchers – am doing progresses, I will build up the full picture. I am as determined today to carry on with this work as I was twenty years ago.

CHAPTER ELEVEN

MY SPIRITUAL JOURNEY

Ever since I saw my first UFO, on that bitterly cold night more than twenty years ago, my life has been dominated by my quest to find out the truth. This is still my approach: the habits of a lifetime are ingrained, and though I may have been retired from the police for several years, I still have a pragmatic detective's outlook. I am, essentially, an investigator, and I thrive on being able to piece together the full picture from leaked documents, obscure official statements, and the evidence of witnesses.

But there is a whole other dimension to my work, one I did not anticipate and by which I am continually surprised. My own contact with an alien intelligence has added a profoundly spiritual context to my life. I was always a nature lover, but I was not introspective. I never thought too deeply about the whys and wherefores of the universe: I was not religious, nor had I studied any form of spiritual enlightenment. I was a very down-to-earth, practical person whose life revolved around family and job.

Now, to my astonishment, my mind is often flooded with uplifting thoughts, messages that spring unbidden into my brain, and which are expressed in a poetic, emotional language that bears little resemblance to my own everyday speech. I believe that the messages are given to me telepathically, by the aliens with whom I have had contact, and who are, in some way, guiding me in my work. Several times I have been told I am a 'teacher', and I believe they see me (and others) as conduits

237

through which to pass on their fears for the future of this planet.

I know that there are more than one race of aliens with an interest in earth, and that some, but not all, are friendly and well disposed towards us, perhaps in the same way that we are towards our domesticated animals. They care about us and our development, and they care about our environment, particularly as we now have the technology to wreak so much damage on the world in which we live. When I am asked why aliens and UFOs are suddenly such an important subject, I point out that there is evidence of their visits to earth throughout human history, but that there may well have been an escalation in interest since we developed the means of total self-destruction. The dropping of the atom bomb at the end of the Second World War was a clear signal that we have the capability to wipe out the human race, but perhaps not the maturity to handle such power. The intelligences that are watching over us, studying us, must have realised that now, more than at any other time in our evolution, we need to be taught to protect and value our fragile environment.

My increased spiritual awareness is not unique: most abductees experience a similar awakening. People who have close encounters always tend to develop psychic ability; they become more artistic, have a deeper understanding of nature, are more protective of living things. We also – and I think this is perhaps the most fundamental aspect of our enhanced appreciation – realise that the human race has endowed itself with too much self-importance. We overvalue ourselves and our part in the huge cosmic scheme of things. We are only a very small and insignificant part of this universe, no more significant than any other living thing, whether it is an animal, a tree or a blade of grass. The earth is a living organism, and everything that is on it and part of it needs to be able to co-exist in harmony and mutual respect with everything else: man's arrogance, in assuming he is superior, is what has attracted the attention of our extra-terrestrial brothers. We are in danger of getting the whole planet out of balance, with possibly disastrous consequences.

The abductees I have taken through hypnotherapy have all, in some way, expressed a greater knowledge of ecology, even if they have been reluctant to accept what one of them refers to as 'the teaching'. This is very much in line with other, serious research into abductions. Professor John Mack says in his book:

'The other important, related aspect of the abduction phenomenon has to do with the provision of information and the alteration of consciousness of the abductees. This is not purely a cognitive process, but one which reaches deeply into the emotional and spiritual lives of the experiencers, profoundly changing their perceptions of themselves, the world, and their place in it. This information concerns the fate of the earth and human responsibility for the destructive activities that are taking place on it.'

He, too, found that this new awareness is conveyed telepathically, and that most abductees have undergone great personal growth, often changing the whole nature of their lives: finding different jobs, different subjects to study, different groups to belong to. His subjects, like the ones I have studied, have a more holistic, less materialistic approach to life after discovering the truth of their abductions.

My life has certainly been fundamentally changed. I have discovered, almost against my will, a deep involvement in an investigation which I doubt will be completed in my lifetime. I know that I will not see all my questions answered, but I think it is important to pose them, and to try, in whatever way I can, to uncover the truth.

INDEX

241